RICK JAMES
Musical Genius

A Dozen
Top Ten Hits

Ten Albums with
Motown Records

Advances of
More than
1 Million Dollars
per Album

Twenty-Five
Top Forty Singles

Six Gold and
Multi-Platinum
Albums

"You and I" / "Mary Jane"
"Bustin Out" / "Give it to Me Baby"
"Super Freak" / "Cold Blooded"
"17" and More...

The Catalog of Rick James Hits Reads like a Highlighted
History of Popular Music over the Past Two Decades

SEX & DRUGS
FUNK & SOUL

NAKED!
RAW!
UNCUT!

"MEMOIRS OF A
SUPER FREAK"

"Midnight Cruises down Sunset Boulevard traveling for *Sex Partners*. Hosting the *Open Ended Orgies* played out behind the walls of Rick's sprawling Mulholland Drive estate where *Crack Whores, A-List Celebrities* and *Psychic Vampires* cavorted through interludes that often Ended in Acts of *Shocking Violence."*

The Confessions of Rick James

"Memoirs of a Super Freak"

The Confessions of Rick James

"Memoirs of a Super Freak"

By
Rick James

Colossus Books
A Division of Amber Communications Group, Inc.
Phoenix
New York   Los Angeles

The Confessions of Rick James
Memoirs of a Super Freak

By Rick James

Published by:
Colossus Books
A Division of Amber Communications Group, Inc.
1334 East Chandler Boulevard, Suite 5-D67
Phoenix, AZ 85048
amberbk@aol.com
WWW.AMBERBOOKS.COM/RickJames

Tony Rose, Publisher/Editorial Director
Yvonne Rose, Associate Publisher/Senior Editor
Yvonne Rose, Cover Design
TR & YR, Photo Concept

Samuel P. Peabody, Associate Publisher
Pittershawn Palmer, Copy Editor
The Printed Page, Interior Design & Layout

© Copyright 2007 Jin Jin Productions, Inc.
ISBN#: 978-0-9790976-3-8/0-9790976-3-0
Library of Congress Control Number: 2007920322

Dedication

This book is dedicated to my beloved mother,
Mable Betty Gladden and to all the musicians in the world.
God bless and keep you, to my family, my friends,
my fans and my foes, God bless you.

Acknowledgment

I praise God. If not for his grace and mercy
I would not have made it this far.

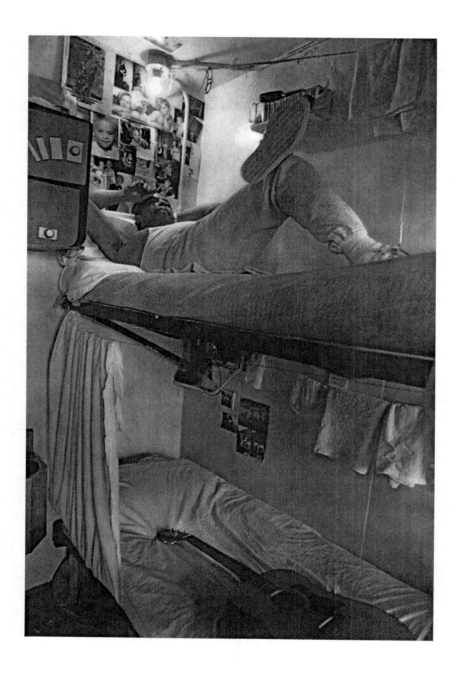

Preface

To all the Super Freaks, Super Geeks, and Super Tweaks, keep on tryin', and to the Brothers and the Sisters who say they just can't stop, stop your lyin'…

All the names and events in this book are true…

It is about 7:30 Friday evening, October 22, 1993, in my six by eight cell in the Los Angeles County Jail. There are no windows here, just dismal grey iron and concrete, and I don't know if the day was filled with rain or sun. The reason or reasons for my incarceration are of no importance at this time. What is important is that by writing my life's story I might help change or make a difference in someone else's life. Then my purpose on this planet would have been fulfilled.

Rick James

Contents

Introduction
Sex and Drugs and Rock and Roll

There is no modern myth more potent or seductive. The dream of rock stardom, of unlimited adulation and unbridled excess, exerts a fascination that has sold countless books, sparked scores of movie and television productions and fueled endless speculation: is the scene backstage, in the back of the limo and back at the hotel suite really as wild, as shocking and as scandalous as the whispered rumors suggest?

The answer to hear Rick James tell it, can be simply summed up "You ain't heard nothin yet." While the superstar's customized version of the old saying might be "sex and drugs and funk & soul," the fact remains that no rock icon, no overnight sensation, no rags to riches tale or saga of sin and redemption can come close to the incredible life, lived to the hilt of James Ambrose Johnson, Jr.

Simply put, in the super freaky world of Rick James the sex is steamier, the drugs more potent, the consumption more conspicuous and the music more explosive than any of a dozen other celebrities, dead or alive.

To fans of sassy and savvy urban music, the name Rick James will forever be associated with the mainstream emergence of Funk—that bottom heavy blend of rock and soul that sparked a multi-racial musical revolution in the 80's and continues to be a prime component in everything from rap to raves, punk to progressive rock. In direct line of decent from James Brown and Motown, Little Richard and Jimi Hendrix, Rick James almost single handedly pioneered a Funk fusion that reached across racial boundaries and united a massive international audience in a get down celebration that resonates to this day.

It's a claim backed up by his extraordinary track record a dozen Top Ten hits; ten albums with Motown, advances of more than one million dollars per album; twenty five Top Forty singles; six gold platinum and multi-platinum albums; a musical family that included such major hit acts as The Mary Jane Girls, The Stone City Band, Teena Marie and others, all masterminded by this diversely talented and multi-faceted artist. Rick James' live act set new standards for showmanship and spectacle and his prodigious creativity in the studio puts him among a handful of popular music's true innovators. Everyone from Michael Jackson to Prince to any of a dozen of today's gangsta rap poets owes an artistic debt to this true original. "You And I," "Mary Jane," "Bustin' Out," "Give it To Me Baby," "Super Freak," "Cold Blooded," "17," "Ebony Eyes," the catalog of Rick James hits reads like a highlighted history of popular music over the past two decades. Small wonder that among the numerous trophies that adorned his mantle was the music industry's prestigious Grammy Award.

But Rick James' reputation revolves around much more than his incredible recorded output. At a time when pop's biggest stars were known as much for over the top lifestyles as top of the chart hits, Rick James went further and faster, with more flash and panache than virtually anyone else in the checkered history of the music scene. A legendary sexual athlete, a brazen drug user, a celebrity constantly at the center of conflict and controversy, Rick James lived the rock roll lifestyle with a vengeance. And paid the price.

For the millions who know Rick James through his music, there still are more who only know his name from the lurid headlines generated by his 1993 criminal trials—headlines that screamed charges of assault with a deadly weapon, aggravated mayhem, kidnapping, drug possession and even torture. As with every other aspect of his outrageous saga, when Rick's karma finally caught up with him, it was under the relentless glare of public scrutiny. With his personal demons on display for the whole world to see, Rick's fall from grace was as steep and dizzying as his climb to the top.

A stiff prison sentence followed his felony convictions and Rick James seemed to have crashed and burned once and for all. The horrific details of his crack cocaine addiction, his insatiable appetite for kinky sex and his penchant for making powerful music business enemies—from MTV to Motown Records—were all magnified under the pitiless media microscope and, his proven talents notwithstanding, his career had careened uncontrollably into oblivion.

But, through the lessons of a lifetime of perseverance, Rick James had learned to never say never. Publicly disgraced, a convicted criminal, bankrupt and destitute, with true friends he could count on the fingers of one hand, he nevertheless saw opportunity where others would find only despair. He used his three years behind bars to make some of the best music of his career and to write, for the first time the astonishing story of his rise and fall, determined to confess the unvarnished truth in every detail, naming names and sparing no one, least of all himself, in his own amazing tale on a life of sex and drugs and music that changed the world.

The result is *The Confessions of Rick James—"Memoirs of a Super Freak"* by Rick James which promises to be one of the most honest and unflinching looks at life in the fast lane ever written. With *"Memoirs of a Super Freak"* Rick James has written the ultimate tell-all confessional with the emphasis on the 'all.' Alternately titillating and soul searching hair raising and heart breaking, *"Memoirs of a Super Freak"* is everything a major celebrity memoir should be; a long look behind the tinsel curtain of fame into the private lives and closely guarded secrets of the glitterati: an unflinching bare-knuckled account of who did what to whom in bed, on stage, and between the legal lines. The stars with walk-on parts in the Rick James story are on the A list just, as the incidents and anecdotes he relates are on the blacklist. *"Memoirs of a Super Freak"* in short makes for some very juicy reading by a man who once called himself "the black Marquis de Sade."

Of course no account of the life and time of Rick James would be complete without a celebration of his music, and in *"Memoirs of a Super Freak"* for the first time, he reveals the in-studio stories behind his biggest hits, from the inspiration for "17" to the off the cuff bass riff for "Super Freak" that would become the hook heard round the world. A delight to the many fans of Funk and a rich resource for any history of modern pop, the musical facets of Super Freak offer a rare glimpse at the creative process of an authentic original.

Yet remarkably, what is most openly revealed in the pages of this often poignant biography, is the restless search of a man looking for love, and truth, in all the wrong places and discovering, along the way, wisdom, compassion, self esteem and spiritual awareness.

It was a process that would bring Rick James to the brink of madness and back, miraculously, to the bonds of a caring and connected family life, in an odyssey that underscores his lifelong quest for the ties that bind. The all too typical product of a broken ghetto home deserted by his father and left largely to himself by a mother too busy making meager ends meet. Rick, early on, developed a deeply rooted desire for the security and support that only a family can provide. Across the years that followed he would try to create that family for himself—first through his strong creative links with fellow musicians, many of whom he not only discovered, but nurtured and sustained throughout their careers; then through a series of intense and ultimately self-destructive love affairs, as he searched for fulfillment with women interested, only too often in his superstar status; then as the architect of an impressive business and entertainment enterprise, with scores of employees and the inevitable coterie of hangers-on, yes-men and professional friends.

Along the way, Rick's star status would increasingly estrange him from his real family, an extended clan of brothers and sisters, cousins and kin all caught up in an internecine web of paranoia and betrayal, jealousy, and double-dealing that would eventually rob him of the one thing all his adulation and accomplishments could never provide—a sense of belonging. That void at the center of his life would eventually drive him to the depths of depravity, as he looked for a yet another family among the pimps and players the drug dealers and hardcore hustlers that gathered around him like moths to a glittering flame. The bitter ironies that defined his life have been played out time and again in tales of the rich and famous—the very talent and charisma that drew so many into his orbit would finally isolate him from the human touch he so longed for. But rarely has the age-old cautionary tale been so starkly drawn, or in such harrowing detail.

The end came with two high profile assault cases the details of which will be revealed for the first time in *"Memoirs of a Super Freak"*—a term in prison where surprisingly, Rick finally made a connection among the lifers and three time losers who shared his hard time behind bars. It was a de-facto family whose unlikely friendship and loyalty provided him with a chance to reevaluate his life and lay hold, once again, of his destiny discovering rich inner resources in the process.

And waiting for him on the day of his release was the one woman who can lay undisputed claim to living out the vow she would make on their wedding day, "For better or for worse." Former call girl and crack cocaine addict, Tanya Hijazi has shared many of the darkest chapters in the Rick James saga: midnight cruises down Sunset Blvd., trawling for fresh sex partners: hosting the open ended orgies played out behind the walls of Rick's sprawling Mulholland Drive estate, where whores and high rollers, slumming celebrities and psychic vampires cavorted through nightmarish interludes that often ended in acts of shocking violence: running scared through the back alleys of South Central LA, while TV screens flashed the mug shots of a fugitive rock star and his beautiful-partner-in crime: descending into the nether realms of cocaine insanity, when days bled to weeks behind windows covered in aluminum foil: facing the consequences as Rick's co-defendant in the trials that put them both behind bars.

Yet through it all, Rick and Tanya's love endured and, following their release and parole the couple slowly, and often painfully, began to build a new life together, centered this time around their young son Tazman. It was Rick James' last chance—and he held on for dear life.

It's there that *"Memoirs of a Super Freak"* both ends and begins. After all the sexual capers and drug delirium, the fortunes won, lost, and won, the double crosses and dangerous liaisons, what comes across most powerfully in *"Memoirs of a Super Freak"* is the voice of a man who learned, the hardest way, from his mistakes and survived to tell the tale, with humor and humanity, an open heart and a vibrant soul.

"Memoirs of a Super Freak" comes at a time when the artist himself had re-emerged triumphantly into the spotlight. Signing to Mercury Records in 1997, he released the best selling "Urban Rhapsody," his first new album in almost ten years, and reintroduced himself to

audiences with a subsequent national tour. Just before he passed away in 2004, Rick had completed a new album, scheduled for release in May 2007. The single "Deeper Still" on Stone City Records, dropped February 2007, and was immediately added to radio in over thirty markets. The film rights to his life story have been sold, with a theatrical release set for 2008.

As the poet William Blake once wrote "The road of excess leads to the palace of wisdom. In *"Memoirs of a Super Freak,"* Rick James will walk that road one step at a time, one more time, with us.

—Davin Seay

Chapter One
The Beginning

I was born James Ambrose Johnson Jr. on February 1, 1948, in Buffalo, New York. In those days Buffalo was a booming town with plenty of nightlife and plenty of jobs. One could always do an honest day's work at Bethlehem Steel Corporation, Chevrolet Motor Company or several other corporations Buffalo was famous for.

The nightlife also had plenty of openings—illegal jobs such as dope dealing, prostitution, numbers running, pimping and playing. The Jazz and Rhythm & Blues clubs swung all night and into the morning, which is probably one reason I chose to be a musician. On any given night you could walk the streets of Buffalo, and hear some of the greatest Blues and Jazz entertainers in the world—I mean cats like Miles, Coltrane, Wes Montgomery, Arthur Prysock, Etta James and Jimmy Smith, all playing at the many night spots of Buffalo. God, it was fantastic, and the old-timers said the scene echoed that of New York City during the Harlem Renaissance.

I was raised in a family of eight, four boys and four girls. My brother Carmen is the oldest, my sister Camille the second oldest. I am the third. Roy is the fourth, Cheryl the fifth, Alberta the sixth, William the seventh, and Penelope (Penny) is the baby. I have often wondered how my mom managed to raise eight crazies like us, especially since most of the time she was raising us on her own.

I was named after my father, of whom I have only vague recollections. He was about five foot nine, a good-looking brother with Indian blood. At night he would wear a woman's stocking over his head to keep his hair pressed down tight when he slept. He was a womanizer, especially after he'd had a few drinks. He and my mother went out frequently, and mom would come home crying. From my bedroom I could hear them fighting, and it usually had something to do with another woman.

He was never the kind of father I used to hear and read about, the kind who took his kids to baseball games and went fishing with them. Instead he worked six days a week at Chevy Company, and when he wasn't working, he was drinking excessively. We never talked much more than hello and goodbye. When I think of him, I think of the constant fights. He would beat my mother, and I'd sit at the top of the stairs with my brothers and sisters, crying, wishing I was grown up so I could kill him.

My only warm memory of my father is of me sitting on the edge of his bed, watching him as he dressed up for a Shriner's meeting. When I'd ask him what the Shriners were, he'd just laugh and say; "It's just a club, son, just a club." He'd have this big cigar in this mouth, and he'd puff away at it, as he got dressed and left, adjusting his Shriner's cap to the perfect angle.

Both of my parents looked distinguished. They would kiss us all goodnight, and tell us to go to bed, and they'd be off. Mom looked elegant in whatever she wore. I thought she was the most beautiful woman in Buffalo. She'd prance around like a model, and we'd just laugh. But when they returned home, the fights would begin. One of my happiest memories was the day Dad walked out on Mom and us and never came back.

Chapter Two
A Child's Heart

My mother was one of the kindest, most considerate, hard working women I've ever known. If God had allowed me to pick the mother of my choice, it would have been her. During my youth, she was the greatest disciplinarian I've ever known. Only five foot five, she was like a giant to me. Mom was born in Akron, Ohio, and came from a long line of girls. She was the youngest and the shortest. Her nickname was Freddie, but after she married my father, he made her drop it and she became just Betty.

Mom was a hard-working woman who always maintained two cleaning jobs. She did this because she said it looked good if the police every suspected her; you see Mom's main income came from running numbers for the Italian mob. I was never really proud of that while growing up. The other kids would say their mother was a secretary or a saleslady. But I couldn't say, "My Mom works for the Mafia." Never the less, it was a way to make a lucrative living, and Mom kept eight children fed and clothed, which is all that really mattered.

My brothers and sisters and I were raised most of our lives in housing projects made for low-income families. I knew we could afford to move into a real home and I would constantly ask Mom when we were going to leave the projects, but she would never say. Whenever Mom or one of us kids had a dream, she would ask us what it was about, then grab her dream book, look it up and play that number. Most of the time she would hit it straight, and when she wasn't hitting, she'd just skim off the top of the gangster's money. They'd never know, and if they did they never said anything to Mom. They all loved her, and she made them lots of money.

The first place I can remember living was the Wullert Park Projects in the black area of Buffalo. Most of us were born there. It's also where I lost my virginity at the ripe ol' age of nine. The girl's name was Nancy. She was fourteen. I remember doing it in the basement of one of the buildings. She was a friend of my sister's and I knew she liked me. It's funny, but when a man loses his virginity, most tend to act like they have been fucking for years when in fact we—or I—are as nervous as could be. When I pulled out my thang I honestly didn't know what hole to put it in. I'm glad she helped.

So here I am, this nine-year-old kid, hopping up and down. Just when I was about to come, I got up and ran to the corner of the basement. I felt like I was going to piss. Nothing would come out, so I went and lay back on top of her, and started going up and down again. This time I decided I wasn't going to get up whatever happened. The whole experience was pretty interesting, though it would take a little time before I would learn to enjoy it.

One year we had an eclipse of the moon, and all us kids were told to stay inside 'less we go blind. Anyway, Stevie Wonder was my idol at the time, so I got me a Harmonica and some sunglasses and stood in the courtyard to watch the eclipse. In my nine-year-old mind, I wanted to be blind like Stevie. I never told anyone that story, except Narada Michael Walden, a friend of mine and a great drummer. I told him because he had just described doing the exact same thing.

Me and my brother Roy always hung out together. We called ourselves Texas Jim and Roy Rogers, and we were inseparable. There were two bedrooms in the apartment, and me and Roy shared one, sleeping in bunk beds. The girls shared the other bedroom.

My older brother Carmen was never around much when I was growing up, even at that time he had already spent many of his years in and out of prisons. I never knew the details of his life, except he had a violent temper that kept him in trouble with the law. He was a master of martial arts, and once I heard a policeman refer to him as a three–time loser and killer. I didn't care what he had done, he was my brother, and as much as I hated him for the way he made my mother suffer, I still loved him. He was very caring of Mom, and whoever hurt my Mom was in serious trouble with Carmen, he especially hated my Dad. Carmen and Camille have different fathers to the rest of us, and we never met Carmen's Dad. But I did meet Camille's once. His name was Homer; he was half black and half white, and a serious alcoholic. When Mom left him, he was devastated. His life became one of alcohol and drugs. Sounds like another mothafucka I know.

Anyway, for the most part we were a happy family. The household was pretty much run by my older sister Camille. She was the one who made us clean up, make our beds, take out the garbage and so on. Camille wasn't big, only a hundred pounds or so, but she was tough, when she hit you, you felt all the power of her thin frame. She was very pretty with long, black, wavy hair, and she had a constant stream of admirers and boyfriends.

My mother had her first child at thirteen, and though this meant she never finished school, she could add, subtract and multiply, and remember numbers like a computer. I was always amazed at her ability, especially since math was my worst subject in school.

Mom hustled hard to take care of her family; she kept our refrigerator packed and we usually kept two cars, and always had nice clothes on our backs. She raised us strict Catholics, keeping us in Catholic school most of our childhood. The Catholics were strict, and I always felt I didn't belong there. Every Sunday the whole family went to church together, eventually I even became an altar boy. However, the priest busted us on drinking the wine from the Tabernacle, and the end came during one of my trips to the confessional booth, when I explained how I had secret desires of having sex with a nun.

One day Mom made us pack all our belongings, loaded them up in a trailer behind her new Edsel, and told us we were moving out. I was about ten or so, and I remember asking with anticipation where we were going. Mom just smiled. We knew we were finally going to have a real home with grass and trees and everything, and we couldn't wait to see it.

Chapter Three
Welcome to the White World

The Perry Projects were all-white housing projects. However, the inhabitants were not just white, they were the most racist white folks I had ever encountered. The drive across the Swan Street Bridge was like driving to another planet. As my siblings and I watched out the car window, the faces changed from all black to all white. The Perry Projects were very similar to the Wullert Park Projects, except the buildings were shorter. Across the street from where we now lived were real houses with trees and back yards, we took some comfort from the fact that we were at least getting closer to our dream of a real home.

As we stumbled out of the over-loaded Edsel onto the pavement, every white face in the neighborhood was staring directly at the five little black kids holding onto each other for dear life. Today this memory makes us laugh hysterically. My Mom directed us into what was going to be our home for the next five years. I would become a lot closer to my family in these years; they would be my entire life.

The first time I heard the word *Nigger* used by a white person was in our new High School. Walking in that first day felt like a nightmare, we were the only black faces in the whole school, and the word *Nigger* followed us wherever we went. There was a white gang at school, and every day Roy and I would meet after class and run our asses off until we got to the safety of our little home. We'd slam the door, gasping for breath. Camille would soon follow us, her clothes ripped and dirty. We would ask what happened and she would just say she had to kick some girl's ass for calling her a nigger. Camille always liked a good scrap.

Mom got tired of me and Roy running home crying, so one day she met us after school and confronted the gang. She asked which boy

13

wanted to whip her sons, and two of them jumped out immediately. Mom made me fight the first boy, and I had this secure feeling because she was there. I whipped this boy's ass almost to submission. Then Mom asked Roy "Whose after you?" and Roy began kicking another white boy's ass.

After it was over, Roy and I felt pretty good about ourselves, and we were left alone from then on. Later I heard that the mothers complained, but nobody wanted any part of Mom.

I remember asking my mother what *Nigger* meant; she just said "Don't use that word in my house." But every time we'd get a whuppin', she'd call us "*niggahs.*" It would take years before I completely understood what she meant.

Chapter Four
Love Thy Neighbor

Whoever said, "Love thy Neighbor" did not have neighbors like ours. While Roy and I continued winning battles at school and gaining friends, our neighbors were another story. They would throw rocks in our windows, and burn crosses. Sometimes I would ask Mom why we didn't move away. Even though we were crying in fear she would say "Nobody's gonna run me out of my house. Nobody!" And that would be that.

On our corner was a store run by a very friendly, very fat Polish man. There was always this gang of tough white teenage boys hanging out there. They would just hang around, combing their greasy hair and messing with people, especially girls. They all looked like characters out of the move *The Wild Ones*, and some of them even had motorcycles. They smoked cigarettes, which I hadn't started to do yet; and they all carried switchblades.

One day Camille went shopping and they knocked over a bag of her groceries and started kicking her food around. She started to fight all of them, but was stopped by the store owner, who made sure she got home safe.

When Mom saw how upset Camille was, she grabbed a long knife in her hands and headed for the door. I'd never seen her so mad; she started walking at a very fast pace towards the corner store. When they saw Mom, some of the gang just flat-out fled. Toby, the leader, a short, well-built boy with a serious crew cut, hung around for a minute till Mom started cussing out him and his whole gang. The whole neighborhood could hear, and she didn't care. The funny thing about this whole incident was that they were all of a sudden just little kids. Not one made a sound; they just stood there looking pitiful.

After Mom had finished, she left just as fast as she came. When she walked in the house she broke down crying and told us to go play. Then she picked up the phone. The last thing I heard her say was "Carmen, I need you." All I could think of was, this means trouble.

Chapter Five
Time for Some Respect

As a kid, I loved Mom's record collection. Billie Holiday, Sarah Vaughn, Dakota Staton, Billie Eckstein. I would sit and just listen to them. Jazz always had a strange effect on me, and I loved the melancholy sound of it. It would put me in a trance, and I felt like I had already lived the stories these singers sang about. I seemed to know their phrasing and chord changes without ever having heard the tune. Sometimes when Mom went on her numbers runs, she would take me along; especially when she knew she would be stopping at a bar with live music. She encouraged my interest any way she could.

I was only nine or ten, but the people who ran these Jazz and Blues joints never cared. They just loved to see us come in. I would ask to sit in on drums, and I remember the proud look on Mama's face when she'd watch her son kickin' on drums to her favorite tune. People would ask, "Where did he learn to play like that?" Mom would just smile and say "Didn't you know my son's a genius?"

Now, it had been a few weeks since I had heard Mom's call to Carmen, and I had hoped that maybe things had been forgotten and nothing was being planned. Carmen had just gotten out of prison for the third time, and whenever Mom brought up his name, Roy and me trembled. His name usually came up when we were being bad. Mom would say: "I'm gonna call your brother. Just wait 'till he gets here." That would always straighten out Roy and me for a while. We knew how hard Carmen could hit.

One night I was lying in bed when I heard guys yelling and screaming outside the house. The noise went on for twenty minutes or so, then there was a knock at our door. It was Carmen, and a friend of Carmen's called Ray, and my father. Carmen was short, about five foot eight, with high cheekbones, and a muscular build. He always wore a process. Ray was a muscular, dark-skinned brother, who had become friends with Carmen in prison.

Turns out that Toby and his gang had exchanged words with Carmen, and had ended up jumping Carmen, Dad and Ray. Well, Carmen always carried nun-chukkas, brass knuckles and a Chinese knife. From what I understood, he had used all of them on Toby and his boys and hurt them real bad. All Carmen had was a bruise over his eye and some bloody knuckles.

Carmen gave Roy and me a hug and asked if we were behaving. We both nodded yes simultaneously. Neither of us acknowledged my father until Mom said "Don't you see your father?" I wanted to say "No!" Carmen and Ray stayed over for a few days just to make sure everything was all right, then left as quick as they came.

A couple of days after the rumble, Roy and I went to the corner store where Toby and his boys hung. The Fat Man asked if we heard what had happened. He said that Toby and his boys had got what was coming to them, Toby was in the hospital along with four out of his gang, beat up pretty bad by a black gang. He was smiling as he talked. Me and Roy just walked out the store trying hard to hold back our laughter. By some gang, he had said. We couldn't help but find it funny that the Black gang was really just our big brother Carmen. That'll teach 'em not to mess with the Johnsons.

After the Toby incident, our lives became instantly better. Our neighbors finally became neighbors. I always thought that it wasn't so much respect that they now had for our family. It was fear—and fear was better than respect.

Chapter Six
Sports, Gangs

By now I was thirteen years old. My life consisted of baseball, football and of course, girls. I was a bubbly kid, always looking for new ways to get in trouble. Girls thought I was funny in school, kinda like the class clown— anything for a laugh. I would sit in class and when the teacher would turn her back I would fart, or throw something. I just wanted to have fun and see people laugh. People would say to my Mama, 'that boy Jimmy is a natural fool,' and Mom would say 'I just hope he makes some money with it.'

By this time, a few more black families had begun to move into the projects and we immediately befriended them. I can remember this one particular black family that lived right across the courtyard from us, a really nice family of three children, two girls and one boy, Nate. Their mother had died some years earlier and their father, who drove a bus, was raising them alone. He gave me my first boxing lesson and I looked up to him like a Dad. He also took me to my first professional football game. I've always remembered him, even to this day.

Roy and I stopped hanging out so much. He had been involved in a terrible accident. Mom had bought the two of us this beautiful ten-speed bike, our very first. One day while Roy was out riding, an ice-cream truck came out of nowhere and hit him, dragging him under the wheels for God knows how long. It left Roy in a cast for almost two years. The cast covered both his legs up to his waist. He also had a severed ear, which the doctors managed to put back on. He almost lost his life, and Mom was devastated by it.

Those years were difficult for all of us. I was alone—my brother and partner was hospitalized and between her two jobs, running numbers and visiting Roy every day, I barely saw my Mom. I felt I had lost her. Although I knew it wasn't his fault, I still resented Roy for my sudden loneliness. Feeling neglected, I started to skip school. I would just walk around singing to myself and by the time I realized it, I had walked right out of the city.

Rick and his mother, Betty, share a playful moment

I started to feel that Mom blamed me for Roy's accident. He had always been the smart one, and I was the one who always led him into trouble. I felt hurt and angered by her disapproval. Sometimes, when I felt that I just had to get away from home, I'd steal money out of her purse and take a Greyhound to New York City. From Port Authority Bus Station in Manhattan I'd walk, not really knowing where I was going. Usually, I'd end up in Greenwich Village, going from coffeehouse to coffeehouse, afraid and lonely. When my money was gone, I'd work up the nerve to call my mother. She would usually scream at me and then send me to a friend's in New York who could give me the bus fare home. When I got home a whipping was waiting for me, but I was too tired to care.

I continued running away until one day the police caught me while hiding in the bathroom of a Greyhound bus. I was put in a juvenile home for a few weeks. Mom finally came to get me, she asked me why I was running and what it was that I hoped to find. I told her with tears in my eyes, that I didn't know, I just wanted something more out of life. She would look at me with a bewildered expression and start to cry. I hated to see her cry, especially when it was because of me.

After returning home from Juvenile Home I found Roy was slowly getting better. I made some new friends, and I started a little singing group with them. We'd stand on the street corner singing acapella and drinking wine out of a brown bag.

Singing and terrorizing the projects was the ultimate groove. We'd fight other gangs, and steal bicycles, even if the rider was still on 'em. When I wasn't out on the streets, I spent time listening to records with my friends. We'd play Frankie Lymon, Sam Cooke, The Drifters, even Elvis. I loved being alone listening to my jams. I'd put on my records and sing at the top of my voice. I even had this broom I played like a guitar—but that axe was short lived once Mama found straw all over the house. I'd get a butt whuppin' and that was that.

I began skipping school again, taking long walks alone just daydreaming. I dreamed of being a big star and having all this money and how proud Mom would be. I would be a star or die trying—that was it. There was no other way.

Those were troublesome days for Mom to. When I look back now, I know it was because she had no man in her life, and was lonely. Loneliness would turn to anger, and she would take it out on us, beating us with an extension chord. The more she beat me, the more rebellious I got.

My gang bangin' got more intense. I rarely came home, either staying at our little clubhouse or one of the guy's houses. One day my gang got into a rumble and a boy was shot. I was arrested and put in a juvenile home for a few months, but eventually the judge dropped the charges because the boy lived. My mother was furious at me, and when I got home, she wanted to give me a beating. But I was too old for beatings, and when she got out the iron cord, I just caught it and held it, preventing her from continuing. My mother looked bewildered and then broke down and cried. I hated to see her cry but I was not going to be beaten again. Ever.

Chapter Seven
Oh Happy Day!

Mom finally met someone we all liked. His name was Elliot Gladden, but we all called him Al. Al was a quiet man with a stern aura around him, my mother was a few years older than he was, but he loved her to death. One day I awoke and found Al sleeping in my Mom's bed. She rushed me into the kitchen like a girl trying to hide something and told me her and Al were getting married. I was happy for her, it was just good to see her smile. She bore him a daughter, who she called Penelope Alicia Gladden, Penny for short. Penny was so beautiful, and our shared love of her helped bring us together as a family. The first time she managed to stand up and walk by herself, we were all standing in the kitchen with our arms stretched out, calling to see who she would walk to. Well, she just opened up this beautiful smile and walked right over to me.

Al was a good father—hardworking and diligent to Mom's needs. He only had one problem—he drank too much. When Al came into the picture, our family finally became a real family. Al was strict, but in a quiet way. When he spoke, we listened.

We stayed in the Projects for about a year more and then we finally moved into a house with trees and a back yard. We now lived right under Al's parents, and they didn't much like Mom or us. They were fat—not just fat—obese. Every one of them must have weighed over three hundred pounds—Al's mother, father, his brother Joe and sister Shugg—all of them were massive except Al, who barely weighed one hundred and sixty pounds. When they moved around above us it was like an earthquake shaking the walls. Looking back, I can't help thinking how funny it was knowing that they were looking at us with distasteful faces, while at the same time, unbeknownst to them, we were looking at them with equal disgust. They were very holier than thou people, always going to church and then coming home to treat us kids in a very un-Christian way. Penny and Al were the only members of our family they really cared for.

Years later, Rick formed the Stone City basketball team.

I was now about fifteen and going to high school wondering what I would be when I grew up. I had joined the local Boys Club where I was becoming a pretty good basketball player. The great Bob Lanier of the Detroit Pistons was center on our team. I was also on the swim team and football team and I was considered to be a pretty good jock. Roy, always a year under me, was determined to be a lawyer. I was still unsure of my life vocation, but whatever it was, I'd be the boss.

Chapter Eight
Failures Make You Stronger

I was now a freshman at Bennett High School. Bennett was a prestigious school with mostly black and Jewish students. It was a very hip prep school and I wanted to be the Big Thing there, 'cept I didn't know how I was going to attain this goal.

My first year, I tried out for the football team at halfback position. My number was thirty-two, after my hero Jim Brown. I had excelled at this position before I got to High School. While at practice one day I took a handoff and came gunning around the right end when this oversized white linebacker grabbed me by my helmet, picked me up and crushed me to the ground. I fractured my jaw in two places. That ended my football career.

I tried basketball since I had played first string with the Boys Club. But even there I didn't make the varsity team. Hurt, but not completely discouraged, I tried track. My hundred-yard dash wasn't fast enough—so I took up pole vaulting. I was a miserable failure at that.

Being good but not good enough was not in my MO in life. I had to be the best—I could never settle for second place. I had tried sports and failed, so now I'd try music. There's no way I could fail at music, no way. Like Mom always said, music was in my blood. The image of a saxophone kept sticking in my head. I decided to learn sax and be the next Coltrane.

So one day I ran out of class up to the music room, out of breath. I ran right into Mr. Hillard, the music teacher. He grabbed me and told me to "Slow down, Junior." I told him that I wanted to play sax, and he led me back to the music room and told me all the saxes were gone. It was not my day, I thought. There was a brother playing drums in the corner, practicing rudiments. I walked over to him and asked if I could use his sticks. I started playing away, mostly out of frustration. Mr. Hillard stopped me and asked where I learned to play, and I told him that I had taught myself. He decided he would teach me the true art of drumming. Finally, I was in music.

Learning drums was more of a task than I thought it would be. When I was young, Mom would just take me to a night spot and I'd get behind the traps and play. The band always liked me sitting in and so did the people. It was just something that came naturally to me. But now it was complex—rudiments, time signatures, polyrhythms, stick rolls, and muscle exercises for your fingers. I started to struggle against the ideas that Mr. Hillard was trying to teach me, and I actually found myself getting bored with music. Sometimes Mr. Hillard would find me after school singing on my traps just playing, and we would sit down together and have long talks about music. He told me I had natural talent and I could go a long way—but I would have to study composition and theory for about ten to fifteen years. I told him I felt music should be simplified, and that the most important thing was that music should just groove. Mr. Hillard had been a graduate of Julliard and was very set in his ways. He would just shake his head and walk away. One day I'd prove him wrong. Until then, I'd continue to study and be bored.

I didn't like anything confining or regimented. That applied to people, situations and, most importantly, music.

Chapter Nine
Victory

Bennett's Talent Show was coming up. It was a major event every year and I was determined to win, but how? I still wasn't comfortable with my voice, except around close friends. The only thing I felt I could do was sing and play drums at the same time, and that meant I had to figure out how to incorporate the two. I remembered Little Stevie Wonder's bongo playing on "Fingertips." If he could sing and drum, I could too.

At that time I had no idea how great he was.

The night of the show, I was so nervous that I went into the bathroom and threw up. The auditorium was packed with family, friends and schoolmates, and I didn't want them to laugh at me. The judges called my name, and the lights went down, I was center stage, alone. A spotlight hit me and I started off with a bongo beat, then I began to sing out this African sounding chant, something like Little Stevie Wonder. "Everybody say yeah!" I asked the crowd to sing along and they did. As they sang, I picked up my mallets and my tom drum and played this funky beat on the tom, switching to rim beats. I would stop and chant and then go back to this tom rhythm, playing a very ethnic groove.

The crowd chanted louder and louder until the auditorium seemed to be moving. The chant and the rhythm seemed voodoo-like. I don't remember how long I played, maybe twenty minutes, before I started dipping off the stage while the audience continued the chant I started.

It took a while for the principal to calm down the crowd, and nobody was surprised when they announced the winner—James Johnson, first prize. I walked out and accepted the award. The crowd started yelling,

27

"More, more!" So I began the beat again. If more was what they wanted, more is what they'd get. The principal wasn't real happy about me winning. He knew me by name for being the school troublemaker and having been written up so much. But tonight was my night and there was nothing he could do. The feeling of the crowd singing and the sight of people dancing in the aisle cast a magic spell on me—a spell that would never be broken. And I wanted more of that magic—much more. I made a pact with myself. From that day on music was my life.

Chapter Ten
The Change

After the talent show, everything seemed different. (I was fourteen years old). When I arrived at school on Monday, everyone congratulated me. It was like one day I was nobody, and the next day I'm this star, at least at Bennett High School. Cliques that were closed to me were giving me open invitations. Girls were smiling and almost throwing themselves at me. I could always get action before, but now I could get top-of-the-line, seniors and juniors. What a change! I loved every moment of it.

There was this girl I had been trying to talk to since I came to Bennett. From friends, I found out her name was Dorinda Carter. I finally got up the nerve to ask her for her phone number. She gave it to me without hesitation and we started dating. Dorinda was a very shy lady and I was completely opposite. We would see each other after school and I'd carry her books and walk her home. She was my first girlfriend.

After Dorinda, I started seeing three or four girls at a time. I hear Dorinda still has feelings for me, but I had to quit seeing Dorinda because she was too sweet and I wanted to play around. That excuse and macho attitude would follow me the rest of my life.

Chapter Eleven
Time to Move on

Living under the Gladdens was never my idea of having my own house, because we were constantly being told by Mom to watch our every move. We lived on Ferry Street, in an upper-middle class black area called Cold Springs. The day Mom told us we were moving out of the Gladdens, our house almost jumped off the block for joy. We ended up only moving about four blocks away on the same street; but at least we weren't under the Gladdens any more.

My life didn't change much from the move. I had been kicked out of Bennett for missing school too much. I tried everything; even sending my Mom to the principal, but no deal, they didn't want me back, period.

My brother Roy was doing very well. His legs were healed and he was at the top of his class in High School. I was proud of him. Camille had a couple of babies and was living over the old fish store on Ferry Street with their father, Jimmy. Carmen had gone back to prison, for reasons I don't know. Cheryl, Alberta and Penny were growing bigger every day. My little brother William was almost as tall as I was.

I enrolled in the most delinquent high school in Buffalo, East High. I'd heard they would hang the principal upside down out the windows. I mean, this school was rough, and all the ghetto gangs were enrolled there. I joined the band, playing trombone in the orchestra.

I had a few friends there and usually kept to myself. I was also playing drums in the Brown Cadet Corp. It was an all-Black marching band with riflemen and the whole works, bugles and pretty majorettes. Even before I joined East High I had seen the Corp marching, with their sharp uniforms, white hats, and big drum sound, and I wanted to be part of it. We won many competitions with our funky drumbeats and hip moves. We were sharp, I was rockin'. That was one of my most memorable experiences while growing up in Buffalo. I was about sixteen years old and was soon kicked out of East High—yes, the worst school in Buffalo didn't want me. It wasn't cuz I was stupid, because I wasn't. I just didn't like what they were teaching, and I was in search of something, I just didn't' know what it was. I guess I always had this feeling that my life was going to be bigger than High School. I went to one more high school called Grover Cleveland, mostly with Italians and Blacks. After leaving there I was through with school forever.

The Vietnam War had begun. Malcolm X was a hero, and Stokley Carmichael and H. Rap Brown were all talking revolution. Since I wasn't going to school, my draft status was at the point where I could be drafted any day. I dreaded the thought. Me and my crew were very Black-conscious, and we loathed the idea of fighting in a war for white America.

The house we lived in was big—big enough so everyone had his or her own room. It was right next to an after-hours joint, a place where people went to gamble, drink, smoke pot, fuck hoes and whatever else they wanted to do. I had these guys I hung with constantly: Danny Peeler, Bubbles, Moses, Truly—they were still going to high school, although I wasn't. We'd meet after school and drink beer and smoke grass. We were like the neighborhood hippies. We all had Afros, these round glasses and far out clothes with third World colors. When I look at kids now in the Nineties it's like they are trying to look like us.

Mom gave me the room in the attic and I fixed it up with couches, stereo, black lights, incense, pillows on the floor, this whole trip. Of all the guys I mentioned, Danny was the closest to me, maybe cuz we were both Aquarians and liked the same things. We were inseparable. When you saw one, you saw the other. If one got into a scrape with someone, they had to deal with both of us. We'd buy all the latest Jazz cuts and Rhythm & Blues cuts, get some weed, play our jams and just laugh. I mean we would crack ourselves up. It was a great time in my life, a time I thought would never end.

Chapter Twelve
Black and Proud

The year was 1963, and Junkies seemed to be nodding on every corner. Friends of mine who could have been great ball players or politicians were strung out. My boys and I hated junkies, and made a point to keep them far way from us.

The Black revolution was a movement sweeping the country. Riots were breaking out everywhere: LA, Watts, Philly, Detroit and, of course, Buffalo. Fires and gunshots were heard throughout my neighborhood, and we found it an exciting time. I watched as some brothers threw rock s into this big furniture and stereo store. People were running inside, taking everything they could get their hands on. I was no different. Danny and I walked right through the front glass and grabbed the biggest and longest stereo with TV and bar, and carried them motherfuckers out. Friends later told us how funny we looked carrying this long–ass stereo across the street and up the stairs to my house, laughing all the way. We made another trip, sold most of the stuff and bought grass enough to last us all summer.

On the street where I lived we had four major night spots where you could hear live music: The Bonton, The Revilot, The Pine Grill and The Royal Arms, all Jazz clubs where at any given time you could see Miles, Stanley Turrentine, MJQ, Pattie LaBelle and the Blue Bells, Jack McDuff, Chico Hamilton—the list went on and on. We used to press our noses against the window and watch these bands. I don't know what Danny and them were thinking, but I was dreaming of one day playing my own music in a spot like these, or maybe even somewhere bigger.

Malcolm Erni was a black minister and a good friend of my mother's. People in the neighborhood thought he was a fanatic, mostly cuz of the way he looked. He was a tall man, with a high yellow complexion and these thick glasses—I mean they were thick! He knew more about politics and Black culture, stemming from Africa, than any man I've ever met to this day. He would come see Mom, mainly to play numbers with her. He'd grown fond of me, and we would walk and talk for hours. Sometimes he would stand on the corner and preach about how Jesus was a Black man, and Moses and King David were the twelve tribes of Judah, all part of the Black race. I would listen attentively. What Malcolm said always made sense, and gave me a great feeling of pride.

One day Malcolm told me he was starting an African culture center where blacks could learn history—not the white man's history, but the truth— Black history. He would come by my house and we'd sit for hours. God, Malcolm taught me so much about my race. Sometimes it was too much to take in. I wasn't hanging out with Danny and the fellows much during these times. As Malcolm taught me more about Black History and Nubian culture I became really proud of my roots and heritage. Malcolm knew I was a natural revolutionary, which is why he wanted me to have this information. I was living as a ghetto hippie, with racist overtones, and going to the Afro Center to learn Swahili and Black history.

By then I'd started wearing Ocbotoms, which is an African shirt that usually consists of earth colors. I was also playing conga drums for the Center. We had a dance teacher from New York named Banjiowolla.

The Center began to come alive. The community subsidized it, with help from the State. We'd do concerts for the community, and one year we were invited to the World's Fair to perform. It was an exciting time for me, and I was learning a lot.

A woman named Amopuza Enze, a dance teacher for the girls, came from the African Ivory Coast. She was beautiful. Malcolm brought her to stay at my mother's house. I fell in love with her the moment I saw her. As I watched her dance, I was under a constant spell. She was in her early thirties, short, with a defined bone structure and this cute Afro. She was articulate, as well as talented. She would always compliment me on my playing. I became close with her son, Ty. He was a conga drummer and a motherfucker. We'd play for hours sometimes.

He taught me a lot. He knew I was in love with his mother, and he would just smile and say every man was.

One day we had a picnic on the beach. The entire Center was there. We brought our drums and plenty of food. We camped and partied until nightfall. It was really nice until we heard a scream—it was one of our dancers running toward us. When she got into the firelight, we saw that she was all bloody. The next thing I knew all these torches were coming our way. It was a crowd of white guys, too many to count, coming toward us.

Malcolm immediately gathered the young: me, Ty and the other teenagers. I didn't want to go. I wanted to rumble! Fuck it!

I was mad. But Malcolm ordered us to run through the trees to where the bus was. We did as we were told, for Malcolm was a non-violent man. As we ran I could see Afmet, our flute player, pick up a stick or something and yell to the other guys to protect themselves. I could see a few fighting in the distance. I was worried about Afmet and hoped he was all right.

We made it to the bus and crouched down in the seats. Everyone followed suit. Amopuza covered Ty and me with her hands. I could see torches and feel the bus being pushed side to side. My memories went back to the Perry Projects and running home from school, and all I could think of was that if Mom were there we'd fight the white motherfuckers.

The police came and escorted us back into the city. The bus was quiet, no singing, no chants, just the sound of weeping. How could they do this and get away with it?

That night something changed in me. I began to understand what Malcolm and Elijah Muhammad had been saying about white people being indeed devils.

Chapter Thirteen
One Bad Habit

After the incident at the beach, I kinda drifted away from the Center—not for any specific reason, it was just I had had enough and I missed hanging out with Danny and the guys. When I came back, things were a little different. Some cats in the neighborhood who I knew were heroin addicts were hanging with the guys. I had heard that Danny was messing around with Stuff, but I didn't believe it because he'd always been so down on it. When I got back on the scene I found it was true. He had a mild Jones, so did Moses and Truly. Bubbles wasn't hanging out so much cuz he didn't like the whole scene.

Anyway, I started chippieing, which means fuck around a little bit, first snorting, then skin-popping. Before I knew it I had a scab.

Danny and I would walk around looking for places to break into. We even had our ol' ladies let us break into their homes so we could get money for a fix. It got way out of hand. Once I went to jail for burglary and Mom had to have Malcolm come and get me out. I told Malcolm I had a Scag Jones, and not to tell Mama.

We figured the best thing to do was to cold turkey somewhere, and figured the best place was my auntie Louella's in the Bronx, Lou was a registered nurse and my mother's oldest sister. She lived in a neighborhood in the Bronx that was kind of like Spanish Harlem, and had a trombonist boyfriend. She understood about drugs and turkeying, and I knew she would help, but the main thing was she wouldn't tell Mom.

Arriving in New York was a strange experience. I was already starting to feel withdrawal symptoms, sweating and feeling chills at the same time, with a terrible knot in my stomach. It was the worst experience I've ever felt.

Lou locked me in an empty bedroom with just a fan while I turkeyed on my own. She fed me soup and checked on me regularly, and after a week, I was feeling more like myself. I always trusted Lou, and to this day I don't think she ever told Mom. For that she has my deepest gratitude.

After I got well I tripped around New York for a while, then went back to Buffalo....

Upon seeing my mother, she told me I'd received a new Army classification and was two steps away from Vietnam, and she wanted to know what I was gonna do about it. I didn't want to go to Nam cuz I was schooled by Malcolm that the war there was manipulated by the United States for political gain and it was no place for a Black Man. But I had to do something, so I did—I called Malcolm.

It was really good seeing Malcolm. He was glad I was off heroin, and I told him I'd never mess with it again. He asked me what I planned on doing with my life, if going back to school was an alternative. I told him no. He also was the first one to tell me that Danny had been arrested for robbery and was facing six to ten years in prison. I was grieved to hear it. Moses was selling heroin and an all out junkie. I wasn't surprised. Bubbles was still in school and Truly had gotten married. As Malcolm talked I couldn't help but think that if I'd stayed in town, I'd probably be in jail too. As we talked about alternatives, I sat in a daze. My life and my friend's lives were crumbling right before my eyes and there was nothing I felt I could do about it. My best friend in the world, Danny, was now a straight-out junky, and I wasn't going to go back to that, and I felt like I was alone and isolated from my old friends. At the same time I was disappointed by the pacifism and turning the other cheek shit of Malcolm and the Afro Center, and no longer saw it as a place of inspiration and encouragement. I was militant; I wanted to fight the injustices that I saw around me.

Malcolm mentioned how he knew some guys who had joined the Navy Reserve. By joining the Reserve, one could stay home, finish school, get paid and not go to Vietnam. It seemed like a good way of getting out of the war. Little did I know I was going on the adventure of my life.

I joined the Reserve, passed the test, and two weeks later I received a sea bag full of Naval gear, my career in the Armed Forces had begun.

Chapter Fourteen
Funk Uncle Sam

I was told to report twice a month, if I remember correctly. The first time I reported I had my stripe sewn on upside down. I think that must have been an indication of how my brief stint in the military was going to turn out.

I had joined The Duprees, a little singing group. We practiced daily. We did a lot of Motown tunes mixed with all the other stuff out at the time. When I wasn't singing with The Duprees, I had a little Jazz group I played drums for. We'd rehearse at my house in the basement, hoping to get a gig playing around in the local clubs. We had flute, sax, piano, bass and drums, and did tunes by Herbie Hancock, Coltrane and other Jazz artists.

While devoting my time to music, I had forgotten about my naval obligations. One day I got a letter that said I had to report for forty-five days punishment, active duty. My Mom cried as if I was going to 'Nam itself, but in my innocence, I thought it would be like a vacation.

Arriving at Great Lakes Naval Base was a scary feeling. It still had not dawned on me that all this military shit was for real. Getting off the bus we were told to line up according to size. The weather was freezing cold, and we must have stood out there at least an hour, freezing our asses off, while we were given orders as to where we'd be bunked. The barracks held about seventy-five of us, mostly teenagers from all over the United States. The only guy I knew was a kid named Gary who lived across the street. He was such an asshole, and a complete ass kisser. We were taught to spit shine shoes, how to shout, load and unload an M-1 and M-16 (which I already knew from my stint in the Brown Cadet Corp—I could do it blindfolded, which I found out later we had to do).

When we first got to the Naval base we were marched to a barber and he shaved us bald. Then we marched to a sink where we had to shave—I mean I had absolutely no hair on my face. So here I am shaving with this officer standing over me yelling at the top of his voice. It was the stupidest scene you could ever imagine.

We were taught to march, shoot, and to survive in the water using every part of our uniform for survival. That was cool, but most of the experience sucked. We were called "forty-five day wonders" by the knuckleheads doing ninety days active duty.

Once I was selected to sentry duty in the barracks. That consisted of watching the barracks for six hours with an empty rifle. Well, with my character, I was not the ideal one for this assignment. I watched for a while, then went to sleep. Some time later I was awakened by a kick, I immediately jumped to attention. By the time my commanding officer finished chewing me out, the whole barracks was awake.

I was sent to a week in Mickey Mouse. That's like a jail where you wash floors with a toothbrush, and eat nothing but potatoes. I did the week, then met the commanding officer of the base—lucky me. He immediately started spurting off about how important it was not to fall asleep on duty, because we could have been attacked. I almost wanted to laugh, especially since I had an empty gun. He went on to tell me how I would never amount to a Navy man. Nevertheless, I graduated and finished my forty-five days. I was never so happy to see my family and sleep in a real bed.

However, upon returning home I received bad news on top of bad news. First Danny was convicted and was serving time in Attica. Moses had died, supposedly he had sold some bad dope to somebody who had come back to collect. Moses was shot in the ass and bled to death because he didn't want to go to the hospital. It sounded like Moses. He was a good dude, and I missed him.

I started to see guys in the neighborhood who had returned from 'Nam, and their behavior scared me. Most of them had turned into junkies, and acted in the same way, like something had been taken out of them while they were over there. They had been turned into killing machines, walking around in their military shit with big ass stereos, and I did not want this to happen to me.

For the next few months I made sure I attended Naval meetings. I auditioned for a few talent shows sponsored by WUFO Radio in Buffalo. I even won one, singing a song called "Stand by Me" by Ben E. King. I got a chance to sing it on the radio, and even won a trophy plus five hundred dollars. I never thought I could make so much money singing. It was great getting paid for something I enjoyed. That was such a groove.

I began missing more Naval meetings. It was a joke to me. I never took it seriously. One day my Mom received a government letter, stamped and everything, which said I had to report to Rochester Naval Base and wait for the Enterprise Aircraft Carrier. I was going to Vietnam.

Mom cried. The girls cried. I even cried. I couldn't believe I was going to Vietnam. The day before I was to leave, Mom gave me a small party. All my friends came and wished me luck. I was going to need all the luck I could get.

Chapter Fifteen
Oh, Canada

Riding the Greyhound to Rochester I felt like the loneliest guy in the world, like a failure who was going off to a strange land to die. And for what? A silly-ass country where I and my people were persecuted? It wasn't right. I would never even get a chance to live my dream of becoming a musical wonder. Where did I go wrong?

Arriving in Rochester with my sea bag over my shoulder was a sight. I was a frail, skinny kid. Everything on me looked big. I checked into a hotel near the base and showed the guy at the desk my orders. He gave me a key for a small room with a bed, and that was all I needed. I immediately fell asleep.

After I woke up I went to the base, and the Captain read my orders and told me to report there at 6:00 am. The following day I awoke and called downstairs. It was 10:00am and I was late! I hurried and got dressed in my Navy blues and ran out the door.

I entered the base; I could see the blood in the Commander's eyes. He was pissed. He made me chip paint in a shower until 3:00 am. Chipping paint was a long, hard, tedious job that hurt like a mother, because the paint chips jumped off the wall, hitting me in the eyes and face. When I finished I had paint everywhere. Before I left, the Commander told me if I was late again, I'd chip paint till dawn. All of a sudden the Enterprise seemed like a million miles away. I called my Mom and asked her to send me a little money. She asked how I was doing. I told her things were fine, so she wouldn't worry. She was relieved. I also told her I was waiting for my ship to come in, then I'd be off to 'Nam. After that I fell into a deep sleep.

When I awoke the next morning, it was 11:00am. I looked at the clock I had borrowed from the desk and almost had a heart attack. All I could think of was chipping paint until dawn, forever. Suddenly I heard a knock and someone slipped something under my door. It was a telegram money order from Mom for fifty bucks. God had heard my prayers. I cashed the money order, went to the bus depot and bought a one-way ticket to Toronto, Canada. AWOL was my only alternative. Fuck this military shit! I had to go seek my destiny. It was now or never.

On the ride to Canada I stared out the window wondering where this adventure would take me. I was happy and nervous at the same time. But at least I'd be free. No more chipping paint and taking orders. That's all that mattered for me right then.

I was going on seventeen in a strange city. I had heard about Toronto from Canadians I'd met in Buffalo. They always seemed like friendly whites, not at all like American whites. Often they would tell me to come to Canada, because Blacks were so much better treated there than in the States. I walked about Toronto dressed in my Navy blues with sea bag over my shoulder, looking like a lost boy. People seemed friendly enough, smiling as I walked by. I didn't have much money left—a little over twenty-five dollars—and it was dark. I had always been fascinated by the Beatniks of Greenwich Village, so I decided to go to York Village, where I knew their Canadian counterparts would be hanging out. I asked a stranger where the York Village was, and he gave me directions. It was a Friday night and the streets were packed with tourists and village people. I could tell them cuz they all looked like beatniks.

Yorkville Village was on the same scale as New York's Greenwich Village: coffeehouses, artists drawing on the street, and outdoor cafes. It was very European. The Beatles had invaded the States. Cassius Clay was on his way to becoming the heavyweight champion of the world. Bob Dylan was a folk hero. And Rick James had arrived in Toronto. (It was 1964)

I walked up and down Yorkville looking at everything like a wide-eyed kid. It was beautiful, and all the people seemed so friendly. It was too good to be true. While walking with my sea bag over my shoulder I was stopped by these four drunken white American tourists. They began pushing me around and calling me names. I thought again of Buffalo during my youth. I started to get mad. I threw down my sea bag and pushed one guy back.

Just then three other white guys came walking down the street. They were wearing nice sharkskin suits. Although they were white, they were acting kinda Black. One of them stopped and asked me if I was having any trouble. I said "No." Then one of the guys who'd been hassling me said "Yeah, we're going to kick his black ass!" So one of the guys in the suit said "What the fuck did you say?" Next thing I knew, the guy who came to my rescue punched the guy who'd been hassling me square in the face. He fell down; his mouth busted wide open. Then my rescuer asked the other three assholes if they wanted some too. They shook their heads, picked up their friend and hurried away.

That was my introduction to Pat McGraw. We would become great friends. The other two white guys were Garth Hudson and Levon Helm. They were in a band called The Hawks, a white Rhythm & Blues band that played steady at a bar called Le Coq d'Or. They backed a rough Country Blues singer called Ronnie Hawkins. Garth and Levon's group would later play behind Bob Dylan, and go on to enjoy life as a group called The Band.

Pat asked if I was all right. I told him yeah. Then he introduced himself and his two friends. He asked where I was headed, and I told him I didn't know. I think he saw I was in distress cuz he asked if I wanted to come with them, and I did. We went up to this coffeehouse on Avenue Road, which was in the Village. As we walked along, everyone seemed to know Pat. He was what they called a Rounder—a Canadian term for hustler. We went to a coffeehouse where we had coffee. Garth and Levon excused themselves because they had to get back to their gig.

So me and Pat hung out. He asked if I was AWOL, and I told him I was. He laughed and patted me on the back. He seemed glad. He took me to another coffeehouse called El Patio. It was under the ground, a four–piece band was playing and the place was packed. The doorman let me and Pat in without waiting, and we found a table. The group played all R&B tunes, and they were good, but the vocals were terrible. I sat with Pat singing along with some tunes. Pat asked me where I'd learned to sing like that. I told him I sang a little back home. He told me to wait, then leaped up and whispered something into the bass player's ear. Next thing I knew the bass player called me up to sing.

I was so shocked that Pat had to force me to get on stage. When the band asked me what I wanted to do, I asked if they knew "Stand by Me." They did, and asked what key I wanted to sing it in. I said "E." As they began to play the crowd was still noisy. But when I started singing the noise died down until it was really quiet. When the song was over the crowd clapped and yelled for more. I looked at Pat. He was smiling like a proud father. I did another song, I think it was "Summertime." Anyway, it went over very well. When I was finished, the club had to close. The bass player came over to me and Pat and introduced himself. His name was Nick. He had blond hair and high cheekbones, and from what I could perceive, girls loved him. He gave me his phone number and told me to make sure I called.

Pat took me to the apartment he shared with Shirley Matthews, a Black woman. She was a singer in a very big Canadian band. Pat gave me a spare room to sleep in and told me he'd see me in the morning. I was happy, I felt I had found a friend.

The next morning I woke late to find Pat was already dressed. It was afternoon already. He told me he had to go meet Shirley for lunch and asked if I wanted to come. I said sure, put on some Navy dungarees and shirt. All I had was Navy clothes.

Shirley was a slender black woman in her late 20's, very attractive and very nice. Pat told her I was AWOL. She said, "Well, if you're on the run, you're gonna need a name. We'll call you Rick—Ricky James Matthews." She said Rick was her dead cousin's name, and from then on I was Ricky Matthews.

Pat loaned me some money, told me he had business to do and gave me the key to the apartment. He and Shirley left. As I walked around the

Village I seemed to fit right in wearing my bell bottoms. I always like to dress different, so this look was kinda cool.

I called Nick later that day. He invited me over to his apartment, which was right on Yorkville—116 Yorkville. I remember it to this day. His apartment was spacious with abstract paintings and art college degrees everywhere. When I arrived he was painting while a foxy nude girl with long blond hair modeled. I'd never seen anything like it. He asked me to sit down and offered me a glass of wine and a joint. It was good to smoke weed.

Nick excused the girl, then came right to the point, saying: "You sing good, man. How would you like to join my band?" I told him I would. He said to come to this local coffeehouse called El Patio for rehearsals that day, and that night I would start.

At rehearsals I jammed with the band, Richie on drums, Nick on bass and Mike on guitar. Nick asked me where I was staying. When I told him I was staying at Pat's apartment I got the feeling he didn't approve of Pat. Nick was a serious beatnik type, and Pat was a serious player, and I guess they were too different to really get along. Nick gave me some money, about seventy-five bucks, and told me after the gig to find a new place.

I couldn't wait to tell Pat and show him the money. He got me an apartment in the same building. So now I had a new name and my own place. I was on my way.

Chapter Sixteen
Whole New World

I was pumped and ready to work. The other band members seemed very excited to work with me, maybe cuz they didn't like Nick's voice. Soon after I joined, we changed the name of the band to The Sailor Boys. We all put on my dungaree jean stuff that I had got from the Navy. And the funny thing was my bell-bottoms and sailor hats fit all four of us fine.

We played all over Toronto as The Sailor Boys and gained quite a following. Fans would come wearing sailor stuff. It was quite a fad. The band started relying more on me as times went on. Nick and I were the closest of friends—or so I thought.

I started playing harmonica about this time and was becoming quite good. I became known all over the Village as Little Ricky. There were great players then struggling just like me in the Village scene—cats like David Clayton Thomas (who later would sing lead for Blood, Sweat and Tears), Gordon Lightfoot, Joni Mitchell, Kenny Rogers, The Band and Neil Young. All of us had one main goal: to be famous one day.

I began to see less and less of Pat. I heard he went out west, got in trouble and went to prison. I often tried to find him just to thank him, but to no avail.

The year was now 1965, and I had been in Toronto for two years. I hadn't seen Mom since I arrived though we would talk on the phone and she would tell me how everyone was. She also said the FBI were looking for me and the phones might be tapped. So we communicated mostly by letter. She was just happy to know I was okay.

Nick and I started feuding. I'd say that most of it was ego because he felt he had lost his band to me. I didn't care one way or another.

The English Invasion had taken off in the United States and Canada. Groups like The Rolling Stones, The Beatles, The Kinks and the Dave Clark Five were taking North America by storm. Most of the groups in the Village either wanted to look like these bands or sound like them. The English sound did have a certain vibe to it. You couldn't help but have to check it out.

I had begun listening to a lot of Classical and Folk music, along with Blues and Jazz. Being in the Village opened up all kinds of new musical experiences in my head. My favorite Jazz albums were Miles Davis' *Sketches of Spain*, Coltrane's *My Favorite Things*, all of Bob Dylan, and deep Country Blues stuff like Elmore James, Robert Johnson and Reverend Gary Davis. I would listen over and over to these albums. They would have so much to do with the future of my musical direction.

Being with The Sailor Boys was starting to grow old. I was tired of doing just R&B. I was getting into writing music, and I wanted to experiment. Nick had his own ideas in mind. Behind the group's back, he took a job with Jack London and the Sparrows. Jack was from Liverpool, with a strong Liverpoolian accent. They dressed in suits and tried to come across like an English band— and they were successful at it. They got a Canadian record deal and even had a hit record in Canada.

Bruce Palmer, Jack's bass player, was well known in the music scene. He decided to join us, saying he "Needed some funk," in his life. We acquired an organ player named Goldy McJohn. Mike was on guitar, Rickie on drums. With Nick gone and these new cats, I became really inspired. We did Jazz, Rock and Funk mixed together with hip arrangements of Top 40 stuff. Every club we played was Standing Room only, and our reputation was spreading all over Toronto.

The whole band would get high together. We smoked a lot of hash— weed was really hard to get—and sniffed Amyl Nitrate (like the locker shit people sniff today, but more powerful).

The band was making three hundred to four hundred dollars a night, which at that time was a lot of money, though by the time we split it we only got about forty bucks a night. We would play from eight until two, but didn't mind the hours. We were just happy to be playing somewhere.

Chapter Seventeen
The Mynah Bird Days

One night while we were playing a local club, this strange man came up to us. He said his name was Colin Kerr and he owned a Mynah Bird shop in the Colonnade, which was the most exclusive department store in Toronto. He said he wanted to manage us, and that he could make us stars overnight, but that we'd have to clean up some. (We were a pretty scruffy looking bunch: bell bottoms, boots, dark round glasses. I always thought we looked hip).

Anyway, we went to the Mynah Bird Shop to talk. He was from England, and we were tripping on his mannerisms, the way he talked, so proper and all. He had lots of money and was willing to spend it on us—and that's what mattered.

Colin (obviously) was a big fan of Brian Epstein, The Beatles manager. I say that because of the way he did things. First he got our hair cut in this strange style with an upside down V in the front. Then he made us wear yellow turtlenecks with black leather jackets, black pants and yellow boots. We looked like fucking Mynah Birds! It was funny as hell.

But fuck it! If he was going to pay the bills, we'd try it. Colin was a trip. One day he told us we were going shopping, so he had his limo take us to Eaton's Department Store, the largest department store in Toronto. So here we are in this department store, just walking around, when all of the sudden we see Kim, Richie's girl, with these other girls we knew, pointing and screaming at the top of their lungs—"The Mynah Birds!" Colin shouted for us to run.

So we ran all through the department store, knocking over things and all of the sudden hundreds of girls were chasing us. Colin led us to the limo and we all jumped in. By that time the car was surrounded by girls—a complete mob scene. Traffic was jammed. It was incredible—girls were screaming and crawling all over the limo. The police came and escorted us away. The limo took us back to the Mynah Bird Shop. Half our clothes had been ripped off our backs. Colin just stood there smiling. He told us to wait until tomorrow's news came out.

The next day we made the front page with pictures and everything:

Rick with Neil Young of Crosby, Stills, Nash and Young fame in Toronto

"Rock group causes riot. Thousands of girls mob downtown Toronto."

And we didn't even have a record!

Colin pulled this stunt two or three more times. Each time it worked. It got to the point we didn't even need our girls to start it off, just our presence would start a mob scene. It was just like The Beatles.

Rick with the Mynah Birds

Colin wouldn't let us work anymore. All we did was rehearse and rehearse. He paid us all a nice salary, more than we had ever made. But we were getting bored with not performing. Finally he took us into the studio to cut our first record. His brother wrote the two songs: "Mynah Bird Hop" and "The Mynah Bird Song," a ballad. We recorded all day and night, trying to get these two songs down, take after take. Finally, after a hundred takes, we finished.

We did this big TV pop show out of Hamilton, Ontario. When we arrived, there were girls everywhere. Colin had me sing the slow tune, "The Mynah Bird Song," to a blind Mynah Bird. He gave this big long rap about this blind bird before I sang, then put the bird on my hand and I sang to it while it shit all over my hand and dug it's claws into me. What a fucking day that was. I wanted to throw this little fucking bird out the window.

All this was gearing up to our first live gig as The Mynah Birds. We sold out four shows at the Colonnade Theater, but we never heard the music because the girls were screaming so loud. We did a few more gigs, then decided this was not our groove. We left Colin Kerr, but kept the name and the costumes, which we burned.

From then on we would make our own kind of music, and dress the way we pleased.

Chapter Eighteen
Starting Over

The year now was round 1967 when The Mynah Birds and I were in the midst of changes. So were other groups in the Village Scene. Nick had somehow gotten Jack London kicked out of his group, and had hired John Kay, this cat was hanging around the Village doing a one-man Blues trip. I had seen John on a couple of occasions and always thought of him as a nice guy. John and Nick shared Nick's apartment on Yorkville with these two gorgeous chicks named Uta and Solveigh. Uta was thin with this Twiggy hairdo and always wore these mini dresses that left nothing for the eyes to desire. Solveigh was even colder looking. Man, she was a hot bitch! Looked just like Sophia Loren—stunning. I always thought they spent more time with each other than they did with Nick and John. But hey, that's the way it was in those days—love the one you're with.

I sneaked across the border once in that time with a young Jewish cat named Morley Schelman. Morley was a filthy rich Jewish boy who looked just like Sal Mineo. Matter of fact, I had met Sal with Morley and we all hung out, tripping around local clubs and smoking this great weed Sal had. Sal and Morley had been friends and lovers for a long time, kinda like soul mates. It was funny watching them try to hide their homosexuality from me. Morley knew I wasn't gay and didn't want to blow my mind. We never talked about it. I never had a problem accepting someone's sexual preference.

Anyway, Morley and I flew down to New York City. I always said if you have to see New York, see it from the top. We stayed with his parents in a beautiful apartment on Park Avenue and took limos everywhere. Morley always carried a bag of cocaine—and in those days it was the real shit, none of this laboratory shit like today. I had only had coke a

couple of times before, and considered it a rich man's drug. I liked it a
lot, but could take it or leave it—at that point. One night while Morley
was out tripping, I called Jake, a friend of mine who I hung out with in
Toronto. He had a group called Jake and the Family Jewels and was an
excellent guitar player. He was a short, white boy with this incredible
Afro. He stayed in the Village with a Black chick named Bunky who
was also in the band. They were the happiest couple I'd ever seen.

Rick James & Hot Lips

Anyway, I met Jake and we went to the Night Owl Cafe to see some more
friends called The Lovin' Spoonful. The Spoonful did this Folk-Rag-
time–R&B thing that I found really interesting. I knew Zally, one of the
cats from the village scene who played guitar and sang along with John
Sebastian, a great harmonica player. A cat name Joe Butler played drums
and Steve played Bass. They had a lot of fun when they performed and it
made me long to be back with my band. After The Night Owl Café, we all
hung out, talking ol' times, playing guitars and getting high. It lasted for
two days. Finally, I told Jake I had to go back to Canada.

On my way back to Canada I couldn't wait to tell Bruce of this new
music I had heard. I got back in Canada with no problem, and immediately called Bruce. He came over and I told him about this new style
of music I had just heard, this mixture of acoustic and electric: Folk,

Blues, Jug and Rock all rolled into one. It was fresh, and I knew it was going to be big.

But first we had to change group personnel. I wanted a new guitar player, someone who could play Folk and acoustic stuff. At this time, seeing I wasn't playing every night, I had a chance to hang out a lot. So me and other muzos would get high and go club hoppin'. At this time I was seeing Elke, a German chick.

Elke was ten years older than me, and very, very hip. She was the first girl I ever gave head to. I had been seeing her for about a year and a half, and when she wasn't working as a waitress at El Patio coffeehouse, she was with me.

Elke, Bruce and his ol' lady Dale and I started club hopping. We knew all the owners in the Village, and they would let us in for free. We were all like family. We went down to a club called The River Boat to drink espresso. There was a cat named Neil Young opening up for David Rae, a friend of ours. Neil had something special about him. It wasn't his singing 'cause that part was very underdeveloped. Matter of fact, Neil sucked as a singer. But his lyrics and chord changes were beautiful. When he finished I immediately asked him to join The Mynah Birds. He said he had

Rick with White Cane

heard of us, and wanted to think about it. I asked him where he was staying and he told me over at Joni Mitchell's place on Avenue Road. I knew Joni and often she would let folk singers who were new in town stay and crash on her floor. Me and Mark, Joni's old man, were very close. Mark was a frustrated Blues singer who traveled around on his motorcycle with just his guitar, kinda like a minstrel vagabond. Joni loved the fuck out of him. But he never could stay in one place too long.

After a few days, Bruce and I went by Joni's. She lived over a coffeehouse called The Purple Onion. She was kinda homely looking and very quiet. Sometimes I'd drop in at The Purple Onion and catch her performing. She was, and still is, one of the greatest lyricists I've ever heard.

Neil was glad to see us. He had talked it over with Joni and another folksinger, Vicky, and they were both glad for him. He moved in with me and we began writing songs for the group. Neil's a Scorpio, like Joni, very passionate when it comes to music and romance and writing with him was fun. He also taught me a lot about playing guitar.

One night at one of our gigs, Morley came by with a bunch of people. One of them was John Craig Eaton. He and his family were the richest people in Canada. They owned (and still own) Eaton's Department store, one of the largest department stores in Canada. Morley and his friends were all high and having a good time. Morley told me he brought John Craig and his friends to see us for possible financial backing. Well, we played our set and loved every minute of it. John Craig and Morley came to see us a few more times. After each gig, John would smoke pot and become looser and looser. We were like his escape back to his youth. He was a conservative like his family, but around us he had a good time.

One day Morley told me he wanted to manage the group. I knew this was coming. He told me he would get us a record deal and get John to back us financially. He came through with both.

Chapter Nineteen
Motown, Here we Come

John Craig bought us all brand new equipment, guitars, drums, the works. We rehearsed up at his mansion. It was incredible, to say the least. Neil and I were writing some great music featuring a twelve–string guitar with Rock guitar melodies, and strong harmony hooks.

I remember the first gig we did with Neil. He took his first solo and leaped forward, playing away in that machine-gun style of his, very fast—but his guitar cord had come unplugged and he didn't realize it, and kept playing away. Boy, we fell out laughing. Neil would have these epileptic fits and we would have to keep him from swallowing his tongue, it was scary. It was like having this emotional baby and you always had to watch him. Neil and I were both very emotional and volatile, and when I had to get on his ass about shit, I kinda knew where he was coming from.

Morley had taken a tape of us to Motown. They liked it and signed us to a contract. We were all excited.

Before we left for Detroit I told Morley I was AWOL from the Navy. He flipped out and started screaming "Why didn't you tell me before?" I had no answer. He arranged for me to drive over the Windsor border in a car with a friend of his while the band flew directly to Detroit. I was nervous when we crossed the border. The Immigration man asked where we were from and I said Detroit. Morley's friend said Canada, and he was going to spend the weekend with me. No problem, we were let through. I was happy to see the guys, and they were relieved to see me.

Detroit was a weird town. It had no village section, and the brothers all wore processes with iridescent pants, Stetsons, Mohair and sharkskin.

My groove caused stares wherever I went. My hair was down to my shoulders and I wore corduroy bell-bottoms, mod jackets, and dark, round glasses. Brothers and sisters would stare. They didn't know where I was coming from.

When we auditioned for the Motown people on West Grand Boulevard, I was scared as hell. But I always would look cool. We had to play live in front of Smokey Robinson, Holland Dozier and Holland, William Mickey Steveson, Jeffrey Bowen and, of course, Barry Gordy. There were also ladies present, one was Tammi Terrell.

We did our set and they were all smiles. So was Morley. It seems Motown wanted to cash in on the English movement and Rock thing, and we were going to be the ones. As we played, they took notes. I didn't know what they were writing until after. Morley told me how they loved our original stuff, but they wanted to make some small changes in the studio.

We recorded about ten tracks. Mickey Stevenson, who wrote "Dancing in the Streets," "Heat wave," and other huge hits for Motown, was like our producer, along with Jeffrey Bowen, who produced The Temptations. Hitsville, the studio at West Grand, was this little house with an eight-track studio in the back. There was lots of security around cuz everyone wanted to know how to get the Motown sound. If they had only known how rustic it really was!

Mickey Stevenson taught me a lot about structure and voicing. At first Neil and I were apprehensive to let them fuck with our music. But after we tried some of their ideas, we were both pleased. Our first single was a tune Neil and I wrote called "It's My Time." It had an up-tempo, infectious melodic groove with a twelve-string theme that made it catchy. The whole company was ecstatic. We had a photo session where Tammi Terrell showed up. She used to just look at me smiling and say, "Ricky, you are too much." I was totally shy in her presence, cuz she had been a favorite of mine. Afterwards, we walked around Motown and were introduced to The Isleys, The Temptations and Marvin Gaye. They all looked at us and said, "Where did you get those clothes?" Little did they know they'd be dressing just like us in the years to come.

Chapter Twenty
I Surrender

From Detroit, the band flew back to Toronto. I flew to Buffalo to see Mama and tell her the good news. Buffalo hadn't changed much in three years.

I didn't call Mama for fear the phones were tapped. When I got home everyone was glad to see me. Roy was now on his way to college. Cheryl had a baby girl. Alberta (also know as Birdie) was bigger and prettier than ever. Penny was staying with the Gladdens. Al wasn't doing to good; He'd been in a couple of car accidents because of alcohol, and Mom was worried that if he kept it up he would surely die.

Mom and I spent a lot of time together while I was in Buffalo going to Jazz clubs and talking. I hadn't realized how much I had missed her. She seemed happy about the Motown situation, but afraid that eventually I would have to give myself up to the FBI. I told her not to worry—as if that would help. I stayed for about a week, and Mom drove me back to Toronto. Getting over the border was easy, especially with Mom.

I showed her around the Village, and all my friends liked her. She kept saying I needed to put some weight on my bones. (I only weighed about ninety pounds and was as thin as a rail.) I didn't tell her I was doing speed and popping pills every day. I didn't know how she would react to that. It just wasn't time yet.

When I got back Morley and I had a falling out over money. He had bought a brand new motorcycle and a new house. I knew it was our money, either from John Craig or from Motown. I had to kick his ass once when he jumped in my face talking shit about it. Neil, Bruce and

I were happy he was out of the picture—but along with Morley, John Craig was out too.

We wondered about Motown. It wasn't long before we found out. Neil and I called Motown and they told us they were holding back on releasing the single because of my military obligations with the Navy. They also told me that when the obligations were over, I'd be welcomed back to Motown. Neil and I both cried cuz we knew I'd have to surrender to the FBI and go face the music. Morley had ratted me out to Motown.

Mom drove up to get me and the following day we returned to Buffalo to give myself up. Bruce, Neil, Elke and friends all wept as I walked out of the door and got into Mom's car. Neil and Bruce told me they'd wait for my return. It seemed like the saddest day of my life.

The night we returned to Buffalo, Mom took me to see Miles Davis at The Royal Arms. Miles was great, as usual, with Tony Williams on drums. The Quartet was kickin'. It almost took my mind off what was to come the next day when I surrendered to the FBI. I couldn't believe it; I felt I was right back where I'd started.

Mom called the FBI early the next morning. Two white guys in suits showed up at the door and asked for me. Mom cried as they put the handcuffs on me. I was afraid and confused, mostly because I didn't know what to expect. We flew to New York where I was taken to the Brooklyn Naval Brig.

The Brig was at the top floor of the Naval Base, a lock–down facility with Marine guards. When the doors slammed shut behind me the nightmare began. I was literally dragged into the supply dorm, where I was told to stand at attention while one Marine after another walked up to me and punched me, calling me "boy" and "traitor." They especially made fun of my hair and the way I was dressed. They called me "faggot" and every other name they could think of. The head of Supply was a thick, Black giant called Corporal Dixon. He seemed empathetic at times, then at other times he was just like the rest. After they gave me clothes I was escorted to a barber where they cut off all my hair. I was bald headed, and God, I was pissed off. I spent the next two weeks learning the rules and regulations of the Brig. Then I was assigned to a dorm with forty other guys. We awoke at six am every morning, did push-ups, jumping jacks, sit-ups and other exercises. By the time the third month kicked in I weighed one hundred and sixty pounds—all muscle.

Corporal Dixon asked that I work in supply with three other brothers. Most guys in the Brig were in for either AWOL or for serious crimes like shooting someone or shooting themselves to leave Vietnam. Working Supply was an easy job, the easiest in the Brig. We also had our pick of the best gear—clothes, that is. Everyone wore the same thing. Your shoes had to be spit shined, your pants creased, you shirt starched. Working in Supply was cool. We smoked cigs all day and listened to the radio. Dixon found out I could sing and he loved to hear me belt one out. His favorites were Billy Stewart tunes and the O'Jays.

When I went to the court martial hearing, they wanted to charge me with desertion, which could mean life in military prison. Desertion was the intent not to return to military duty. But seeing I gave myself up, all I was charged with was being AWOL. I had been in the Brig for about seven months and still didn't have a court martial. Time seemed to go by quickly, especially working in the Brig. Eddie and this dude we called Doc hung out all the time. Eddie was half Black and half Puerto Rican. Doc was just plain Black.

One day while reading a teen magazine I noticed pictures of a band called The Buffalo Springfield. And there they were: Bruce Palmer, Neil Young, Steven Stills, Richie Furay, and Dewey Martin. They were named as part of the California sound. There was also a picture of a group called Steppenwolf with John Kay, Nick St. Nicholas, Goldy McJohn, Dennis Edmonton and Gerry Edmonton—all my old Village buddies getting ready to do well. I was happy, sad and pissed, all at the same time. I decided I'd been in the Brig long enough. Here they were, both my groups, and I was locked up.

Chapter Twenty-one
The Escape

For months Doc had been bragging about ripping off this dispersing ship for over thirty thousand dollars in cash. He said his mom had it stashed for him and he gave her about half and had at least fifteen thousand left. Eddie and I had heard this story for months, but now it was different. I wanted out, and so did Eddie and Doc. But how? Every Sunday the three dorms went to the kitchen for movie call. We laid plans for escape during movie call.

I had told them all about Canada, and they were excited about going. The only thing stopping us was money, and this huge iron door at the back of the Brig.

One Sunday when we were all in the Supply dorm Dixon told us he was under the weather and was going home early, and for us to close it down after movie call. This was the perfect time. The mess hall was in the front of the Brig and all three dorms were there. Doc, Eddie and I decided to roll this clothing cart, which made a lot of noise down the hall while two of us kicked the shit out of the door. We took turns at rolling the cart. It didn't take long before the door was busted open.

An alarm went off, but it was too late. We hurried down six flights of stairs, put on our hats and calmly walked out the front gates of the Naval base. We turned the block at Flushing Avenue and hailed a cab.

Doc was from Brooklyn so he knew the fastest way to go. He gave the driver an address and when we got there he told me and Eddie to wait. He ran in and was gone for a while. Eddie and I were starting to think Doc had been lying to us when all of the sudden he jumped in the front seat and threw us a brown bag filled with hundreds. We each took five.

We were free!

We took the cab to Manhattan, got a hotel room, then went out and bought clothes. We were sharp. Doc made some calls and his ol' lady came by with two bad-ass bitches. Then he called a friend of his and bought some drugs—coke, weed and heroin. I didn't know it, but Doc was really into scag. I snorted and smoked, but I didn't fuck with the scag. I was proud of myself. We spent about seven grand that week. Then I told them we had to split before we were caught, so we booked flights to Toronto.

It was no problem getting into Canada. We just told them we were only going for the weekend. We went to the Village and checked into a hotel. I called Elke and told her to bring some friends. She came with two gorgeous white chicks. Doc and Eddie were happy. Then Elke and I disappeared. We must have fucked for three days straight. It was so good to see her.

Elke told me I shouldn't show myself around, because she had heard through a friend that the police in Canada had been advised I might be coming. That's when I decided it was time to split.

We stayed in Toronto for a little over a week, then Doc, Eddie and I flew to Montreal.

We hung out in Montreal for about a month, basically just getting high and fucking bitches. It started to get boring quick. I talked to Mom, and she said there were FBI agents everywhere, but if I gave myself up soon they'd go easy on me.

Doc went back to New York, where his habit started to get the best of him. Eddie decided to stay in Montreal and become a pimp. I decided to go stay with Elke for a while, then give myself up.

I went back to Elke's for a month, mostly staying in her house and playing guitar and writing songs. Mom would call and tell me what was going on with the Navy. She said that Louis Stokes, my cousin who was a Congressman for Ohio, had written a special letter on my behalf, and that checking on my history with the Navy, it seems they were as anxious as I was to have me out. They told mom I'd probably have to do a couple years with a dishonorable discharge. I thought that was a good deal, so I told Mom I'd give myself up, and I did.

This time when I arrived at the Brig in Brooklyn I was like a star—the one who broke out of the Brooklyn Brig. I was escorted to CellBlock Confinement out of Population. I didn't mind because I knew it would all be over soon.

Not long after I got my court martial (where I was given less than two years), I got a general discharge under administrative conditions. Because I was underage when I joined, I only had like six months to do. The Powers That Be wanted me out of the Brig, I think for political reasons: I was famous for my escape.

Doc wasn't so lucky. Upon his return he was arrested and brought back to the Brig, where he jumped off a window and later was found overdosed from scag. It really fucked me up. Doc was my friend. Eddie, I heard, was still in Canada pimpin' and doing well. Most of my time I spent in my cell writing songs. It was hard without an instrument, but I managed it.

One day a gunnery sergeant showed up and asked me would I go to Portsmouth Prison to finish my time. He said I would have more time cut off my sentence if I agreed. I said, "Yes."

Portsmouth was a Naval and Marine prison in Portsmouth, New Hampshire. When I got there I was told not to tell anyone how much time I was doing because it might cause animosity among the inmates because I was short—on time, that is.

I worked in the kitchen. At night while in my cell I would sing to the prisoners. They'd scream and clap after each song. I felt so sorry for some of them. Here they were, most of them young like me, locked up for doing something stupid like trying to get out of Vietnam. There's no need to go into who and what their crimes were. I like to think their only crime was not wanting to fight for a country that didn't give a shit, in a war that didn't matter.

After I got out of prison I went back to Buffalo. It was good seeing my family. But I had changed and nothing seemed the same. I felt I could-n't relate to my ol' friends anymore. Buffalo seemed small, like a country town. People seemed shallow. I can't put my finger on it, but something was happening in me that I didn't understand. I was home less than a year, then told Mom I'd have to be moving on. I was in search of something.

I went to Toronto thinking I might find what I was looking for there. But all I found was the Village had changed and it was a whole new crowd. Most of my friends had gone: Joni, Nick, Bruce, Neil, even Elke. She went back to Denmark. Toronto seemed lonely. So I did what everyone else had done—I went to California.

Chapter Twenty-two
California Bound

When I arrived in California I had this incredible warm feeling all over me. The sun was bright. There were palm trees everywhere, mountains and beautiful women. I felt I had finally arrived home.

Bruce and Dale picked me up at the airport in a red convertible Mustang. The top was down and it was a beautiful day. We drove to West Hollywood, where Bruce and Dale had a house on Clark Street. Bruce was telling me about the band him and Neil were in. They had just released an album and had a single that Neil had written called "Nowadays Clancy Can't Sing." When I first heard it I wanted to laugh. It sounded like a piece of shit, although I never told him so. Neil was so proud. I knew it was going to flop, and it did.

Neil took me over to Steven Stills' House. He seemed likable enough—but he had an arrogant side I spotted immediately, like this was his show and he wanted everyone to know it. Richie Furay, another band member, came over. I really liked Richie. He was very happy-go-lucky. Then Steven, Bruce and I drove to Laurel Canyon to see Neil.

Neil lived in a log cabin in the hills. When we walked in he was wearing all this Indian shit. He saw me and we just hugged each other. He was really glad to see me. We talked for hours, reminiscing about old times. Steven sat laughing with his guitar in his hands. He never let it leave him.

Bruce decided it was time to leave but wanted to make one more stop. I said goodbye to Neil and we left. While at Neil's I detected an undertone of animosity between Steve and Neil, like a hint of ego, which I couldn't understand. Later I would find out.

Then we ended up at David Crosby's, who was a friend of Steve and Bruce. He was playing in a group called The Byrds. They did a lot of Dylan tunes and, like "Mr. Tamberine Man", I kinda liked them. They had sweet harmonies and used twelve–string guitar a lot. David was quite cool. We all sat and talked. David had this great weed. They also had this clear acid. I was offered some, but said "No." I didn't think I was ready for acid—not yet.

It was night and everyone decided to go to The Whiskey A Go-Go to see a group called Love. I remember getting there and not having enough money to get in. David came out of nowhere and said "Don't worry 'bout it." David was a good dude with a big smile. We would become friends. Our friendship has lasted till this day.

The opening group was called The Daily Flash. They kind of reminded me of the Jefferson Starship. Then Love came on, to my surprise, they had two Black dudes in the group. The lead singer's name was Arthur Lee and the guitar player's name was Johnny Echoes. I was not at all impressed by Love, although Arthur did have this certain charisma 'bout him, and the crowd loved it. I just thought if they loved this, wait till they see me.

After the show, Arthur and Johnny came over to where David, Bruce and I were sitting. They eyed me carefully, as if to say "Whose the new kid in town?" All I could think of was "You'll see, motherfuckers. You'll see."

My first day in LA had certainly been an interesting one. I had met a lot of people, and I was checking it all out. While staying at Bruce's, Johnny Echoes from Love and I became close and hung out a lot together, which was good cuz Bruce spent a lot of his time rehearsing with The Band, and I needed to see things, meet people.

I also started to hang with Steven Stills a lot. His house was a good spot to meet people, especially chicks. One night after spending about a week at Steven's, I was crashed out on the floor and I felt someone staring at me. When I jumped up here's this dude with his wrist cut, just watching the blood going "Wow, isn't this beautiful?" I called Steven. He got out of bed where he'd been with this chick he was seeing named Nancy and ran into the room. He screamed "What the fuck happened?" I said "I just woke up and there he was sitting in a lotus position watching his blood, going 'Wow!'" His name was Jim Morrison.

After bandaging Jim, Steven told me to look out for him, then went back to bed with Nancy. Jim and I talked until morning, drinking rose wine out of the bottle and laughing.

The next day Bruce came over with Dale. Bruce wanted to take me to Disneyland. So Jim Morrison, Steven, Bruce, Dale, Nancy, Johnny Echoes and I jumped in Steven's wooden station wagon and drove to Disneyland. When we got there they wouldn't let us in because of a dress code.

So we went to this place where they had bumper cars and drove them till night. It was so much fun that I felt like a kid again. Then we went back to Steven's where we ate and played songs. I was really starting to dig LA.

The following week was going to be a big week for Bruce. They were playing The Whiskey, and The Doors opened for them. I'd finally get a chance to see Bruce's group Live. I had heard they were hot. I didn't even go to rehearsals because I wanted to wait and be surprised.

That night Johnny and I hung out tough. He introduced me to this hot Black chick named Jade. She was into reading Tarot cards and thought she was a witch. It was cool. I just loved her sex. Jade had lived with this singer from England named Donovan, who I also met at Steven's. I wasn't impressed. He thought he was Bob Dylan. He was funny, and wrote cute tunes, "Catch the Wind" was a beautiful piece of music.

Charlie Green and Brian Stone managed Buffalo Springfield. Bruce told me they were interested in me. After meeting them, I decided they were just a bunch of New York pimps, and I refused their offer.

Chapter Twenty-three
Acid Time

The night Buffalo Springfield opened at The Whiskey everyone was there. I met so many people I can't even remember. As I sat upstairs with the band playing one of Steven's acoustics, Morrison walked up to me with this strange smile on his face. He sat next to me, humming as I played. I thought Jim had a strange voice and I couldn't wait to hear his band. They had no record deal, but they were shopping for one.

Jim and I smoked a joint. He asked me if I wanted some mints. I said, "Yes." He smiled and said "Open." I did, and he threw this little blue mint into my mouth. I should have known then what time it was, but I wasn't thinking. At first the mint was sour, but the more I sucked the sweeter it got. I thought nothing of it.

The Doors were a four–piece band with a bitchin' drummer, a real good keyboard player and a good guitar player. Jim was a whole different trip and I didn't know whether or not I liked him. He recited poetry a lot and seemed shy on stage. The Doors were my first encounter with theatrical rock. Until then I had always thought that a singer was a guy with a wonderful voice, I had no idea about stylists and attitude. Jim was a stylist, but at that time I just looked at him as a terrible singer, even though I admired the musicianship of The Doors. They had a Rock and Roll Jazz Fusion Sound. I knew Jim had a little something-something going on, but I didn't think he had a voice.

I started to feel strange. My fingers became numb and everything seemed bright and funny. The music seemed to go on and on forever. I was alone and didn't know how to get from the balcony to the downstairs—and didn't care.

Jade had been looking for me. All she could say was "Wow, Ricky, you're fucked up!" And I was. But I liked it. That fucking Morrison! I'd get him later.

I don't remember much about that night other than it was the most wonderful feeling I'd ever had. Jade and I made love on this ol' couch in the dressing room while Springfield was on. People came in and out, but I didn't care. I was free!

When I saw Bruce and Steven again they were all in the dressing room and it was filled with people. Jade and I sat in the corner. I played guitar while Jade sang. Bruce came over and sat with us, making these faces. All I could do was laugh hysterically. Morrison came over with his ol' lady. Everyone was stoned and nobody cared.

My first acid experience had been a good one—although I still hadn't really heard Buffalo Springfield!

The next night we all were at The Whiskey again. This time I didn't do acid and I sat downstairs, paying close attention. After hearing The Springfield I was totally impressed. They sang well, harmonized great, and the songs and musicianship was superb. I was especially impressed with Steven. He had a lot of soul for a white boy, and I was sure he would go far. Neil was cool, but Steven had fire.

I hung out in LA for eight or nine months, dropping acid and having fun. While hanging out with Steven and Nancy, I met a guy named Jay Sebring. Jay had become a multimillionaire with Sebring's Hair Products. He was very good friends with Steve McQueen, along with Sammy Davis, Jr. and one of the owners of The Factory, the hottest club in LA. He was short, handsome and very debonair. Jay had fallen in love with Nancy and had started to hang around the scene. Nancy was more Beverly Hills than Hippie, with her long black hair and full lips…she looked like she had a little Black in her…and she moved in similar circles to Jay. However she was still Steven's groupie. Jay would invite Nancy and Steven to all these Beverly Hills parties. Steven hated them, but Nancy and I would go, we'd dance and just have fun. It was like I was chaperoning Nancy for Steven—he trusted me with her. But the more we hung out, the closer we got. One day I told Nancy to ask

Jay to back me and I would bring a group down to LA that would blow all the other groups away. She did. And, just as I thought he would, Jay said "Yes"—providing Nancy went with me to Canada. I couldn't have planned it better. Steven agreed.

Nancy and I went to Canada. Our objective was to find the right cats and bring them back to form my group. It would be easy, plus Nancy was there.

Chapter Twenty-four
Busted

On the plane ride to Toronto all I could think of was how great it would be in LA with my own band. I already knew the cats I was going to bring down. We'd kick everyone's ass. Nancy was a beautiful girl, nineteen years of age with black wavy hair, long shapely legs, thick, perfect lips and large melon-shaped breasts. Jay had given her about five thousand dollars. We had weed and a few hundred dollars worth of coke. On the plane, we kept going in and out of the bathroom, sniffing. Finally, we went in the bathroom together. Our eyes met at the same time and we became animals, all over each other. We made love with her sitting on the sink. I fell to my knees and gave her head, when she came it tasted like wine, I must have drank a quart of it, it was so exciting. I had ripped her dress and she didn't care. We both knew this was coming, we had both tried in our own way to prevent it but it was impossible. When we got to Toronto, we rented a suite at the Queen Elizabeth Hotel. No sooner than we got in the room, we were at each other like animals again. I was in love with Nancy and she with me.

We talked about how we would tell Steven and Jay. We both decided we would play it by ear. Anyway, fuck it. Both of them had plenty of other women.

The group I wanted was playing at a club in the Village. There was a table set up for us and everyone knew me and was happy to see me. The group's name was the "Ooppicks." They were tight and funky, plus they looked good. Me and Nancy held hands while she nodded her approval. The owner, a woman, told me that someone wanted to talk to me. When I walked outside, two big white dudes grabbed me. I tried to resist but they told me they were the police and to get in the fucking

car. I did and they drove away. That was the last time I'd ever see
Nancy.

As I sat in the cop car. I almost started to laugh. One minute I'm with
the most beautiful woman I'd ever seen and the next I'm stuck in some
police car going down to the station. The two cops were silent. All they
had said was, "Welcome back Ricky." They were both sarcastic motherfuckers. They took me to the station and asked me a lot of questions
about former friends of mine, dope dealers and such. I told them I
didn't know what the fuck they were talking about. Then they asked
me about some clothing store in Toronto that was robbed. I told them
I still didn't know what they were talking about. Unfortunately, this
was not quite true. Before I had split for Cali, I had broken into a very
Mod boutique in the Village. I had taken French corduroy suits, English mod clothes, fly-ass shirts, pants, all this shit. I wasn't wearing
gloves, cuz it was a spontaneous thing, so I'd left fingerprints all over
the joint. All the time I was in Cali, the cops were looking for me, and
as soon as they knew I was back, they jumped. Then they took me to
my hotel, The Royal York, where they had confiscated some of the

clothes, a few of them still had price tags on them. Dumb, dumb, dumb. I was charged with possession of stolen goods and Breaking and Entering. When they took me back to the station, they took me into this empty room and told me to strip. When I was naked, they commenced kicking my ass. They punched me and said shit like, "All you niggers come up here and fuck our women, we'll show you." I tried to fight back but these motherfuckers were too big. Most of the punches were body punches, I guess they didn't want to show bruises in case the Judge might see. When I went to court, I was pissed. Man, was I pissed. I didn't have a lawyer and refused a public defender. I told the Judge the cops had kicked my ass, and I wanted something done about it. I also told him I was innocent of these bullshit charges. He asked me if I wanted my case to go to High Court. I said, "Hell yeah." I thought that if this case went to High Court, I could get out on bail. Wrong.

I was remanded with an Immigration hold. No bail because I was from the States. I finally got a lawyer, a friend of mine named Stan Wiseman. He told me the next time the high Court convened was nine months away. I almost died. Nine fucking months. Here I am in the Dawn Jail, a jail facility that had been condemned by the City. They were building a new part, but it wasn't finished. I was in the old part of the jail, cells you open with a key, two bunk beds, one little pot to shit and piss in, wood floors that you got down on your knees and had to scrub every morning. I was fucked. The only good thing about the whole experience was that I learned how to play bridge. Whoopee!

Nine months went by and I was released from jail, time served, and deported. Man, was I glad. I never thought I'd be glad to leave Canada. Man, was I wrong.

Chapter Twenty-five
After The Fall

The Immigration people dropped me off at the border where my Mom picked me up. I was really happy to see her, but something inside me died. I felt no motivation. It seemed my world had crumbled. I couldn't even call Steven and Bruce, I was too embarrassed. I just hung around the house moping. One day Mom said, "Why don't you go back to Motown and make some music?" So I called Mr. Seltzer, the Motown lawyer, and he sent me a ticket to Detroit. The people at Motown were glad to see me again and they all were willing to work with my development as a producer. I felt being an artist was out of the question. There were just too many great singers there. Motown put me up at a place called the Lee Plaza, a hotel right up the street from the studio on West Grand Boulevard. I spent most of my time learning, and I had a lot to learn. I wanted to be a great producer, and in order to do that, I had to study from the great ones. Norman Whitfield took an extra liking to me. He used to like the way I dressed. Norman had become one of the best producers in the world with The Temptations, Marvin Gaye, The Supremes and the Four Tops, just to name a few he had written and produced. I watched Norman like a school kid watched his teacher, picking up points on production.

I also attended a lot of Holland, Dozier & Holland sessions. These three cats had written and produced more hit records than The Beatles. I would visit them in the studio, and just watch in amazement how they would put material together. The way they constructed was just beautiful. It was like watching magic wizards, hit after hit after hit. I started building friendships with some of the artists—Jimmy Ruffin, the Originals, Edwin Starr. Me and Jimmy Ruffin got especially close. Jimmy was the brother of the late David Ruffin, with whom I would have a strong friendship in later years. Jimmy had huge success with a record called "Broken Hearted." He was offered lead singer for The Temptations but he rejected it and turned his brother David onto the gig. Well, the rest is history.

Once while staying at the Lee Plaza, I met this cute white girl from Toronto, of all places. We became very intimate. She stayed at the Lee Plaza with another girl, who was seeing Jimmy at the time. The four of us became the best of friends. Jimmy was married at the time with kids, so this affair was a real secret thing to him. One day, Jimmy told me his girl wanted to go to work for him and how would I like it if my girl worked too. In that way, we could pimp them together.

Well, I knew nothing about pimpin', and quiet as I kept it, I don't think Jimmy did either. We took the girls to Canada where they worked. We made good money, but I thought the whole experience was too inhumane for me. I had feelings for her, and the idea of her selling pussy was not at all what I wanted my life to be about. By the end I had three or four women working for me, and it was strenuous. Pimpin' is a twenty-four /seven job, and in my mind I was going to be a big star and make more than all these hoes put together. I put an end to that experience quick and vowed never to pimp again. Motown moved me to the Hilton downtown and I still hadn't done a session yet. But I didn't mind. I was living good and got a check every week just for learning. It was cool. After the pimp episode, I cut Jimmy loose and hardly ever saw him again. I think he knew that lifestyle was not my groove. I was sorry I had done it. I knew that I would make more money than that. It was tiresome.

Calvin Hardaway, Stevie Wonder's brother, and I had gotten real close. Calvin was an experienced writer and producer. We spent most of our time burning records and analyzing them. We also smoked a lot of bud. Our favorite composers at this time were Burt Bacharach and Hal David. I loved their stuff. Jose Feliciano had just come onto the scene with California Dreamin and we were really into him.

At that time, I had this woman who was a hoe, named Pat. She was older than me by about six or seven years and she was gorgeous. She would come to my hotel, which she couldn't have gotten into if I wasn't staying there, come to my room, jump on my bed and say, "Well little buddy, what do we do today?" I would usually be writing music or something. She would smoke a joint then say, "I'll be right back." She would leave my room with no money and start at the top floor of the hotel turning tricks. By the time Pat would come back to my room, she'd have a bosom full of cash She was a special lady and she taught me a lot about life. One day, she came to get me and we walked. It began to rain and I jumped in a building so I wouldn't get wet. She just took her shoes off and started turning with her arms spread, just turning in circles. Wow, she looked so beautiful. She told me how she had a daughter going to private school and that was her world. She had left the biggest pimp in Detroit, Bummy Turner, to be alone and she did quite well. She told me once, "Rick, everyone's a hoe, 'cept some sell it and some give it away." I would always remember that.

Pat and I never had sex—not that I didn't want to. But my respect for her was like that of a sister. She would take me and Calvin to all the hottest after hours spots. Everyone knew and respected her. She had this girlfriend named Pussycat, who was about ten years older than me. Pat had fallen for Calvin and Pussycat for me. It was a funny scenario. They called us their buttons, a word older hoes use for their young spouses. Pussycat and I became sex partners while Calvin and Pat fucked around. Pat would tell me "Rick, I really like Calvin," which made Calvin extremely nervous. She would also say Pussycat really liked me, which made me extremely nervous. Pussycat was a retired hoe who kept about ten cats in her home. She had made a lot of money, and all she did now was travel and play cards with other retired hoes. Calvin and I decided to leave them alone and fuck with some chicks our own age.

We hadn't talked to Pat or Pussycat in about two weeks. Pat would call and I would tell her I had to go to the studio with Calvin. He'd be there with me, with his finger over his mouth. Man, it was funny. One day while we were in my room fucking these two chicks, Pat and Pussycat came to the door banging away. They said they had guns and to open up. Me and Calvin looked over at each other while fucking and stopped at the same time. We put our hands over the girls' mouths while Pat and Pussycat cussed us from outside the door. After a while, they both just left. Man, they were mad. Pat later came by and apologized for her behavior and told Calvin she set him free. Was he relieved. I never saw Pussycat after that, mainly because I was too scared.

Motown signed a new group called Bobby Taylor and The Vancouvers. It was a white band, with Bobby Taylor a black singer. He could really blow. The guitar player in the band was named Tommy Chong, later to be in a comedy duet called Cheech and Chong. Tommy Chong wrote a song called "Does your Mama Know About me?" a song about an integrated couple. He was Chinese and his ol' lady was black. They had a cute little baby girl named Rae Dawn Chong. She would later become a pretty good actress. Anyway, Motown assigned the band to me as my first project. I wrote and produced this song called "Out in the Country."

I remember walking into Motown for my first session. Man, I was scared to death. All the original cats were there. I mean the veterans—Earl Van Dyke on piano, Dennis Coffey, Eddie Bongo on congas and Dupree on guitar, Pistol on drums and the legendary James Jamerson on bass. Wow, it didn't get any better for session players. I walked in with Paul Riser, my arranger, and I just stood there. The cats just joked and played around like I wasn't even there. Jamerson walked over to me and said, "Kid, if you want these cats to play, you gotta take over." Finally, I screamed, "Hey!" and they all became attentive. I said, "My name's Rick and this is my first session. I've only got three hours to get it. I know who all of you are, so if you don't mind, help me and let's get this motherfuckin' track cut." I looked at Jamerson and he winked and smiled. The session turned out great. "Out in the Country" was supposed to be their second single. Motown just put it on their album and I was hurt and disappointed.

Norman Whitfield told me in confidence, "Rick, you might as well try to do your thing somewhere else." I asked him why and he said, "All you'll ever be here is a tax right-off. There are too many obstacles in your way." He went on to say I was much too talented to suffer through Motown's political bullshit. I had an idea what he was saying.

At that time, I was hanging out with this bass player friend of mine named Greg Reaves who understudied James Jamerson. Frustrated like myself, Greg would take acid with me and we would listen to Hendrix and The Beatles. He was the only cat who thought like I did and dressed like I did. We connected when we first met. I had told him all about LA and it sounded good to him. We were both tired of Detroit. So we decided to go west.

Chapter Twenty-six
Going Back to Cali

When we arrived in Los Angeles, we checked into a motel on La Cienega and Santa Monica. We had very little money and no idea how we were going to get any. One day, while walking on Sunset, I ran into this friend of mine named Eddie Singleton. Eddie was a good-looking, older man in his mid-forties who had worked with Barry Gordy in the beginning of Motown. He had met this woman named Ray and fallen in love with her. Ray was Barry's ex and from what I heard, Barry got extremely jealous of Eddie and blackballed him in the industry. He was now in LA, trying to get his shit together.

Anyway, he remembered me from Detroit. I told him that me and Greg were in LA. to start a group but we were running out of money and would soon need a place to stay. He invited me and Greg to stay at his house in the Hollywood Hills, which he shared with this brother named Cassius Wheathersby. Cassius booked all the talent for *The Dating Game*, so you can imagine all the bitches that were coming in and out.

Personally, I never liked Cassius. I always thought of him as an Uncle Tom. He loved Eddie's drawers. Whatever Eddie said was OK with Cassius. Eddie had this way with people. Everyone liked him so I don't know what I would have done without him being there for me.

I started hanging out with these two chicks named Pam Louise and Nancy Leviska. Pam was a tall black chick who modeled. She was a Leo, six-foot-one and stunning. Nancy was a Cancer, blonde and very free-spirited. The three of us hung out a lot and would become the best of friends.

Greg and I started this group called Salt 'n Pepper with these two cats: Steve on drums, (who coincidentally played with Nick St. Nicholas in a band called Time after Nick was kicked out of Steppenwolf), and a guitar player named Mike. Mike was quiet-natured, but man, he could play guitar. Ron Levin managed us. He was a Beverly Hills gay boy, who spent more time dressing up and going out than managing us. He would later be murdered because of his involvement in an organization called the Billionaire Boys Club, a story that made front–page news across the country. Ron made a lot of promises he couldn't keep but he helped us a little financially.

Although I stayed at Eddie's, I was spending a lot of time at Pam's. She had this little bungalow filled with candles and Persian rugs, where she read Tarot cards and considered herself a witch. I never could understand my personal connection with witches—it was uncanny. There was a married couple who lived next door to Pam. They had wild parties on the weekends with acid, coke and weed and the parties usually turned into orgies. I had gone to a couple of parties with Pam and it was strange. If I wasn't with Pam, making love and tripping on acid, I was with Nancy, making love and tripping on acid. They would confront me about each other and I would just laugh. I wish I could have gotten both of them together at the same time, but it never happened.

One day, Nancy and Pam were missing for about a week and I began to worry about them. When I finally saw them again, they told me they had spent the week partying with Sammy Davis, Jr. and Barry Gordy. I was a bit jealous at the thought of losing my two favorite lovers—especially Nancy—Barry Gordy had taken an extra liking to her. In later years, she would have his baby, Stephen, and Barry would put her on Easy Street.

Me and Pam continued to hang while Greg had some chick he was seeing. Salt 'n Pepper had basically broken up, mainly because I lost interest. I just wasn't ready to make music yet. There was too much fun to have.

Me and Pam had a couple of friends who threw orgies, and one weekend, we went to visit them. While I was there, and Pam was off fucking or something, I happened to see this pretty little brown-skinned angel. As soon as I saw her, something happened. I asked her what she was doing there and she said Pam and the couple invited her. We sat on the steps during the whole party talking. Everyone was fucking and getting high, and we just sat on these steps, looking into each other's eyes. We left and went to her apartment. Making love with her lasted days and days. Her name was Seville Morgan.

One day Eddie told me and Greg that his old lady was coming from Detroit to stay with him and he wanted us to stay at an apartment that belonged to one of Eddie's girlfriends who was out of town. Troy Donahue lived next door and he and I became good friends. He had this dog the size of a horse named Gaylord. I'm sure Troy was gay even though he acted macho.

Eddie stopped by one day and told me that I knew the girl whose apartment we were staying in. He told me her name was Willow Timms. I told him I didn't know a Willow Timms but he said, "Yes, you do," With this funny smile on his face. "She's also known as Pat."

"Pat from Detroit?" I asked. I was completely blown away. Eddie and I both broke out. We called Pat and the first thing she said was, "You can't run—promise little buddy."

I fell out. She told me not to go anywhere 'till she got back. Wow, what a small world.

Some time later the phone rang. When I answered, a voice said, "Is Pat home?" The voice seemed familiar. He asked me, "Who is this?"

I replied "Her brother."

Then he said, "Tell her Johnny called." I thought nothing of it.

Pat finally came home. She hadn't changed a bit, still crazy as ever. Now she was in love with Eddie. She told me she was not hustling anymore. She said now she had sugar daddies. We snorted coke and reminisced. She asked me if she received any phone calls and I told her they were written down. I told her Johnny had been calling a lot. She jumped up and said, "Oh no, I forgot."

She got on the phone and starts talking, laughing with her hand over the phone. "Yes baby," she'd say. "Why sure, baby, Ok, I'll be right here waiting." She then hung up and busted out laughing.

I said, "Who was that?"

She said, "Johnny Carson." I thought I had recognized his voice.

"Somebody's got to pay the bills," she continued. She added that he was on his way over and I would have to leave for a while. I didn't mind. I had seen her work before and they didn't get any better than Pat.

I was seeing Seville more and more. I could tell we were falling in love. Seville had the ability to cook her ass off. I mean, there was never a time when I didn't wake up to a serious meal. That's how she kept me there. Whoever said the way to a man's heart was through his stomach was right.

We decided to move in together. It was the first time in my life I had ever lived with a girl. We got a nice one-bedroom apartment on Alta Loma with a pool and beam ceilings. It was my first nice place. Greg moved in with us and the three of us were like a family.

Chapter Twenty-seven
C.S.N.Y.

It was the year of Woodstock. Peace and love was everywhere. Most of my time was spent lounging around my pool listening to music with Greg while Seville and Greg's ol' lady would barbecue or whatever.

I had run into Jay Sebring and explained to him what had happened in Canada. He told me I should have called and he would have helped me. I told him I was too embarrassed. I asked about Nancy and he said he saw her for a while but then she disappeared. Such is life. He asked if I needed anything and I told him how me and my old lady had spent all our money just to get into an apartment. He loaned me a couple grand. I'll never forget that, Jay was a good man.

Me and Seville went out to celebrate our new fortune. I took her to the Troubadour to see my friend Richie Furay's Country & Western Rock band, Poco. They were really great.

While we were backstage talking to Richie and meeting the band, Steven Stills walked up. We hugged and I introduced Seville to him. Later we went to Steven's house. He had purchased it from another friend of ours named Peter Tork who was in The Monkees. Steven was enjoying his new found success with his group called Crosby, Stills and Nash. He told me Bruce Palmer, my ex-bass player, was their bass player and he thought Bruce was doing too many drugs and would I talk to him. At this time I did not have a drug problem at all, when I did cocaine, it was a special time, and I was never a heavy drinker. However, now that Bruce had some money and success, he was drugging out constantly.

He said they had tried out a lot of bass players including Harvey Brooks and had finally settled on Bruce. Steven was concerned because they were getting ready to play the Woodstock Music Festival and they were going to play the Greek Theater for a week or two with Joni Mitchell opening. Apparently, Bruce was starting to forget chord change and shit. It didn't sound like Bruce to me. He could always play no matter what shape he was in. Steven thought if I talked to him, he might straighten up. I told him I would try.

Bruce stayed in a log cabin, High in Topanga Canyon with his ol' lady, named Sally. Dale and Bruce had a baby together but she got tired of the whole scene and went back to Canada. I couldn't wait to introduce Greg to Bruce. They were both like brothers to me. Bruce had no idea Steven had sent me. Looking at Bruce, I could see Steven was right. When I walked in, he couldn't believe his eyes. It had been years since we had seen each other. I introduced Greg to him. Bruce started telling me all about the group—how many records they were selling. He was very excited to be a part of it. After all, they were considered a super group. I never told Bruce about Steven's concern. I just quietly checked him out. Bruce decided to go to Steven's but he was fucked up. He wanted to drive but I managed to get his keys from him.

When we got to Steven's house, Steven pulled me aside and asked if I had talked to Bruce. I told Steven to give me a chance, I was still checking out Bruce's behavior. Eventually, we all went into the rehearsal room, a cool ass space that had been soundproofed with Persian rugs. I sat on the drums, Bruce played bass, Steven played organ and Greg played guitar. We jammed for a few hours, but Greg never touched his usual instrument, the bass.

The next morning there was a knock at my door, and when I opened it, I saw Steven Stills and Graham Nash. I was kind of curious to see the Number One band in the country standing there, and wondered what they could want with me. They asked if I wanted to go to lunch, I said "Sure," and we headed down to The Source, a health food place on Sunset. Steven and Greg sat down with very serious looks on their faces. They explained to me that they could no longer tolerate Bruce and would I mind if they tried out Greg. I said no, I'd talk to Greg for them, we finished our food and they dropped me back home.

When Greg came home, I sat him down and told him what had happened. First he said he didn't want to leave me. I told him joining the Number One group in the world was the opportunity of a lifetime, and that he and I could always do something together later on. Greg and I loved that first Crosby, Stills and Nash album. We would sit around by the pool listening to it all day, loving the flavor of the music. That first album had been huge, and it had made Crosby, Stills and Nash into a Supergroup, but now they had to Show and Tell, because their fans wanted to see what was behind the hype. Woodstock would be the first time they had played together, and Steven, David and Graham were nervous, they only had a week to go, and Bruce, the bassist, was running around forgetting his parts. After we talked, Greg nervously agreed to join the band.

Later Steven drove us to this house on Shady Oak. Dallas Taylor, the drummer, was there to greet us and we all went into the rehearsal room. I took a seat on the floor and Steven gave me a joint and a bottle of pure pharmaceutical grade coke. I knew Greg would blow their asses away. He had this Jamerson style of playing—plus we had listened to the Crosby, Stills and Nash album numerous times and Greg knew the changes upside down. Steven didn't realize that.

Dallas started playing this beat, Steven sat at the organ and began playing and Greg joined in. Greg put some shit on their asses I know they weren't ready for. Dallas just smiled. Graham came in smiling, picked up a guitar and joined in. David walked in. It was good to see him. He looked at Greg with this big smile on his face, then bent down and hugged me. He just said, "Thank you Ricky." He picked up his guitar. It was magic. I could finally see what the hype was about. Neil came later, his hands waving in the air. He was wearing this big smile.

Crosby, Stills, Nash and Young were complete.

I just laid on the floor, fucked up, I was happy for Greg.

Chapter Twenty-eight
On My Own

I never saw much of Greg after that. He moved up to Steven's, which gave me and Seville time alone. I would still go to Steven's on occasion and just hang out. Me and Ty, Steven's sister, became tight.

The group recorded a second album called *Déjà Vu* and changed their name to Crosby, Stills, Nash & Young, featuring Taylor and Reeves. At least one of us had hit the big time.

Things started to get bad between me and Seville, mainly because I wasn't doing anything productive. I needed to make some money and fast. I began to hang out with this older black dude, Ron, from Chicago. He was a real Mack Daddy and a serious Player. He wore a big gaucho hat and leather clothes. He was a super-fly light skinned brother. He lived with this white chick in a million dollar home at the top of Mulholland. He dealt in counterfeit money, heroin and cocaine. He said he liked my style and we became constant buddies. I would hold drugs for him and he would throw me a grand here and a grand there.

One day Ron came by and told me he was going away for a week or so and asked if we would hold some shit for him. He gave me a bag of coke and told me I could do as much as I liked. He had this contraceptive filled with this brown shit—I found out later it was heroin. Well, Ron stayed gone quite a while. The large bag of coke had almost diminished to nothing by the time Ron came back into town. He asked me if I had his shit and I told him, "Yes, all of it."

I felt bad that I didn't tell him most of his coke was gone so I came up with a brilliant idea to put flour inside the coke bag to compensate for the loss. Bad idea.

I had also sold a bunch of his heroin to musician friends. I knew it was wrong but I needed the money. When he came over to my house, I know he sensed something wasn't right. He just picked up his stuff and left. He never called after that and I felt I had lost a good friend.

There was shortage of weed in LA and everyone was looking. A friend of mine, Dale, who I used to cop from, told me he needed ten keys. The only one I could think of was Ron. I called him and he seemed really happy to hear from me. I asked him if he knew anyone with ten keys and he said he would get back to me. Later that day he called and said ten keys would be no problem. So I called Dale, who lived in the canyon next door to Eddie. Dale asked if I knew the guy. I told him yeah. I'd bet my life on him.

Ron drove over to my house. Dale waited inside the apartment. Dale gave me the money, about five or six thousand, I can't remember. Anyway, Ron opened his trunk and I could see the keys wrapped perfectly with cellophane. There was weed in between the cellophane. I had already smoked a joint of it, and it was the bomb. Ron told me he couldn't give me all the keys I wanted cuz some had to go somewhere else. I think he gave me about five. He even let me pick them out. I gave him the money, he smiled and drove off. Dale came, saw them and was pleased. We drove to Dale's house to really check them out. Upon opening the packages all we found was newspaper with grass sprinkled over it to make it look right. Ron had ripped us off for exactly what he felt I had ripped him off for, no more, no less. He could have sold us all the phony keys. But he had his own integrity as a Player, and took only what he felt he was owed.

Dale asked where he lived. I told Dale I wouldn't fuck with Ron if I were him. We drove up to Ron's place but he wasn't home. Dale was pissed but he knew I wasn't involved. He forgave me and we parted ways. I wouldn't see Ron again until about a year later.

Me and Jay Sebring started to hang out again. He loved Seville's cooking, and she enjoyed cooking for him. One day Jay told me he was coming by my house to pick up me and Seville cuz he wanted to take us to see some friends of his for a weekend of fun. Me and Seville had gotten fucked up the night before snorting coke and drinking wine and when Jay came over I wouldn't get out of bed. I can remember him standing at the end of my bed trying to wake me up, but I was too gone to talk, and just waved at him.

Seville said "He can't move Jay, he can't get up. You'll have to go without him."

I managed to say, "I'll see you when you get back, Jay."

Jay smiled and shrugged, "Your going to miss a great time, Rick." Then he walked out, and I fell back asleep.

A few days later I read he had been murdered along with Sharon Tate and others. I was shocked. All I could think about was that I was supposed to be there. I remember thanking God. I also remember thinking of Jay and how nice he was. Why Jay, I wondered. After Jay's death I realized how precious life was, here today and gone the next.

I ran into some friends from Canada—the group me and Nancy were gonna bring down. They had done an album for Capitol and it didn't do very well. Their manager was an asshole who was ripping them off. When I started to hang out with them, the group told me they were broke and felt the bass player, Neil, and his girlfriend were in cahoots with the manager.

Neil's girlfriend's name was Lynn Carey and her father was McDonald Carey the actor. I asked the group why they didn't get rid of Neil, his bitch and Morley the manager. They said they had no equipment because Morley owned it all and Morley was paying their rent at a hotel. They asked for my help and I told them they would have to stand on their own two feet. Be men and get rid of these people. They decided they would, and finally, they did.

Me and Seville decided to split up, just for a while. I needed time to think. Here were these three musicians about to be kicked out of their hotel. They had listened to me tell them to get rid of their asshole manager. They had no equipment, no money and soon no place to live. I guess I felt responsible for them.

Chapter Twenty-nine
The New Salt 'n Pepper

Steven Stills gave me a couple thousand dollars and I gave the guys some money to pay a weeks' rent at the hotel. But how long would that last? One night we all took a walk around Hollywood, just to take our minds off the pressure. We stopped at a hamburger take-out called "Orange Julius" on Santa Monica. While we stood there eating, these chicks came by and gave us this piece of paper. They were really fine, so we decided to check the paper out. It said something about Buddhism and chanting. There was a number with a Beverly Hills address, so we decided fuck it, what did we have to lose?

We were using a friend of mine's van. His name was Chris and he was a road-man for CSNY. He was also a good bass player. We drove to the address. When we entered the house we heard this loud groan. It was one of the strangest sounds I've ever heard. It never stopped.

Inside, there were all these people sitting on the floor, eyes closed, chanting. Someone told us to sit down and we did. After the chanting was done, people got up one by one and started telling the others these stories of what chanting brought into their lives. They were all bubbly and smiling. Each one told of how they wanted this and that and after chanting they received it. Some had beads like rosary beads only different and a Gohansen, a little altar that you pray to in chanting.

We listened to everything and when they started chanting again, me and the guys looked at each other and started chanting, too. We knew exactly what we were chanting for.

After we were through chanting, we had this kind of natural high. We had all chanted for a house, musical equipment and success. We were all in accord. As soon as we got to the hotel we chanted a few hours more. The next day Eddie Singleton called me to see how I was doing and I told him I had a group but we had no equipment. He told me he knew a black R&B group who were going to Japan for about eight or nine months and needed someplace to put their equipment, I almost fell over. They had a Hammond B3 organ exactly what my guy played. It was uncanny. Eddie said it would be perfect. We could keep the equipment and use it. But we still needed someplace to stay.

That night I saw Pam who told me that Nancy was living with Barry Gordy. I was happy for her. I told her what I was up to and if she knew anyone who had a house for rent. She told me a friend, a new actress named Katherine Ross, was renting out her house in the Valley. The house was private with a separate garage that could be converted into a rehearsal studio. I couldn't believe it! Equipment and a house all in one week. We thought about chanting some more, but we never did.

We called the group Salt 'n Pepper. I just loved that name. I always thought a band with a name like that couldn't go wrong. At this time I was still experimenting in sounds and textures. This group could do it all, Classical, Jazz, Rock, Funk, Latin and Country. They were technicians.

I was writing different shit in those days. The band consisted of Hammond organ, guitar bass and drums. I was playing guitar, congas and percussion and sometimes I'd switch to bass. I spent most of my time experimenting. I just wanted to try new sounds, new grooves. There was so much I wanted to say and I had so many ways to say it. I was digging playing with these cats because they were real musicians. I was doing rock and roll, blues… all that shit.

The keyboard player was named Eddie Roth. He was an organ wizard and he could really play the foot pedals, something a lot of organ players don't do. There was no music Eddie wasn't up on. He also played a hell of a flute.

David Burt played guitar. Jazz and Rock were his forte. Pit him against Ali Dimeola and John McLaughlin and I bet David would win.

Coffey Hall played drums. Being a drummer myself, I know drummers. This boy could backstick on a bottle top. He could do rolls with one finger that would take cats three hands to do.

Chris Sarnes was a bass player who was like a rock, steady and earthy. He taught me a lot about the merits of simplicity in music and the bass.

So you see I had a lot of room to stretch out. Everywhere we played in LA we fucked audiences up with our musicianship. In those days I wasn't writing grooves, I was into technical shit. We wanted to show off the group's individual musicianship and that's what we did.

When the group Yes first played at the Whiskey A Go Go, we opened up for them. By the time Yes came on, we had three standing ovations. After the show Chris Buford, their drummer, was getting lessons from Coffey, and their guitar player, Steve Howe, was asking Dave shit. We made those motherfuckers work all week. Their manager told me after the gig was over he had never seen a band make his boys work so hard. It was a great compliment. Our musicians were seriously qualified.

While playing in Topanga Canyon, Neil Young used to come see us all the time. I played one of his compositions called "Cinnamon Girl," which blew him away. It was quite a different arrangement than his. He made his manager, Elliot Roberts, come see us. At that time Elliott had Jackson Browne, Joni Mitchell, CSNY, America, and was getting ready to take on the Eagles. He signed us, but he never had enough time for us. So he gave us to Bill Graham to handle.

Bill flew us to San Francisco where we played the Fillmore with Jethro Tull on their first American tour. We opened for a lot of acts in those days—Allman Brothers, Boz Scaggs, Chicago, Fairport Convention, BB King– and we still didn't have a record deal. I was beginning to think we 'd never get an album deal.

One day we got a call from Phil Walden who managed the Allman Brothers. He was interested in signing us and Atlantic Records was interested in us as well. I was geeked. They had seen us with the Brothers and liked what they saw.

Phil sent one of his go-fors from Macon to sign us. The guy was named Bunky Oddems—is that a Country name or what? He looked just like his fucking name. Anyway, Atlantic sent the legendary Tom Dowd to our house to hear our sound. Tom was renowned for his production work with Aretha Franklin, Otis Redding, Sam and Dave, Wilson Pickett and The Allman Brothers. However, in my mind he was an engineer turned producer. I felt he only had so much talent. I mean the acts were motherfuckers and so was the studio band—the Atlantic Rhythm section. You can't beat 'em. That white boy just fell into a good thing.

Anyway, he came to our house, listening with his fucking ear right up to the amplifiers and he was looking under the drums. I was wondering what the fuck he was trying to find. Finally, he shook his head and said, "Yeah."

I was not impressed by the famous Tom Dowd. He was being ridiculous. I don't know what he was up to. Our bass player, Chris and I had some disputes so I fired his ass. I hired this awesome bass player named Ron Johnson. Ron later played that bad-ass Carlos Santana and Buddy Miles, *Live in Hawaii* album. Ron was an Aries and just like his sign, he was filled with fire. Now we had the complete group.

We headed for Miami to start work on our album, but we needed some things first. The house we rented had no air conditioning and we needed a rental car. We also needed some special equipment. While buying our equipment they had to call Jerry Wexler, another Atlantic producer, off his fucking yacht to sign our order. He was pissed that we were interfering with his yacht time. I almost told him to kiss my Black ass. That was equipment we needed.

Whenever we needed money we got a run around from Phil Walden. Finally, I told them if they were gonna treat us like slaves, *fuck them*! Phil Walden was zooming us. I don't know to this day how much we got as an advance, cuz we never saw it. They let us out of our contract.

After only a month in Miami, we were back in LA.

Chapter Thirty
Papa Rick

Salt 'n Pepper continued to play, but once we were back in LA I was two seconds away from saying fuck it. I mean I really felt like packing it in. Seville and me were back together and we were very happy. It seems absence does make the heart grow fonder.

We moved off Alta Loma into a cheaper place in Hollywood on Yucca and Argyle—a little studio. We didn't have much furniture, but with Seville we didn't need it. She'd find boxes and shit on the street and by the time she was finished it looked like a million bucks. She always kept lots of flowers and plants around. She was a hell of a woman.

One day Seville came home from the doctor's and told me she was pregnant. I was never happier. I had wanted to wait 'till I was rich and famous to have kids. Well I wasn't rich and I damned sure wasn't famous, but I accepted the challenge and responsibility. My daughter Ty was born. She was beautiful. I used to watch her sleep for hours. She was Daddy's little girl. She would look up at me and crack her big, wide smile. Wow! I remember it like it was yesterday. Money was tight— almost nil in fact. Ty was almost two now and Seville had never been to my hometown. So I decided to take my girl and baby home to see Grandma. Buffalo was a welcome sight.

Buffalo had changed. Most of the clubs had closed down. Malcolm had moved to New York, Danny was still doing time. Roy was at the top of his class in college. Cheryl had moved to Cleveland with my uncle and Camille. Penny and William were young adults. Alberta had her own apartment and spent most of her time in church. Al was still having car accidents and surviving–God, he was amazing.

And Mom—well she still played her numbers and ran around like a field mouse. Every one loved Seville and Ty and Mom was happy to be a grandmother for the second time.

We stayed in Buffalo for a few months. Then I received word that Morley Schelman had died in a motorcycle accident and my ex-girl, Elke, was in the hospital dying of lung cancer. I gave Seville an excuse for going to Toronto—business or something. She wanted to stay with Mom anyway because they were getting to know each other.

I drove to Toronto with a friend. It was no problem sneaking in. They had no pictures at the border. It was like two black dudes going over for a few days. Once in Toronto, I went to the hospital where I met Elke's parents and her brother, Henry. They were nice people. Elke had just come out of some kind of coma, her mother brought me in and Elke recognized me immediately. She had lost a lot of weight and her cute little pixie hair cut had all but vanished. The doctor told me I couldn't stay long because Elke needed sleep. She held my hand and I began to cry. I just couldn't help it, seeing her lying so helpless.

She whispered that I had been in her prayers. I told her about Seville and Ty and she cried and said I deserved happiness. She told me she dreamed I was a big star and everyone loved me. In her dream I had a Rolls Royce and a big house with people everywhere but I looked so sad and lonely that she worried about me.

I told her I was a long way from being a star and I still didn't even own a car. She just smiled. When me and Elke were together, I used to tell her I would buy her a Cadillac and clothes when I made it big. She told me in Europe you buy Mercedes and Rolls Royces. When she had told me how much they cost, I was sure I'd never be able to afford it.

I told her she'd be out of bed in no time. She whispered that she didn't think so. I kissed her, told her I'd pray for her and left. Elke died later that week.

Bruce was in Toronto and we were hanging out together. Toronto had changed a lot. The Village was mostly cafes and boutique shops. Most of the coffee-houses had closed down. One night, me and Bruce went to a club called On The Bar. There was a blues band playing. I couldn't remember ever meeting them in Toronto before but they all knew me. They called me on stage to jam and we played for about an hour. I had a good time. They were all good Blues players.

When I sat down, I noticed this chick looking at me—staring would be a better word. This chick was fine—white with big brown eyes, really sexy lips and a serious body. I noticed her checking me out so I waved my finger for her to come sit down. She waved for me to come sit down. This went on for a few minutes, both of us laughing. Finally, she came over and sat down. Her name was Kelly. She was Canadian-English and I was attracted to her in a way I had never been with any other woman—and I had known a few. She left the crowd she was sitting with and hung out with us the rest of the evening.

Bruce, me, Pat Little, a drummer, and Kelly went to another spot and jammed. At the end of the night, Kelly came back with me to where I was staying. We made love every kind of way I can think of. We also created some new ways—I was whipped.

She stayed with me all night and most of the day. Then she left for work. I counted the hours before I would see her again. I had been in Canada for about a week when Seville called and told me her mother had taken sick and would I mind if she and the baby went back to LA. I said cool, I'd meet them there. I would miss Ty and Seville but Kelly had me in this weird trance where all I thought about was her.

I stayed in Toronto for about four months and decided I would stay for a while, illegal or not. Besides, Kelly was there, and we saw each other every single day. For the entire time I was up there we made love constantly. I had told Kelly about Seville, and she sympathized with Seville. I also asked Kelly if she thought I should try to make it work with Seville. Kelly told me I owed it to the baby and I agreed.

Kelly and I decided not to see each other anymore until I decided what to do. Seville and Ty came to Toronto to stay with me in this apartment in a big, old house where I was paying by the week. I told Seville about Kelly and she was not happy at all. She told me of some guy she had met and I was pissed. We tried to make things work but we were faking our feelings. Finally, one day she just left me, baby and all. I was hurt, but hoped she would be happy.

Chapter Thirty-one
My First Big Band

By now I was pretty well versed in a lot of different kinds of music—Blues, Jazz, Rhythm & Blues, Latin, Classical, Folk, Afro, Ragtime, Reggae and Rock. I had played them and schooled myself well. The only music I hadn't experimented with was big band music. I had never had a big band and I wanted one BAD. A band with a fat horn section. I had heard big bands when I was growing up—Gil Evans, Dizzy and his band, Kupra, Benny Goodman and I always loved the sound of horns, trumpets, bones, saxes—just something about it.

Kelly and I had rented this old Victorian house, and fixed it up. We stayed there with Pat Little, a drummer friend of mine who was playing with Van Morrison at the time. A lawyer friend of mine, Stan Wiesman, started to hang out with me regularly. He was a straight looking guy with glasses who had started smoking hash and weed and snorting coke. He was being turned on by sex, drugs and Rock and Roll, so much so he hardly spent time with his wife Sandra and his four kids. Eventually Sandra divorced him because of it. Stan decided he wanted to invest some money into me and a band. So I put together my first big band, fourteen pieces, and it was hot. I called it the White Cane. Some people thought it had something to do with cocaine but it didn't.

Anyway, he flew me and Kelly and the band to LA to get a record deal, and it wasn't long before I did. MGM records signed us and gave us two hundred and fifty thousand dollars, which was OK in those days. The only other group MGM really had at the time was their pride and joy, The Osmond Brothers. Mike Curb signed us personally. He was this white guy whom Time Magazine and Newsweek called a wonder boy because of all the money he made for MGM this particular year.

The only thing I ever wondered about Mike Curb was why in the fuck anyone hired this little fuck and left him in charge of anything. He had this funny little haircut, like someone put a bowl on his head. He had photographs of him and that asshole president Richard Nixon. I always thought Mike had hidden ambitions to be president.

Anyway, Mike signed us. From the first day I met him I felt this ongoing doom. Mike hired this other asshole to produce us named Jimmy Inner. Jimmy was this New York Italian producer. He had tasted fame with the Raspberries Rock band and some other schmucks. I never liked him from the first day I saw him. You can't trust a producer who wears a toupee and grins all the time; Jimmy had this big, Cheshire-cat smile and was known as Jimmy "the Tooth" Inner.

He took us in Village Recording Studios to record the album. We had good arrangements and the band was tight, but, like a fool, I let Jimmy have complete control. He absolutely massacred our music and fucked up the entire album. After that experience, I decided I would never let anyone, especially a no-good, untalented, toupee-wearing schmuck like Jimmy "the Tooth" Inner, produce me. From then on, I'd produce myself.

Needless to say, the album came out and failed miserably. Billboard said they thought the band had great potential with brilliant ideas, but the production sucked. I agreed. We toured with BB King but then I said I've had it. We went back to Toronto with another year fucked.

Me and Kelly moved into an apartment. I had fallen head over heels for her and the feeling was mutual. I would have given my life for her. Her parents never cared for me much. They weren't so much racist, but just felt my life was too up and down for their daughter. I had to agree. She deserved better. Some day I was going to make it, just for Kelly.

Chapter Thirty-two
The Drug Smuggler

Kelly and I did everything together. We were partners in crime. By now I had no job, and the biggest agency in town was mad at me for calling one of their bosses a racist punk. I was right in doing so. This guy did not want to book black people. If he did, why were there so many of us in Toronto out of work? He especially was afraid of me because I would speak out—a fact that would get me in a lot of trouble in years to come. I always was a rebel, and stood up for the under-dogs, even when I was young.

Kelly and I barely paid our rent and hardly had food to eat. Sometimes we would do these scams. She'd get dressed up all sexy and walk into a bank. She would pick out a dude in the Loan department, tell him a sob story, and ask to borrow two to five thousand dollars. She'd tell him where she worked, and that she'd just started there. Meanwhile, the number she'd give him would be to our apartment. I'd answer when he'd call in a very distinguished voice and say "So and So's Place." I then verified she worked there. They'd usually accept that, and give her the loan.

Canadian banks were a lot easier to work than American banks. This scam enabled us to buy a car and pay rent. Eventually Kelly got popped and had to make installment payments to the banks. It taught me to never over-do a good thing.

Me and Kelly were smoking a lot of hashish in those days. It was black hash from Nepal. That stuff was a bitch cuz it was opiated, which really made it strong. Hash dealers couldn't keep the shit and the demand for it was making dealers rich.

A friend of mine named Bill and this black dude named Donny Detroit had smuggled a bunch of this shit and made a bunch of money.

Stan and I were impressed enough with this story to inquire about where we had to go, and what we had to do to score the hash. After a bit of research, Kelly and I decided to go over to India and bring the hash back. We were both wild in those days and weren't afraid to try anything at least once.

Kelly and I arrived in India and checked into the Oshaka Hotel, a large new hotel in New Delhi that had just opened. We checked in and this Indian kid, our bellhop, was a little fast-talking son of a bitch. I think he knew why we were in India. One of the first things he asked was where we were from. We said Canada. He then went on to tell us he had met and done some business with this black guy named Donny Detroit. I told Kelly this world was too small.

Living in India was extremely cheap. We got a one bedroom with air conditioning, and kitchen for less than one thousand rupees a day, which was less than fifty dollars a day. The hotel had a swimming pool and a night-club with food you could eat without catching dysentery.

We gave the bellboy a nice tip. He happened to see a bottle of Chivas Regal and asked for it, I made him promise that if I gave it to him, he'd be in my debt forever. He smiled as he said, "Yes Sahib." That Indian was the happiest motherfucker in the world when he got that scotch. Kelly and I had definitely made a friend.

We tripped around in New Delhi, I had never seen so much poverty in my life. I mean, here were these people starving on the street, while these cows that they considered sacred walked freely, fat as can be, all over the city. Compared to this every black in the ghetto was lucky: we saw children crawling on the street cuz their parents had broken their legs so they could beg. This one family pulled us into their house on a holiday, put flowers around our necks and wrists, and sat us down in front of a TV that showed only the faintest picture through blurriness and static. Everyone in the family was sitting around, smiling, looking at this shit. Cars, buses and these little two-seater cabs were everywhere. The law was if you hit a cow your ass was grass, yet half the people we saw were starving. If nothing else, it made me appreciate America more, even with all the shit I and my people had to deal with.

I would consistently tell my driver to slow the fuck down. I did not want to hit anything over there, especially being a black tourist, traveling with a white chick.

Walking around New Delhi was a trip. Women's faces were covered with veils and these gems on their foreheads. I always thought it was some kind of spiritual thing, but eventually I realized it was just a fashion. We visited the city of Agra and the Taj Mahal, a beautiful mausoleum that was never finished. The story behind it is a beautiful love story. The king built a mausoleum for himself, and covered the wall with gems so he could see it as he went blind. Across the river he built another mausoleum for his beloved dead wife. After it was finished, he had all the workmen killed, so the Taj Mahal could never be duplicated.

One day I was down in the hotel drugstore, getting some lotion or something and the bellboy came in. He said hello to me, then spoke to the druggist. He introduced the druggist to me and split. The druggist waited 'till the store was empty and locked the door. He took me to the back in a room and brought out a glass container filled with cocaine. Pharmaceutical coke made in Germany. It was fantastic shit, at about thirty dollars for a bottle containing two grams. What a deal—and it was legal in India. I bought a bottle so Kelly could see. She was blown away. She just smiled in disbelief at this totally unexpected surprise. In the end we bought every bottle the pharmacy had.

Barry White's first album had just come out and Kelly and I toured India smoking hash and snorting coke and making love. It was a beautiful experience. I bought a sitar while I was there and met the second cousin of Ravi Shankar, who gave me lessons. In India you couldn't help but fall into the spiritual groove. It was part of India. We met this Indian guy who had a clothing manufacturing company outside of New Delhi and we became friends. He helped hook me up with a connection for hash, and I bought about six or seven pounds of hash and fifteen bottles of pharmaceutical coke.

We had to find someplace to put this shit and I decided to put the hash inside our boots. We had a lot of boots. The hash was shaped into little black balls called "Temple balls" so they fit easily. Then we just laid the boots in our suitcase. It looked good. We put the coke into a baby powder container. We poured the powder out and put the coke inside a baggie, then put powder on top.

In the Immigration Depot I stood back to check out the guy I thought was cool for Kelly. I pointed to him and she went over to his line. Then I checked out one for myself and I went to him. My hair was short at this time and I looked like a student. They saw my sitar, smiled and asked if I had a good time. I smiled also and said yes. They let us through, Kelly and I had no problem. We sat on the plane and got fucked up snorting all the way to New York City.

When we arrived in New York, Rockefeller had just passed a law which would go into full effect in about six days. Anyone caught with over a gram of anything goes to jail for life, no bail. I almost fainted. Now we had to get rid of this shit—quick.

We stayed with Kelly's best friend, a model named Jill Hammond. I ran into Calvin, Stevie Wonder's brother. He just came down from the South where Stevie had a bad car accident after finishing *Inner Visions*. Stevie almost lost his life. Calvin pulled him out of a burning car in the nick of time. He was shook up so I gave him a bunch of coke to calm him down and we talked ol' times.

After getting rid of most of the shit. I decided to go to Buffalo to see my family. I had a suitcase full of money. We had to sell the stuff for half its worth on account of this new law but it was better than nothing. Kelly stayed in the Apple with Jill. Mom was happy when I gave her five thousand I owed her. She didn't want it but I told her I had plenty. She asked me how I got it and I told her. She just laughed, and said, "Boy, you're crazy." It was the first time I would tell Mom the entire truth about a situation like that—something I did with her from that moment on until she passed.

While hanging out I met this ex-hoe named Pat. We became good friends. She took me to all the new spots. There was one club called The Padlocks where all the young blacks hung out and danced. The two hot records out at this time were "Funky Stuff" by Kool and The Gang and "Ecstasy" by the Ohio Players. When these two songs played you couldn't get motherfuckers off the floor. They loved that shit in Buffalo, so I decided to make some more money.

I had run into Truly and we decided to promote a concert—two shows with The Ohio Players and Kool and The Gang. I went back to New York City to their agency, Queen Booking. It cost three thousand dollars for both of 'em. Cheap, I thought to myself. If I ever had an R&B hit you can believe I'd never work for three thousand dollars. Anyway, the two shows were a complete success. I sent Stan his money, paid off the bands and bought a brand new 350 Mercedes cash and drove me and Kelly to LA.

We had a six-month party in LA, getting high, eating expensive dinners and staying in nice hotels. Then our money got low, I got fucked up one night and totaled the Benz. When I looked around, we were just about broke again. It seemed that when I was broke or on the edge, that's when I would get down and make shit happen.

Kelly was missing her mother and father so I sent her home. I got myself an apartment and bought an ol' Fender Bass and taught myself how to play. I was playing basketball every afternoon at this park on Santa Monica and Vine where I met this guitar player. I went in the studio with him and cut some tracks. This was the first time I ever played bass in a session.

A&M bought the tracks and released a single. The single was called "My Mama" and the B side was called "Funkin' Around." I produced them both, and A&M was so impressed, they wanted me to sign an exclusive deal with them. I told them I wanted first to see how they would push the single, but since I had no album deal, they said they weren't going to promote the single. A&M felt that if they promoted my single, and it hit, they would have no control over the subsequent album. A guy named Harold Childs did that bullshit. In later years, he'd apologize for that mistake.

The single did nothing in the U.S., but in Europe it was kicking ass. So I decided to go to Europe. Sweden was cold when me and Sandy, the guitarist, arrived. My record was doing well there and I wanted to work it. We formed a four-piece band and played all over Europe—England, France and Germany. While being based in Stockholm, me and Sandy both started to get homesick. Sandy fell in love with this chick from Denmark and I was living with a mother and daughter team. The three of us slept in the same bed. Mom was in her thirties and the daughter was about nineteen, and it was my first real introduction to true Freakiness. Their house was in a very nice section of Stockholm. I had been there for almost a year and was starting to miss Kelly. I wanted to go home, but either the mother or daughter stole my passport. They really didn't want me to leave. I went to the airport but they wouldn't let me on the plane without a passport. So they told me I must go to the United States Consulate in Gothenburg and convince them I was American. I couldn't believe it. Now I had to convince the motherfucker I was from the United States.

I arrived at the Consulate where they sent me to this little office where this guy started asking me all kinds of questions like who won the World Series pennant in '65 and what was the capital of New York— stupid shit. I started getting angry, and by the time he was finished I was raging. They put my ass on a plane quick. The plane was leaving and they made the fucker stop just to put my ass on. The plane was leaving and they made the fucker stop just to put my ass on. In retrospect, I really miss that Swedish pussy. It's the best tasting pussy in the world.

I was never so happy to see the United States. Me and Kelly got back together in Toronto and got an apartment. She took a job and I set up a little studio and started writing my ass off. I had this little sound-on-sound tape recorder, where I could put drums, guitar and bass on tape, with a tape on track for vocals.

I wanted to play music again, but I didn't want my own band. I was too frustrated. This Blues group called Mainline asked me to join them. They were one of Canada's biggest with two or three albums out at the time and they were always working. The leader was a white guy named Joe Mendelson, who wrote all their shit. He was a big, husky fellow with a deep, raspy voice. Joe was strange, but likeable, and wanted to pursue a solo career. So I stepped in to fill his spot. The other members were Tony Nolasco, Mike McKenna and a bass player named Harry. One of the unique things about them was that they sat down when they played. I dug that.

The drummer, Tony, and me got a place together and I played and toured with them for about a year. Tony was a dealer, and we smoked a lot of hash and snorted a lot of coke together. This was my first real introduction into constant cocaine use. I stayed with Mainline long enough to save some money and then quit.

Me and Kelly were happy in those days. I figured it was time to settle down, so I asked her to marry me. We went to Buffalo and got married at my Mom's house. We honeymooned in Jamaica, and then spent a few months in Miami in the Coconut Grove area. Those were happy times for me. Someone told me once, "Don't marry the one you love—it spoils shit." They were right. Something changed when Kelly and me got married, I can't put my finger on it, but it changed.

Back in Toronto, we continued to live together, but hardly ever spoke or made love. The whole relationship was getting boring; so we decided to call it quits. Living alone without Kelly became depressing, no band, no work—only loneliness. This guy who dealt coke decided to let me stay at his house, so I let Kelly have the apartment and I moved in with him. When he went away, I would sell coke for him. George Clinton was one of his clients.

The first time I met George was when I was selling him coke. I told him I was a writer and a producer and asked if would he help me get in the business. He said, "Yes." But never did. I swore one day I would pay his Black ass back for building my hopes.

I was making good money dealing coke, fifty dollars on a hundred gram. One day Jimmy introduced me to his main connection. I asked him "Where did this coke come from?" The connection told me "Columbia." I wanted to know how much money I'd make if I went to Colombia and brought it back. He said five thousand on every key. At that time, keys were going for about forty thousand dollars each. They had a guy in Montreal working in a rural mail department. He ran it, so anything coming in from Columbia, he saw and cleared. They'd send it in magazines sown inside, and marked. It was a perfect setup and me and Jimmy decided to go.

Our connection was this little Colombian cat called Rocky who lived in Bogota. He was this young pumped up little Colombian whose father worked in government or something, I had met him in Toronto when he was traveling on his diplomatic passport. Anyway, when we arrived in Cartejena and tried to call him, he had gone on holiday to a beautiful little island called San Andreas. We were very disappointed, but we went to an area called Boca Grande and checked in at the Americana Hotel. Across the street was this little bar owned by a happy-go-lucky guy called Mario. He waited the bar and there were always pretty girls inside. Me and Jimmy went there everyday hoping Rocky would come back soon.

Here we are in this fucking country and neither one of us spoke Spanish. Behind the bar in the corner was a microphone and a guitar. One day I asked Mario if I could play. By the time I finished, people were coming in off the street to see the Black gringo from America.

I played and sang everyday at Mario's and his little bar was packed with young Colombians, drinking and singing with me. One thing I noticed about these young Colombians was that they all had Jeeps and plenty of money. I later found out it was because they all dealt cocaine—big time. I met this beautiful Colombian girl named Yvonne. Her father was a wealthy art collector. Me and Yvonne hung out everyday, snorting and fucking mostly right on the beach. One thing I learnt from this experience was that fucking on the beach is not as pleasant as you may have heard. Sand every fucking place.

One day Mario took me on his boat. He asked me what I was really doing in Colombia. I had told him I was a musician taking a holiday, but now I had to level with him. I told him we were there to buy coke, but our connection had vanished. He told me he could help me, especially for what I had done for him at his bar. Jimmy, Mario and I took a plane to Bogota. On every corner there were military men. Mario told me there would be a revolution here soon. Guerillas would come into Bogota at night and blow things up. It was a trip. We checked into a hotel where I bought some emeralds very cheap.

That night we went to this club at the top of the tallest building in the town. Salsa music was playing loudly and everywhere people danced and shouted. Mario introduced me to the owner, a short, well-dressed dude. We sat down at our table, and Mario passed me a folded-up newspaper. I asked what the newspaper was for. He said, "Just open it."

I did and the whole motherfucker was filled with mother-of-pearl, serious, top-of-the —line, pure coke, about two ounces. He asked how much I wanted. I told him only five keys. He told me that was no problem and even gave me a big discount. Five keys for twenty five thousand dollars. I thanked him and put the keys in a briefcase.

The next day we flew back to Cartajena. Mario took the keys from us so they would be safe. I trusted Mario, he was that kind of a guy. Five keys were nothing to Mario. He dealt in thousands of keys. Me and Jimmy packed and sent the keys to Montreal and kept a couple of ounces each for personal use.

The day we were to leave I had a shopping bag of grass, which I gave to Mario and another friend of mine named Soupy. I wanted to take coke back with me but I was told not to bring anything because US Customs searches carefully. Being hard-headed as I am, I didn't care.

I was in the bathroom brushing my hair getting ready to leave Colombia when an idea occurred to me. The brush was one of those brushes that you could push down like a sponge. It had little red wires for brushes. Well, I put about an ounce and a half in a rubber and tied it up and put it in the brush. I cut around the sponge, opened it and put the coke inside, then glued the sponge back and voila! It was perfect. I put some strands of hair in it just for looks and then threw it in my cosmetic case.

It was a serious stash. I looked like a young student at the time so it was no problem getting past customs. I stopped in Washington to see Roy, and Jimmy went o Canada. Roy was in Georgetown Law School sharing an apartment with his friend Romaine. He was also living with the beautiful black girl named Brenda. Her family was one of the wealthiest in Washington. I spent time with Roy and Brenda.

To my surprise, Roy was snorting coke and smoking weed. He and Brenda were madly in love with each other and I was happy for them. Brenda's family were doctors, and very conservative. Roy couldn't even leave his clothes at her place for fear her family might find them. I never liked her family, I've always hated blacks who acted stuck up, bourgeois niggers I call them.

I stopped in Buffalo on my way to Toronto. Mom had moved and as usual I was happy to see her. Penny was beautiful, about thirteen years old. I even started showing her some stuff on piano that she still remembers. Penny and William, who we called "Head," were the only ones around. The rest had gotten married and moved on except Birdie, who was in college studying to be a minister.

I stayed in Buffalo, hanging out for about a month. I tried calling Jimmy to see if my money was straight from our little trip but I could never reach him. I decided to wait until I got to Toronto. I felt something wasn't right. George Clinton and The Funkadelics had *Mothership Connection* out. George was starting to ride a wave of hits and creating a bunch of clone groups along with it—Brides of Funkenstein, Parliament, and the Funkedelics. A combination of Rock, Funk and Frank Zappa shit. I liked most of the grooves. They had a cool, James Brown sound. But most of the time I could do without George's verbal ramblings.

I listened and felt maybe there still might be a chance for new music to happen. I had run into George again in Buffalo and he bought some more coke. I remember charging him triple for it. I was still determined to get his ass, and that day would come on the stage.

When I got back to Canada I found Kelly. My feelings for her were as strong as ever. I couldn't get her out of my system. I still had coke left so we got fucked up for days. Kelly asked me to move back in so I did, she was my wife.

I called Jimmy every day and all I got was the brush off. Tony, my drummer friend, told me Jimmy bought a brand new townhouse, a Rolls and was spending money all over town. Tony also told me no one knew where he lived but he would find out and he did.

One day, broke and pissed off I decided to get mine. I just woke up raging. I was mad as a motherfucker. After everything we had been through in Columbia, I was still broke. I felt ripped off and betrayed. I found out Jimmy's address and went to his town house, jumped the fence and waited behind the garbage cans. I had this long butcher knife in my hand. I was going to get this motherfucker one way or another. No motherfucker had ever done this to me.

He came out in a robe with the garbage and I jumped out from behind and grabbed him around the neck. He was a skinny motherfucker so I handled his ass like a fuckin' baby. He looked scared to death. There was a girl. I told her to shut the fuck up and everything would be cool. She knew me and complied. Jimmy tried to tell me that the coke was lost. That's when I slapped the shit out of him. The girl's name was Susan, she came in to the living room and shouted, "Ricky, stop."

I said, "Fuck you, he ripped me off."

By now Jimmy was crying like a baby. Suzie screamed, "The coke's in the safe."

I told Jimmy to open the fuckin' safe. He did. There was about a pound of coke and fifteen thousand dollars. I took it all, every bit. Susan's ex-old man was this big biker dude who hated Jimmy. I told Jimmy I figure he owed ten grand more and he better get it.

He asked "How?"

I told him "Sell the fucking car." I told Susan I'd call her ex if she didn't get the fuck out, NOW! She ran out the door half dressed. I told Jimmy if he didn't have my money within a week I'd find him and kill him, and then I left. Jimmy paid me back.

I rented a townhouse in an exclusive part of Toronto and sold most of the coke. I now had a nice bankroll. I sent Mom fifteen thousand dollars and paid back some other people I owed money to. I bought a bunch more instruments and a new Mercedes. I told Kelly about Colombia; so we decided to have a second honeymoon there.

Mario and Soupy were happy to meet Kelly and we had a great time just lying in the sun and getting high. When it was time to leave I had about three ounces with me, so I put two in the brush and one I wrapped in my tie when I tied the knot.

When we arrived in Miami, this black immigration dude pulled me in his office. I was scared as hell. He told me to get undressed for a search. I got undressed, pulled the tie down halfway, took it off my neck and threw it on the floor. I was searched thoroughly. He never undid my tie.

117

Chapter Thirty-three
My Own Record Label

Back in Toronto, Kelly and I started to drift apart again. She moved out and was living with her ex—this strange little motherfucker called Kyle. Whenever Kelly and I broke up, she always ran back to this motherfucker. He was a thorn in my side, and I had had to physically kick his ass on a few occasions. So now I was alone again though I always felt Kelly's leaving was long over due. She took a lot of shit from me—fucking around with her best friends and not coming home at night. If I was her, I would have left a long time ago. Love makes a motherfucker do strange things.

But now this girl who lived on my street had become friendly with me. Her name was Linda Steinhouse. She would bring me food and just be there when I needed someone to talk to. She started to see this guy, Tony, my drummer friend. Tony and I became even closer than before. He was no longer in the Mainline, so he had plenty of free time. We would hang out and jam, and smoke a lot of hash.

I was still trying to stay on top of my heart. After Kelly walked out on me I was crushed. I had a gun, and I was going to commit suicide. I even raised the gun to my head and felt the cold steel. I was emotionally dependant on her. I mean I loved the fuck out of Kelly. Her leaving me was the first time that I couldn't just run away from an emotional situation, I mean there was never any real emotional demonstrativeness in my family, my mother never showed love, so I didn't either. But Kelly could read me, and I couldn't play the situation with her the way I'd been able to with other females. I mean this bitch had my mind fucked up. When she finally left, for good. I was lonely and depressed, out-of-control and vulnerable. I was going to trick myself out with this gun. But me being a chicken-shit and the narcissistic person that I was, I didn't do it.

Tony helped pull me out of it. He always kept me laughing. He always had coke and hash, so we stayed fucked up—getting high and chasing women, that's all we did. We also jammed with other cats a lot. We were a team. One day Tony introduced me to this short pimple-faced Chinese cat. He wore these thick-ass glasses. His name was Aiden Mow, and he was from South Africa. This little weird looking motherfucker could play guitar. I mean he could blow—George Benson type shit—he had it covered. Me and him started to write a lot together.

Anyway we came up with this funky tune called *Get Up and Dance* and it was funky. Tony heard it and flipped out. He said we should cut it, so we did, with the Brecker Brothers on horns. It was a killer. So here we are with this twenty-four-track tune. We decided to start our own label and I called it Moon Records, after my interest in astrology. Tony had some money from hash dealing to set us up, so we had a hip logo made and we were ready to go. We took the record to Buffalo, got an office, hired this black friend of mine named Luther and started manufacturing records. We made a few thousand and put them in the stores from Buffalo to Rochester to Syracuse. Then we took the record to the two biggest soul stations in Buffalo, WUFO and WBLK. For weeks, *Get up and Dance* went up against the latest records in the nightly "Battle of the Bands," and won. Nothing could beat it. It was a great Funk record. The high of success was incredible, and it lasted for about a month, till the day we lost out to another record.

Get Up and Dance continued to be played on WUFO and WBLK, and it went to Number One in Buffalo, Rochester and Syracuse. We couldn't keep records in the store and for the first time I felt my musical career was really on its way. There was only one minor problem—the stores wouldn't pay us. The distribution companies were run by Italian gangsters and these gangsters wanted an album. You wouldn't be paid for one record until you had the next in the stores, and if you didn't like it, you could go see Big Al. The motherfuckers kept our money and talked that shit. I was pissed. An Italian friend of mine told me "That's the way it goes if you're independent."

One day, Tony said "Rick, let's make an album."

I said "What?"

"Yeah, we'll record an entire album and sell it to a major company."

By this time I had written all these songs at my Mom's house and I felt they were ready to record. So I got a few cats I knew and we rehearsed for about two weeks straight. Then we rented this raw little studio that had been built in a barn by Spyro Gyra in the country outside of Buffalo. The recording fees that Tony and I paid Spyro Gyra enabled them to record their first album, which they did as soon as we wrapped. That album subsequently went platinum for them.

The first track I cut was an up-tempo Funk tune with a disco intro called "You and I". Disco was still in at the time, and man, did I hate it. That pulsating beat and that same old same old rhythm and structure used to bother me, and I couldn't wait for the demise of disco. There was something about the simplicity of it that I liked, and the power of the kick drum that seemed to give it a driving pulse, and I can't honestly say I hated all disco. Cats like Barry White, Peter Brown, B.T. Express, and the group that did Disco Inferno kind of turned me on, but a lot of it was bullshit. It was fun going to clubs and dancing to Van

121

McCoy, but after a while I began to think, "God, this has to change." Black music was becoming obsolete, even Rod Stewart was doing "Do Ya Think I'm Sexy." (Which was really kind of fly. Me and Rod have always been close and there pretty much isn't anything he can't do that isn't cold.)

If I had to do disco, I was going to give them a piece of it, then put some funk on their ass. "You and I" may have had a disco intro, but it went pretty quickly into a funk break. "You and I" was about Kelly, and throughout my writing career, all my songs would be about personal experiences and feelings. I had to write from my heart and experiences, and my life with Kelly was the most profound experience I had had till that point. "Sexy Ladies," was about hoes, and I'd had a lot of experience with them, so it was easy to write about them.

I had fallen in love with the *Sergeant Pepper* album by The Beatles. I loved the way it started, with this overture that got the listener anticipating the rest of the album. So I wrote this funky intro to open up the album called "Stone City Bank Hi." Besides Jazz, one of my biggest musical inspirations was The Beatles. I loved them because they were so original. They could tap Classical, Rhythm & Blues, Rock & Roll or Folk and integrate all this in their music and I loved that. I wanted to tailor my vision as a Black songwriter and producer but I also wanted to be able to integrate every kind of music that I liked into my music. The Beatles would often emulate bands they loved. They would do productions where they sounded like The Beach Boys, or The Everly Brothers, or the Marvelettes, and this was very complementary to those groups. In my own work I would do this occasionally and knowingly write a song that would remind people of another group that I had a lot of respect for. The Funkadelic sound on Stone City Bank Hi was a tribute to George Clinton, who I always considered a friend, except when he was refusing to help me back in the early days in Buffalo.

For Side Two, I found three white boys who I knew loved black music. Each one had the style I wanted for the album. I had brought The Brecker Brothers in to play the horns on the first side. But I decided to cut the second side in New York City at The Record Plant. So these three white boys and I, along with three black singers, flew to New York.

Record Plant put me in touch with an engineer named Shelly Yakus, a well-known Rock engineer. Shelly was a groove to work with. He gave me exactly what I was looking for. While I was there, Bruce Springsteen was recording his first album since leaving his manager and the Rock group Aerosmith was also recording there. It was funny, all these groupie bitches sitting in the lobby saying shit like, "I need a new car," and "I want some clothes" looking bored to death, while five limos waited day and night at their beck and call.

With Shelly I cut this up-temp disco kind of groove called "Be My Lady" and a tune called "Mary Jane" a tune with his Rock intro about my love affair with Marijuana and a ballad called "Hollywood." It was written for my Mama, a song telling her I would soon be a star. One day while upstairs in the Record Plant listening to a mix of "Mary Jane," Steven Tyler poked his head in. He asked if he could come in and I said sure. As he listened he danced around and pulled out this huge bag of coke. Then he took out this big ass Bowie knife and dunked it in the coke. He must of snorted two grams at one time. I saw this and freaked. He asked me if I wanted any and I put the knife in and took a little, one and one. I asked, "So this is what it's like to make it?" He answered, "Yeah, Man," with his big ass lips. Man, he had lips bigger than mine. He said the tune was great. I'll never forget it. While walking to the door, he said with this big smile "I'll see you up there." Then he disappeared. I didn't know it then but he was so right. He and I would become the best of friends.

I finished recording that album in all of two months. I called it *Come Get It*, cuz that's what I wanted people to do, and after listening to it, my opinion was, not bad. I felt it might get me in the door at a record company or at least give me the chance to record one more album. There was a cohesive magic to the album, which is something young songwriters should remember, always try to keep the music in your album cohesive. In other words the color, the music, the words, and the story should flow into one another. Not necessarily conceptual, but magical, if that makes sense.

My confidence was still lacking at this point. I had had so many let downs, I was sure this would be another one. But for once I was wrong.

Chapter Thirty-four
My First Single

In 1978 Disco music still dominated the national charts. Donna Summer was the Queen of Disco, and at one point she had four songs in the Top One Hundred. Linda Clifford, Thelma Houston, Taste of Honey and Evelyn Champagne King were just a few women achieving success through Disco music.

The last thing I wanted to be was a Disco Star. I found the music very boring, and I had seen too many disco stars come to a bad end. When Tony and I went to LA to shop my deal, I told him I didn't care who we signed with as long as it wasn't Motown—and I was adamant about that.

We got rooms in the Continental Hyatt on Sunset Boulevard. The next day we began to look for a deal. Before leaving Buffalo, I made a bunch of copies of the album to give to A&R people.

The first place Tony and I went was this building on Sunset that housed about five major companies, including Motown. In the elevator we ran into Jeffrey Bowen, a producer I had met while I was with The Mynah Birds at Motown. Jeffrey asked me what I was doing in town, and I told him I had an album and was shopping for a record deal. I also told him I didn't think the music was compatible with Motown. He said he wanted to hear it anyway. I told him I wasn't sure I wanted to be with the company because I felt so many artists had been ripped off. Jeffrey said Motown had changed, and to give him a chance. I talked to Tony about it, seeing I had given him permission to do the business. I had seen the way Motown worked when I was a kid, and I thought they were very slick and shady, and I was very apprehensive about giving Jeffrey that tape. I did though, because I was pretty sure he would see it wasn't their brand of music at all.

125

In Canada, Tony had always been good at business, so I consulted with him on every move I made. We decided to give Jeffrey a tape and not see any more companies until he got back to us.

It was the weekend, and Kelly had flown down to LA to be with me. I was happy. We'd been separated for almost a year, and I really had missed her. I played the album for Kelly and she thought it was great. She loved the raw feeling, and she said one could tell it was a band and not a bunch of studio cats. I had taught her well.

During my musical career, the one constant has been, I want a BAND sound, raw and live. If you desire a raw feel, without perfection, a feel where there might be a tempo change, or a bad note, or it might not be structured right, but it still flows right, and it feels good—always go with that feeling. And that's what I always wanted, I never wanted a group to sound like a bunch of studio musicians, and I never wanted a slick-ass recording. There were a lot of slick recordings out there. To me, Earth, Wind and Fire, as much as I love them, were a perfect sounding, flaw-less studio group. If you listen to my records, you'll hear a guitar go out of tune and you'll hear some misses. I always kept those little mistakes, because I always wanted a real band feel. With the Stone City Band, you could always tell they were a real band, true players, and not a bunch of hired studio musicians.

That night Jeffrey called while I was asleep. He told me he had played the tape and thought it was an absolute smash. I was happy to hear that—but I had heard that kind of shit before, so it wasn't gospel. I went back to sleep feeling better.

The next day Jeffrey said he had played the tape for Barry Gordy and Suzanne De Passe, and they wanted to make a deal. I told Tony. All of us were happy.

Jeffrey always carried these gram bottles of coke with him, and he gave me and Kelly a couple to celebrate with. I didn't know it then, but every one of those little bottles of coke would be charged to me when my deal money came in; and I would find out that Jeffrey was the biggest snake-in-the-grass motherfucker I'd ever met. Tony was going up to Motown every day negotiating while Jeffrey came to see me every day, giving me and Kelly bottles of blow. I always felt that Jeffrey was also trying to catch Kelly. I never worried much about that, cuz my wife hated the little, skinny, four-eyed, fast-talking creep.

After a few weeks, Tony came to me and said the negotiations were at a standstill and maybe we should look for another company. I asked what the problem was and he just said, "Money." They wouldn't do the right thing. I believed him, till one day Suzanne De Passe called me to her office and told me why the deal was really at a standstill: Tony wanted an override; for every penny I made he wanted two, plus a bunch of other shit. Tony was manipulating the deal so he could own me. When we had originally worked together on *Come Get It,* we had a deal that he would see profits on that album, but he was trying to negotiate to see revenue on everything I recorded for Motown from then on. Unlike most musicians, I was very aware of the importance of publishing and royalty rights. By the time I was talking to Motown, I had been in the business a long time, and I knew that publishing rights were an artist's lifeline, and that you had to hold on to them no matter what. I had seen what happened to groups like The Temptations, who turned to pimpin' their women, while they were Number One artists, and were only seeing a weekly salary, despite being huge stars.

I didn't believe Suzanne at first, till she showed me in print that she was telling the truth. Tony wanted a piece of my publishing, and an override, (money you receive on the back end, without the artist's knowledge), and I was like "Forget that." Tony was beginning to grow a tail, and I didn't like it. Suzanne said she could deal with the matter by simply giving Tony some money and sending him on his way. I agreed, though I was hurt by my friend's betrayal.

With Tony out of the picture, I hired an attorney named Joel Strote to finish the negotiations. Jeffrey was still supplying me with coke. Me and Suzanne and Suzanne's assistant were snorting a lot in those days. Whenever I went to her office, the three of us would get fucked up. It was great times.

I wanted to make "You and I" longer before I released it. So I took the track back in the studio, added a drummer named Ollie Brown, and another guitar vamp, and made it over six minutes, as opposed to three and a half. I added some more vocals on the vamp, singing "Everybody dance on the funk. Everybody shake yo booty's down." By now it was good to go. I received about two hundred and fifty thousand dollars for *Come Get It*. Motown managed to get half of my publishing, but that would return to me in three years. It wasn't an ideal situation, but I knew eventually I'd get my rights back. Out of the four hundred thousand, Jeffrey got a one-time ten percent finder's fee, about forty thousand dollars. And as if that wasn't enough, he told Suzanne De Passe to give him six thousand dollars he said I owed him for cocaine. This motherfucker was crazy. Even if it was true and I did owe him, it would have been less than a grand. So I said if she gave him any of my money, I'd say fuck the deal. I don't know what happened, but I do know he didn't get my money.

Jack Andrews, this little white maniac, ran Motown's mastering lab. The mastering lab is the last place the record goes before it's released. That's where you put the record on wax. And the lab is also where you fine-tune your record: add some highs, some lows and mid-range, make it crisper, or round it off, whatever you want to do. Jack was a very outspoken little motherfucker, especially to the new producers. After putting on "You and I," he played it and his face got all contorted. Then he played it again. This time he told me how my record stunk, how it was too noisy, and how could Motown release such shit. The tape was very noisy, with a lot of hiss, cuz we had recorded it in a barn. I felt about two inches tall. I told him what I wanted done to the record and left with my head down. I was never more embarrassed. All I could think of was the things he said about my record, and how one day I'd show that little motherfucker.

Chapter Thirty-five
Creating An Image

Now that the album was finished, I needed to have an album shoot, and I wanted a hip album cover. Kelly had gone back to Toronto and I was alone.

One day while looking for something interesting to do, I noticed that Olantunji, an African drummer, was appearing in town near UCLA with Massai dancers. I decided to go.

The show was magnificent. Olatunji was as always at his very best. I went back stage to say hello to Baba, which is Tunji's first name. We had met a couple of times in New York.

As impressed as I was with their dancing, the thing that really drew my eye was the amazing hairstyles of the Massai performers. They all wore animal hair braided into their own hair, making these long extensions that they used to create whatever style they wanted; long, short, curly. I was flipped out at all the different styles. I met the girl who kept their hair together and she gave me a history of coiffeurism. She told me that white Europeans actually stole their styles from Africa after seeing the Massai. The warriors believed that they would gain the powers and strengths of the animals whose hair they wore. She introduced me to her cousin Tomani. Tomani told me she could give me any hairstyle I wanted. When I told her I wasn't sure that I wanted animal hair, she just laughed and said "No, real hair!"

The next day Tomani came to my hotel room with bags of hair. My hair was kind of short then, and I told her I wanted it long with beads. She got started braiding the strands with my own hair, and two long days later I had long, beautiful beaded hair. I looked like a Massai warrior. She charged me one hundred and fifty dollars, and I gave her three hundred. Everywhere I went, people stared. They all wanted to know how I got my hair like that—but I wouldn't say. I never gave away the secrets of the braids.

My image was finally coming around. I flew back to Buffalo with my new hairstyle. Everyone in Buffalo freaked. All they asked was, "Rick, how did you do that to your hair?" I would just smile.

This guy named Prez and I were hanging tight in Buffalo, getting high and going out at night to this Italian nightclub named Eduardo's. Eduardo's would hold a Black disco, and "Flashlight" was the most popular record on those nights, with every one doing this dance called the "Freak," which was basically an excuse to get on the floor and touch your partner. The DJ, California St. Clair, was a funny, funny dude. He would play records while sniffing Locker, a form of Amyl Nitrate. He was insane. I asked him to slip my record on, and he said he would.

The dance floor was almost empty at one point. All of a sudden, "You and I" came on. For the first time I would see if people liked it. To me, if they liked it in Buffalo, they would like it everywhere. One minute after "You and I" came on, the dance floor was packed. I mean, motherfuckers were dancing in the aisles. It was like something in a movie. Motherfuckers were yelling and screaming. I knew my shit was a smash right there. California played it about five times, back-to-back. I had to go take the tape from him so he didn't overdo a good thing. They loved it. "You and I" was a hit, at least in Buffalo.

One day a friend of mine named Icky came by my house. He told me this Rock group, Kiss, was playing in Buffalo, and asked me if I wanted to go. I said, "Fuck, no!" I didn't want to see Kiss. He kept asking. Finally, I said, "Yes."

Kiss wore all black, with rockets and pyro going off, loud drums that rose twenty-five feet in the air. While watching, I became mesmerized. All of a sudden the sounds of the band faded, and I actually saw myself on stage with a Black band in costumes and everything. It was such a rush; I had to get out of there. I knew then that my concerts would be like Fourth of July—a big party. I didn't need to see anymore. I knew what my image would be.

Chapter Thirty-six
"You and I"—the First Hit

It was 1978, and summer was around the corner. I knew "You and I" would be out soon, and I wanted to be prepared. Levi Ruffin had become one of my best pals. We had hung a little in school, and I had written a couple of songs for the singing group he was with. He was serious about music, but he had settled down and was married with a couple of children. I told him about the album deal and, if things worked out, I'd need a band and asked if he would be interested. He said yes. He was singing and playing synthesizers. His wife Jackie had done background on my album. So I already had two members of the band. Although I had no band yet, I did have a name for the group: The Stone City Band. I went to see Roy in Washington to share the good news. He was very happy, but he had heard shit like this before and didn't want to see me have any more let downs.

So here I am in Washington, DC, wearing all leather with earrings and long hair. Those straight motherfuckers in Washington didn't know how to deal with me. They just thought of me as some kind of freak, and I was. I didn't care. I looked at them with their ties and silly suits as freaks— closet freaks. Those Washington motherfuckers would come home from their lawyer job or doctor job and as soon as they got behind closed doors, they would snort coke, smoke weed, eat pussy and everything else they could think of. At least my shit is out in the open. I hate closet freaks!

One day a real strange thing happened. This dude and I went to a house party in Washington. I was in this room getting high when someone came in to get me, saying I had a phone call. It was someone from Motown, telling me "You and I" was the hottest record in the

South. Atlanta had started playing it and now people were jumping on it like hotcakes up and down the East Coast. I just held onto the phone with my mouth open. To this day I have no idea how they found the number at the house party to talk to me. It was very strange. Yet all I could really think of was that I was finally on my way. After years and years of struggling, I had a hit record. I had always said if I ever got one hit record my momentum would be unstoppable. Now I would show this world what Rick James was all about. I was on my way.

Chapter Thirty-seven
The Stone City Band

Now that "You and I" was taking off, I decided I needed a band. I wasn't sure how long this dream would last and I didn't want to be a one-hit-wonder. I prepared to stretch it out as long as I could. Levi was a dark-skinned, six-foot Brother who was always my Rock of Gibraltar. He was intelligent and a Leo. I had always had a lot of respect for him in school, because he was a strong, powerful and soulful brother. Now that I was on the verge of success, I wanted somebody I could trust with me and I knew I could rely on Levi. I didn't want to start on this road alone. I wanted a family to be there with me, and as I built my band, I built a family too. Jackie, Levi's wife, was singing back up, and it was good to have both of them in the band. They had been sweethearts in grammar school and had married right after high school. They had three kids and were good people who always treated me right.

Oscar, a six–foot bass player, could play anything, plus he had a great personality, always laughing and making fun. Lanise Hughes, the drummer, was the quietest member of the group, he was like my Ringo, very strong and steady. Nate Hughes, Lanise's brother, played percussion, congas, etc. On keyboards was Ramadon, a Jazz pianist, who could play Funk, Classical and you name it. Finally, on guitar was Allan Symanski, a white boy was one of the best guitar players in Buffalo. That was the band. I never had confidence in my playing, plus I wanted to be a front man, and have the freedom of dancing and having a good time. I didn't want to be constricted on stage by being tied to an instrument, that's why I hired Oscar.

When we flew down to LA I brought California to work as my valet, along with Prez. They were both friends of mine from Buffalo and we were one big, happy family. I gave the band some money and told them we'd be moving to LA when I took care of my business.

While in LA. I stopped by this studio to see Stevie Wonder, who was recording some tracks for his upcoming album. Calvin and his girlfriend Valerie were there. Valerie was a designer and together we designed my first stage costume. It was black with silver lightning bolts running down both sides of my legs, and a red rhinestone heart around the chest area. The boots had silver wings on them. I took my album cover picture with this beautiful Black chick named Bernadette. She was lying down reaching up at me, I was excited. The cover was going to be cool yet sexy and really fly.

I was scheduled to do the Dick Clark Show, and I was really nervous. It was the first major TV show I'd ever done and because the Stone City Band was still in Buffalo I wouldn't have them behind me—just two girls I had hired as back-up singers. I couldn't believe that after all my efforts to create the perfect musical family I would have to face this first big gig alone. Barry Gordy, who wanted to meet me, had me picked up and taken to his house in Bel Air. While riding up to Barry's house, I couldn't help but think on how far I'd come. "You and I" was Number One R&B, Number One Disco, and Top Five Pop. Black FM radio was playing almost everything on the album including; "Dream Maker," "Stone City Hollywood" and "Mary Jane." It was looking like "Mary Jane" would by my next single. The trade magazines were calling *Come Get It* the biggest Black album of the year.

Meeting Barry Gordy was a trip. He was this short, balding little guy with a big smile and a good sense of humor. He made me feel relaxed and said: "So you're the one I've been hearing about."

I said "And you're the one I've been hearing about too." I didn't want to appear too cocky, but I wasn't going to come off as timid either.

I played it off like I was self-assured, but my heart was pounding. I was meeting one of the biggest musical icons of the time. No matter what people say about Barry, he had built Motown and he was a genius. Barry treated me with respect and love, and he's a man with a lot of dignity, but I was still nervous as a motherfucker.

He smiled and said "I think I'm gonna like you."

We talked about a lot things. He said he was looking for great things from me. He said he wanted me to make him proud. I told him I would. He called Dick Clark while I was standing there, and he let me listen in on the conversation. Dick was telling him how he was going to have a live TV show like Ed Sullivan, and asked if Barry could possibly get Diana Ross for a show. Barry told him: "Sure, but I want you to use Rick James, too." Then Barry told him that I was getting ready to do his show that night and to treat me good. Dick said he would.

I was impressed. I left Barry's house liking the guy a lot. He wasn't as bad as I had heard. Little did I know I was due for an awakening.

Valerie called and told me my costume had been stolen out of her car. All that was left were my boots. I was pissed, but I didn't have enough time to be angry, so I went to this head shop and bought a black T-shirt and had "Stone City Band" put on it. Then I bought an applejack hat. Now I was ready.

Dick Clark is one of the kindest, most considerate men in television. It was easy to see why he's maintained such a high stature in the industry. He made me feel real comfortable. He knew this was my first show. I'd always watched "American Bandstand," and I couldn't believe I was

135

actually there. Dick looked as young as he did in his Philly days. He came to my dressing room and told me how much he enjoyed my album. When he announced me, he gave me this huge fanfare. Between "You and I" and "Mary Jane," Dick did his usual interview, except this one went on and on and on. I thought he'd never stop asking me questions. Then I remembered his talk with Barry Gordy.

I had been in the dressing room snorting coke, out of a little Coca-Cola bottle around my neck. As we talked, I could feel my nose running. Dick must have seen it too, but kept his cool. He was probably used to it. Whenever I watch that tape of the show I laugh my ass off. I was sniffing and rubbing my nose. It was hysterical.

The whole country saw my debut on "American Bandstand." Motown told me they received more fan letters off that one show than they ever received before. It made me feel good. My mother and family and my group all got together with big screen TV and watched it in Buffalo. It was final—I was now a star.

Let the Music Play

Studio Time

Rick on Tour

It's Party Time

In the Joint Studio Lantis Hughes drummer, Kenny Hawkins guitar, Rick, Nate Hughe adn Thomas Flye "Super Engineer"

139

In the middle is Anne Mabin, Rick's Secretary and Office Manager in the 1980's with Singer Lisa Sarna (right) and a friend.

Rick with Stone City background singer, Lisa Sarna

Kimberly Hughes, Ann Mabin and Rick in his office at Motown.
He called them his Sexrataries.

Rick and Smokey at Motown

Back-up singers: Lisa Sarna, JoJo Mcduffy and Tabby Johnson photo shoot

Teddy Pendergrass and Rick

Rick and the Pips

Rick with Marvin Gaye

Rick and the Jacksons

Eatin' cake…
    It's all good

Rick with Jim Brown

Backstage with the crew

Backstage at a concert in Buffalo for Rick's group the Process & the Doo Rags. Standing, Linda Hunt, Charlie Murphy and Rick

145

Rick and Friends

146

Angel Corley and Rick on a day off

Rick and Phyllis Hyman

147

Rick James
the Ultimate Performer

Chapter Thirty-eight
Double Platinum

The album was platinum and on its way to double and Motown was already talking about my second album. I had purchased a mansion on Coldwater Canyon that had been owned by William Randolph Hearst. It was a huge motherfucker with a sunken living room, a fireplace that looked like something out of *Citizen Kane*, Spanish Stucco, marble floor, foyer and a winding staircase. It was a beautiful home that I bought with my Mom in mind. I was sure she'd like it.

The band flew into town and moved into the house. The first week they were there was spent getting their hair braided—that was a must. I had learnt from hanging around CSNY and other white Rock groups to never go on tour with your first album and never open for anybody. I was going to stick to that. All kinds of offers were coming in for me to tour, but I just turned them down. Even my band thought I was crazy. I told them I knew what I was doing; I was building a demand, a demand so great they'd have to pay my price, not theirs. And I didn't want people to see us yet. I still had a lot of hits in me and I was in no hurry. "Mary Jane" was out and, like "You and I," it was moving up the charts. Everything was working the way I'd planned.

I had developed a friendship with Art Stewart, an engineer. Art worked mostly for Marvin Gaye in Marvin's studio and had engineered all of Marvin's later albums. I had used Art while fixing up "You and I." And we had developed a special friendship. He was an Aquarius like me and very mild-mannered. I liked and trusted him to the point that I even offered him half production on the stuff we did together.

One day at the studio I ran into Marvin. He was sitting with Art just kicking it. We started joking about who gave the best head. He said he did. I said I did. It went backwards and forwards like this for about an hour. Then Marvin got real serious.

He asked me: "Rick, have you gotten your bonus yet?'

I said "What bonus?"

He said "Your bonus for going Platinum."

I said I hadn't. He said whenever somebody's album goes Platinum the company gives them a bonus. I said I hadn't gotten mine yet. He said that if it wasn't cash, then a Stutz or something.

I began to get pissed. I hadn't received anything and I certainly felt I deserved it.

The next day I got up early and went to Motown. I was mad. As soon as I got off the elevator on the seventeenth floor I bumped into Lee Young, Motown's lawyer.

I screamed "Where's my bonus?"

He looked at me like I was crazy. Then I went to Suzanne de Passe's office and screamed:

"Where's my bonus?"

She calmed me down and said, "Rick, this is something you should talk to Barry Gordy about."

I tried calling Barry but he was nowhere to be found. That was the first time I freaked out at the company—the first of many. I didn't know it then, but Marvin loved to start shit up with the company and their artists. Motown did sometimes give bonuses for huge selling albums, but it wasn't mandatory, and Marvin knew this. He was just trying to rile me up and cause trouble. He knew I had a crazy nature and he knew that I would run straight to Motown and raise hell. Marvin was always like that, a crazy motherfucker, but I loved him to death.

I never got a bonus and Barry Gordy called me up and told me I was out of line and that I lacked tact. At that time Marvin was divorcing Barry's sister, Anna, and he was recording an album that she would get all the royalties from. So I guess he felt like causing even more trouble than usual. Barry did end up throwing some extra money my way, but he made sure I knew that from then on I had to talk straight to him if I had a problem.

It was now time to release my second album. I called it *Bustin' Out*, and I had an artist do a cartoon picture of me busting out of this prison wall. I decided to record it in New York. So me and the band left Buffalo and headed down to the city. I booked a studio called The Village Recording and they put me in this new room that had just been finished.

The first night we cut about three tracks. The whole time we were recording, everything was fine. I mean playbacks and all. After layin' down the third track we went in to listen and heard absolutely nothing. It was gone. I mean I couldn't believe it—no music at all. The engineer called the owner and he came down. When the smoke had cleared, the owner said he was sorry and gave us five days free of charge. I had a photo shoot while in New York and flew back to LA.

Chapter Thirty-nine
Teena Maria

Bustin' Out had received great reviews. The first single was called "High on Your Love," an up-tempo Funk tune. I wrote a ballad called "Spacey Love," which I dedicated to Patti Labelle and the Blue Bells. I hadn't met Patti yet and I couldn't wait for the day. She was my favorite. The song was a cross between Afro and Funk, it was a long number, almost a suite, and it went through a number of variations and changed. I thought she would like it. She and I would later become great friends.

"High on your Love" didn't do as well as "You and I." It went Number One R&B, but the album sold like a motherfucker. I found out one important thing about my sale and air-play: while most artists released a single and got AM air-play, I released a single and got AM and FM air play. FM would play almost every cut on my album, as if they were singles. That enabled me to play a lot of different shit when I started to tour.

I was happy to get back to LA. *Bustin' Out* was finished. Now it was time to start rehearsing for the tour. But first I needed a horn section. My ol' friend Norman Whitfield heard I was going on tour and needed some horn players. I had left Motown years ago on his advice and since then he had done extremely well writing and producing such hits as: "Heard It Through the Grapevine," "Cloud Nine," "Get Ready," "Car Wash," "Runaway Child" and many others. I was as proud of him as he was of me. Anyway, Norman had told these three players the best way to get the gig with me was to learn my shit—and they did. *Bustin' Out* was now at the top of the charts. When Danny Lemelle, Cliff and John Irving came to my house to audition for the gig, they were ready. Enter the Punk Funk Horns.

Before *Bustin' Out* was finished being mixed, Barry Gordy called me early in the morning and asked if I would like to produce Diana Ross. I was thrilled at the chance. He put Diana on the other line and we talked for an hour about concepts. I even had this great concept for the album cover. I was going to have her pictured in ripped up jeans and leather, looking at her old self, dressed up like a Supreme, lying in a coffin

The next day I began to write tunes for Diana. I wrote this funky duet called "Sucker for Love." It would feature me and Diana. She loved the song and she loved my ideas. But as soon as I found out I was only going to do three or four cuts on her, I balked—it was all or nothing.

While walking through Motown one day I heard this beautiful voice. I looked in the office where it was coming from and sitting at the piano singing was this little white chick named Teena Marie. She was shy, even bashful as she introduced herself to me. I asked her what she was doing there, and she said she was signed to the company. We talked a little longer, then I left.

One day I got this call from her manager, Winnie Jones, who asked if I wanted to produce Teena. I said "Send me some tapes," so I could hear some more of her voice. After I heard her, I was geeked to produce her. Never in my life had I heard such a range with so much passion in a white voice. I immediately started writing for her. I was also told this was her last shot. She had spent close to four hundred thousand dollars recording and still no album. I was amazed at how Motown could spend so much without getting at least one tune out of it. Motown really didn't know what to do with her, Barry had signed her as an actress, and singing was going to be secondary for her. They had all these producers writing songs for her that just didn't work, some of the songs sounded good to me, but Motown just didn't hear it. In any case, I finished a bunch of tunes for Teena. I also decided to give her "Sucker for Love," since I wasn't doing Diana's album anymore.

After I listened to Teena's voice carefully, writing for her was easy. The songs just seemed to come: "Déjà Vu," a slow ballad about reincarnation; "Don't Look Back," a Temptations remake; "Turning Me On," "Can't Love Anymore," and Teena's tune, "Have my Cake." I cut "Have my Cake," with Oscar on upright bass and hired some old Jazz cats for real Jazz flavor and authenticity.

Teena lived with Winnie and her daughter Jill and Winnie's live-in lover, Fuller Gordy, Barry's brother. Jill would later move in with Prince and have a part in *Purple Rain*. Prince also wrote and produced Jill's album. The three lived in a very nice house in the Hollywood Hills. Teena had been kicked out of her mother's house in Venice for hanging with Black people, and Winnie and Fuller took her in. She was like their daughter. Teena, being only five feet tall, had the voice of someone seven feet high. I mean she could sing her ass off. I remember once in the studio doing her first album; when she sang I had to punch her in and out—in other words, when she sang I had to stop and start the tape—to get her to sing the song correctly. She would get so frustrated she'd cry. The reason I had to do this was to teach her how not to use all her vocal licks at the top of the song, and how to wait till she got into the tune before she used all her hip tricks. She would come into the control room after I had finished and cry while listening to her playbacks. She finally understood what I was doing.

Teena's album turned out great, we called it: *Wild and Peaceful*. We deliberately didn't put her picture on the album cover, because we wanted to confuse people, and made them wonder whether Teena was Black or White.

When I finished with Teena, Barney Ales—Motown President at the time, a fat, grey-haired Mafia-looking fuck—got right in my face at Suzanne De Passe's wedding and ordered me to finish *Bustin' Out*. When he said "Fuck Teena Marie," I knew he meant business.

During my career at Motown I always felt the presence of organized crime. Having grown up around it in Buffalo with Mom, I knew the Italian groove and it made me nervous. The closest I ever came to having a real problem with organized crime at Motown was with Danny Davis, an older, grey-haired gentleman in his fifties, who headed the Promotion Department of Motown. I always liked Danny. He was a happy-go-lucky fellow whose biggest claim to fame was working with The Monkees in their earlier years.

One day Danny called me to his office. He looked distraught. After I sat down, I asked him what was wrong. He told me he needed to talk to me about a life-and-death situation. He explained to me that because of me, Motown was going to have airplay stopped on all their records. I couldn't believe my ears and I asked Danny to explain. He said he really couldn't at that point, but someone who could would talk to me soon. I was so freaked that when I went back to the studio I cancelled the session and went home.

All that day I wondered how little ol' me could be responsible for big ass Motown Record Company's air play to be stopped across the country. I was totally confused.

Kelly had come to town to see me. I decided we'd be alone so I rented a suite at the Chateau Marmont and had all my calls transferred there. About one o'clock that evening I got a strange call. Kelly answered it, and said it was for me. I told her to tell whomever it was to fuck off. I heard her speak, then she said with a strange sound to her voice, "Rick, I think you should take this." I got up sleepy-eyed and shouted, "Who is it?" This strong Italian accent was on the other end of the line. He told me I was going to be picked up in the morning to talk and I'd best be ready. Then he just hung up. I told Kelly what happened and could see the fear on her face.

About nine the next morning there was a knock on my door. It was this huge muscle-bound, unsmiling Black motherfucker with this bald fucking head, wearing a jogging suit. This dude was a sight. I got dressed, kissed Kelly goodbye and got into this long black limousine that was waiting outside. Inside were a well-dressed, older Italian gentleman and a young Italian in his early twenties. The older guy told me he was glad I could make it. I wanted to tell him "Fuck You," but I had no choice. So I just remained quiet and listened.

He told me the young guy in the car was his nephew, and his nephew had this beautiful girl who could sing. His nephew had introduced her to the snake Jeffrey Bowen to be produced. By the time Jeffrey finished giving her drugs and fucking her up completely, she was through. The capper was Jeffrey had promised the nephew me in exchange! Yeah, he had told the nephew that he'd be able to manage me.

I was shocked—I mean the story was fucked up. This big shot was obviously a Mafioso who probably ran a lot of radio stations across the country, who now wanted me for his nephew.

We had breakfast at the Old World Café on Sunset. Danny even drove by and waved. I listened carefully to every word the big guy said. It was like out of a fucking Godfather movie—an offer I couldn't refuse. He told me that by being with his nephew, I'd never have to worry about money or anything. He told me he'd call me the next day for my answer. He dropped me off at the hotel.

My head was spinning. I was confused, so I called my mother and told her about it. She told me I had worked too hard to just throw it away that easily, and to follow my heart, she'd be behind me, no matter what. I stayed up all night thinking.

Morning came and the phone rang. It was the Mafioso. I just told him, "Hey, thanks for the offer, but I have to refuse." I told him his nephew probably was a great manager, but I had come too far to let go and now I had my own way of doing things. He listened then said, " I can respect the way you feel." He wished me luck in my career and told me he'd handle Jeffrey, the snake, Bowen. I was relieved. Now it was time to get on with my life.

The band threw me a surprise birthday party. A lot of celebrities came, Marvin Gay and his young, beautiful wife Jan brought me some great weed. Most of the people there just wanted to hang out and get a glimpse of the new kid in town. All went well, and the party was a success.

At that time my love interest was a beautiful Black woman named Patti Brooks. I had met her during one of her performances in Hollywood. She was a Disco star and a very good one. She also had this great sense of humor. I always loved women who made me laugh. Her daughter Yvette was also beautiful. She looked like a Black Brooke Shields. She would later become Corvette, a Mary Jane Girl.

Everything in my life was going perfect. *Bustin' Out* was at the top of the charts. I wouldn't want more. Teena and I were spending a lot of time together—nothing sexual as of yet, just strong friendship.

Chapter Forty
The Magical Funk Tour

Teena Marie never got high in those days. She didn't even smoke cigarettes. Even now she'll occasionally have one. Most of the time she just bums off me. In those days Teena and I would sit quietly by my swimming pool and talk about the future, our ambitions, our fears, and shit like that. One day she told me how she thought she might be gay. I asked her what made her think like that. She told me she was developing strong desires for women, one in particular. As we talked I could see how serious she was feeling. Little did I know then but what Teena was going through was only the tip of the iceberg of what was soon to come.

It was now time for me to get a manager. My life was getting too hectic with interviews, TV shows, meetings and rehearsals. I needed someone to handle my business. Shep Gordon was a Buffalo boy who made millions of dollars handling Alice Cooper. Now he had Teddy Pendergrass, and a bunch of other acts. I went to his office to meet him. Shep is a very likable fellow who smoked a lot of grass, fucked a lot of women, snorted a lot of coke and made a lot of deals. Just my kind of guy. He had even started to get into films: Alive Films, named after his management company, Alive Management. I liked Shep for the most part. I'd find out later he was nothing more than a bald-headed Jewish pimp.

Shep basically would sit at his desk smoking weed and let these other schmucks like Joe Gannon and Alan Strahl take care of the business. He thought he was far too rich to get involved, and after doing what little he did, he would have to go to his house in Maui, Hawaii to relax some more. If I had known then what I know now, I never would have let that bald headed son-of-a-bitch near my business. I used to tell Teddy Pendergrass how Shep was ripping his ass off. But Teddy was so busy fucking over people himself—like fucking dude's wives and

159

shit—thinking he was God's gift to the Universe. I just said, "Fuck it, Teddy. You'll see in the long run." And I was right.

By now *Bustin' Out* and Teena Marie were both at the top of the charts and I was finally ready to go on tour. I had a stage design in mind, and I told Shep who called Joe Gannon. Joe was an old grey-haired motherfucker who probably would have sucked Shep's dick if Shep asked him.

Joe came to one—I mean one rehearsal, looked around at the band and left. Joe was supposed to be our stage coordinator. A couple of weeks later I walked into rehearsal and saw what Joe had built: a bunch of wooden backdrops with lights inside of them—cheap looking shit. Joe and Shep charged me over fifty thousand dollars for that cheap-ass shit and thirty thousand dollars to Joe Gannon for "supervision." I freaked. I knew then and there Shep and Joe, and Shep's whole operation, were bullshit. Right then I started thinking of ways to get the fuck out of Shep's contract.

The cross-country tour would visit over forty cities. I was excited. I told the band I thought it would be good if we went to a small city without letting them know it was us and just play a gig for a week or two. The city was Fresno, California.

Fresno was a medium sized town between LA and Frisco, a great warm-up spot. The venues on our tour were two thousand five hundred to four thousand five hundred people. Little did I know it then, but those halls would be too, too small. When Motown gave me a platinum party they had this magician named Alan entertaining the guests. I was so impressed by his tricks that I asked him to open for me on tour.

Our first week in Fresno we played in front of this theater under another name. The theater had built a cool stage for us, and the arena held about five hundred people. With the town being so small, word of our arrival traveled fast. By the time the first week was over, there were crowds around the entire block. The band was in top form, and each night that passed we got tighter and tighter. After the first week we went and played the theater. It held three thousand, five hundred people. We played four nights. Each night was sold out. Chicanos, Blacks and Whites mixed without trouble—not one incident.

After finishing our two–week stint in Fresno, I spent a week in the bed. There was more coke in Fresno than any place I'd been; little kids on the street even sold it. It seemed that Fresno, being between LA and Frisco, was a drop-off point. I mean we stayed fucked up every night, I suffered for it after the two weeks.

We all flew back to LA to relax before we went on the four-month tour. My first royalty check had just arrived for *Come Get It* and *Bustin' Out*—one million, eight hundred thousand dollars. I showed it to this band and then put it above the fireplace. Funk was starting to pay off.

The tour ran smooth, except that everywhere we played there were near riots. The venues were just too small, and every night there were more people out side the arenas trying to get in than there were inside. It was fantastic.

In Boston we played the Orpheum Theater. The only way to enter the theater was through this small entrance at the end of a narrow alley, and we had thousands of kids milling around, trying to get in. After the show, we came out to see that the mounted police had been sent in, and that cops were beating on Black sisters and brothers from their horses. As I watched the cops assaulting my fans I just cried. I felt responsible and promised myself from then on I would only play places that could hold the kind of crowds we were getting. I never broke that promise.

Al Haymon was the promoter of the Orpheum show. He was a young Black brother attending Harvard Law School who promoted concerts on the side to make money for school. He asked me if I thought there was any real money in promotion and I said "Hell yeah! Especially in Buffalo." I told him "Fuck law school" and encouraged him to promote full time. He did just that, and now he is the biggest Black promoter in the world. He's a good brother and I'm very proud to have been part of his success.

After the tour we went back to LA. I bought a brand new Rolls Royce and a Jaguar. Mom had moved into the house. But I had the feeling she wasn't comfortable because the house was too big, plus she had also been unable to find a corner bar in the neighborhood where she could play numbers. One morning we had an earthquake and Mom freaked. Next thing I knew she had packed her clothes and gone back to

Buffalo. I was getting a little tired of LA myself. I wanted to go home. So did my band, so that's what we did.

I sold the house and moved back to Buffalo. I got rid of the Jag and bought an Excalibur that I shipped to Buffalo, leaving the Rolls in LA. I bought a house outside Buffalo in the suburb of Orchard Park, along with fifteen acres, horses, an Olympic-sized indoor pool and a tennis court. I hired a beautiful sweet Cancer lady named Linda Hunt to work as my housekeeper. I'm not sure how I met her. She just appeared at my house one day and never left. She didn't drink, smoke or swear, even till this day, and she's still with me, working as my assistant.

I'd started work on my third album and was enjoying living in Buffalo. I had carte blanche everywhere. The City even named a street after me.

There's a funny story about the house I bought outside of Buffalo. The first owners were a Black doctor and his family. Of course, it was a very racist area. The people in the community burned crosses on the property and wouldn't let the doctor join the country club. When the doctor heard that, he decided to build his own club and added a pool and tennis court for his kids. Eventually, the doctor was forced to move out. The next owners decided to make it a home for retarded people, but the community got together and banned the idea. The owner was pissed. He told the town council that if he wasn't allowed to open his home, he would see the house to niggers. I swear. It's on the city records.

Then I bought the house. Surprise. When I moved in there was a full–color picture of me and my mother on the front of the Buffalo newspaper. The caption read: "Crowned Prince Returns Home." It came out when we sold out the twenty thousand-seat venue in Buffalo during the "Magical Funk Tour." I told my security to drop copies off at everybody's doorsteps in the area so they would know I had arrived and I wasn't Dr. Dunn—do not fuck with me! I remembered back to the night on the beach with Malcolm and Amopuza. Just let these motherfuckers try to burn a cross on my yard!

The tour had gone quite successfully and the whole country was Rick James crazy. It was great. It was now time to do another album. I decided to leave Art Stewart and produce on my own. There were no hard feelings. I just needed a change. I also wanted a new studio to work in, so I called the Record Plant in Sausalito. Sly and The Family Stone had done a lot of work there, so I felt if it was good enough for Sly it was good enough for me. Tom Flye, the engineer, a mild-mannered guy who wore glasses and was extremely quiet, had worked with Sly and also worked with the Grateful Dead, Starship and numerous other Frisco acts. Tom became my engineer and other than the square way he looked, we were extremely compatible.

During the sixties Tom's hair was past his ass. He played Theramin in a Frisco group called Lothar and the Hand People. He also starred in an Andy Warhol film called *Edie*, a film about Edie Sedgwick. So despite the square look Tom now had, he was one of the original freaks.

The band and I had already thoroughly rehearsed in an empty studio. So at The Record Plant we recorded and mixed, finishing the album in thirteen days. The album was called *Fire It Up* and the single was "Love Gun." I also started work on the Stone City Band's first album, called *In N Out*. The band's album was different than mine and it had Jazz, Latin, Rock and Funk, all with different textures than mine.

I had been using the Pointer Sisters a lot to sing background on my albums, and I decided to use them on Stone City Band's first single "Little Runaway." If one didn't know better, they would have thought it was a Pointer Sisters' single. Working with the girls was a great experience. I had always loved them, especially "Betcha Gota Chick on the Side," which was a great record. I really loved Ruth. She was tall like an African Queen and I used to get a hard-on working with them. I'd sit at the console snorting and working away while they'd be smoking co-co puffs (cigarettes with coke inside). They were always a pleasure to work with, and talented, talented ladies.

Everything I touched was turning to Gold and Platinum. It seemed I was the only artist doing Funk and Rock; other groups were trying, but failing miserably. The press and the fans were calling me an overnight success, a boy wonder, all this shit. Little did they know that my story dated back to the early sixties, and the reason I was so good at what I did was because I had mastered it after many, many years. A lot of cats knew how to funk—that part was easy. But very few knew how to put that special vibe on their music. That's what I knew best.

Chapter Forty-one
Me and Prince

Fire It Up went platinum and critics loved it, calling it one of my best works, although I never thought so. The fact that it had been written, recorded and mixed in thirteen days, impressed a lot of the musical press. After *Fire It Up*, I recorded the Stone City Band's second album called *The Boys Are Back*. I think I enjoyed cutting the band more than I did recording myself. The only problem with the Stone City Band was that Levi, the lead singer, sounded a little too much like me, which sometimes confused radio programmers.

I longed to see the Stone City Band become a success independent of their work with me. I always strove to put something really strong and unique on their albums. We would use complex textures, and take inspiration from Latin America and Africa in the instrumentation. But in the end, they never really got the acclaim they deserved.

It was time for me to go back on tour. This time I wanted to go twenty thousand seaters all the way. But I needed an opening act.

There was a record burning up the airwaves called "I Wanna Be Your Lover" by some cat named Prince. He played guitar, and everyone was telling me how a tour with me and him would be great. I bought his album and I really enjoyed it, especially "Sexy Dancer." I thought the kid was pretty funky. So I asked for the company to send me a video on him. I received the video and as I watched him I thought he reminded me a bit of myself, except he didn't move as much. I asked Prince to open up the *Fire It Up* tour.

My stage for the tour was the most elaborate and expensive yet. I had stairs everywhere, moveable lights, and forty-foot lifts for both me and my drummer. I had designed the stage set myself, and it was all white. I had new costumes designed that were really cool and sharp. The band loved them, and we were geeked to get out on the road. We were never so ready for a tour as the *Fire It Up* tour. Our first date was down south. I hadn't met Prince yet. In fact, the only thing I had heard about him was that he was shy. I had hoped he wasn't too shy, or he had no right being on the road with me, that's for sure.

When I walked in through the backstage entrance, Prince was sitting on his group's drums playing some bullshit beat. I sat down on our set where he could see me and began playing some serious shit. He looked over at me and just got his little ass up and walked away. That was my first victory.

I had a feeling this tour was going to be something else, but I had no idea. The first time I saw Prince and his band I felt sorry for him. Here's this little dude wearing hi-heels, playing this New Wave Rock & Roll, not moving or anything on stage, just standing there wearing this trench coat. Then at the end of his set he'd take off his trench coat and he'd be wearing little girl's bloomers. I just died. The guys in the audience just booed the poor thing to death.

The following weeks of the tour weren't very different from the opening date. Whenever I was on stage I'd see Prince on the side of the stage just staring and watching everything I did, like a kid in school. I'd walk over to him during a song and point my bass right in his face, grab my crotch, give him the finger and keep jammin'. He was remembering everything I did, like a computer.

I used to do all these tricks with the microphone—flip it, catch it backwards, you name it. It was a trademark of mine. I also used to do a lot of crowd chants. I'd have my hand on my ear while I called these funk chants to the audience. This was another trademark.

One day I walked into the auditorium, getting ready to go on, and I heard the crowd chanting loudly. I went to check it out. Here's Prince doing my chants. Not only that he was stalking the stage just like me, doing the funk sign, flipping the microphone and everything. The boy had stolen my whole show. I was pissed, and so was my band. This went on night after night, every show I'd see more of my own routine. It got to the point I couldn't do the stuff I had always done cuz Prince was doing it before I came on. It started to look like I was copying him.

Everyone knew what was happening: his management, my management. The atmosphere backstage was not improved by the fact that Prince's band members were not on good terms with my band and my guys wanted to kick their asses. Prince's musicians would stick their noses in the air and not even acknowledge the Stone City Band, even if they were all standing together, waiting for the elevator. My band was the friendliest bunch of guys you ever wanted to meet. They were veterans; everyone liked them. Prince's group was a bunch of egotistical assholes who never even played on a record. The kid did it all; they were just hired players. On the road, you have to have camaraderie, because you are seeing the same people night after night. Prince's shitty attitude and the attitude of his band made it pretty hard some nights.

One day things almost blew up. I was pissed, my band was pissed, and something had to be done. So my management and Prince's management got together, along with Prince and his band and me and my band to have it out once and for all.

First, I met with Prince's manager and told him that if Prince did any more of my show he was off the tour. Even his own manager agreed that Prince was stealing my show. Finally, we all met in Prince's room: Prince, me and our bands. My band, looking like six foot five Black Maasai Warriors with their braids and leather, sat at one end, while Prince's band, in their eyelashes and make-up, sat at the other. Prince's band was afraid, very afraid. Levi and the boys were ready to give an ass-whipping. Prince sat on the bed and hardly said a word. He acted like a little bitch while his band and mine patched up their differences. After that confrontation, things went back to normal—me kicking his ass every night.

Soon after that episode there was a birthday party for me. Prince came, he was sitting at a table with some people not drinking. I walked up to him, grabbed him by the back of his hair and poured cognac down his throat. He spit it out like a little bitch and I laughed and walked away. I loved fucking with him like that. Later on he would fuck with me, but for now, it was all about Rick James.

I always felt our competition was healthy, although I was jealous when he started getting big—more than jealous—I was pissed, because here was this little short ego'd-out fucker who I had a feeling didn't like people of his own race and wanted to be white and taller. I was pissed because I felt his songs about incest with his sister and a lot his stuff wasn't real, and it was dangerous for the race. A writer and a recording artist has to be careful with what they write. We are obligated to at least be real. There have been enough motherfuckers running around talking about devil-worship or gangster rap, whereas I always felt that black people had to be a little more concerned with the influence they had on younger generations. All the power he had became scary when you think of it being in his little fucked up hands. When he wrote "Controversy," "Am I Black, Am I White, Am I Straight, Am I Gay?" me and my band would say "Who Gives a Fuck?" I never saw Prince hang with a Brother or a Sister. In fact his whole demeanor was like that of a short uppity white boy. He would sing songs like "Give Head Till Your Red." I mean that motherfucker probably never gave head in his life.

Chapter Forty-two
King of Funk

A reporter asked me one day what I called my brand of music. For a joke, I said "Punk Funk." Punks were kids from England who were usually poor and who were rebelling against the Queen, the system, bureaucrats and everything. Although we weren't as radical as Punk Rockers, we were rebellious. The title stuck, and after that I was called "The King of Punk Funk." The white critics always want to name and categorize things, so I got the jump on them and named our style of music myself.

Toward the end of the *Fire It Up* tour I began to go to work on my next album. Prince had a synthesizer called an OBX back then and nobody else had one. I loved the way it sounded. So while going to Miami to do tracks for my next album I decided to borrow it without telling the little runt. We kept it for two weeks while we had a break on the tour, used it, and then put it back on his truck. Prince never knew.

While in Miami me and the band rented a mansion right on the Keys next door to one of the BeeGees. Miami was sunny and laid back.

After the tour wrapped, I started to work on my next album. Motown and I were having our differences, mostly about money. I was pissed off and frustrated, which was not a good state to make an album. *Garden of Love,* my forth album, was really laid back, with mostly slow, summer tunes on it. Most of the songs had been written while vacationing in the Caribbean Islands. Every year after I toured I'd go to the islands: St. Croix, St. Thomas, Martinique. I'd take my acoustic guitar, rent a yacht and just cruise. *Garden of Love* was written down there. The single was called "Big Time," and had been written by Leroy Burgess. It was the only song I ever recorded that I didn't write.

Garden of Love had only six songs on it. I usually put eight or nine on my albums—never less. This time, because I was angry with Motown, I only put on six. *Garden of Love* barely went gold for me and I had to cancel the tour I'd planned for it. I found out with *Garden of Love* that success could end any time and you're only as good as your last record.

After *Garden of Love* I was afraid my career was over. The cancellation of the tour had crushed me and I went to Hawaii to think. Shep Gordon had a house right on the beach of Maui, and I needed to regroup. While I was there I had dinner with Shep. An artist was there eating with us. He and Shep talked art and shit but my mind was in another place. This artist thought I had great lips, at least that's what he said. He asked me if he could sketch me, which he did, on a napkin. The artist was Salvador Dali, he handed me the napkin. I looked at it and stuck it in my pocket. Later that day I unthinkingly jumped in the ocean wearing the same clothes from dinner with the napkin and the portrait in my pocket.

While in Hawaii I'd made up my mind about a lot of things: first, I would never cut an album with only six tunes; second, no matter how mad I got with Motown, I would never let my emotions interfere with my music; and third, I wanted to leave Shep Gordon.

When I arrived in LA, all my friends said, "Rick, you got to get back to the Funk, the streets. You got to get hungry again." Everyone said the same thing. It was like a broken record. I had gotten too rich, too fast. I had lost that thing, that ghetto tiger, which had fueled me in the beginning. Instead of drinking cheap wine, I was drinking Cristal Champagne and bottles of Chateau Rothschild. Instead of one bitch there were twenty. Everything had multiplied. I was in the California sunshine, not the ghettos and black snow of Buffalo. Life had become easy and I had become lackadaisical.

My hangout spot was a club in Hollywood called Carlos N Charlie's, a restaurant on the bottom and a club on the top. It was strictly VIP. All the stars hung out there. It was the in spot. I was hangin' out with this guy named Pete Kelly, a light-skinned brother who resembled Smokey Robinson. He was also my coke dealer. Girls liked Petey and he liked the girls. He owned two Rolls Royces and a house in the hills. We were inseparable.

Sunset Boulevard was a hoe stroll. All the prostitutes in Hollywood worked The Strip, and they loved Rick James and I loved them. I would send them roses while they worked. When I'd ride down the street they would whistle and yell my name. It seemed I had something in common with them. And I did—we were all from the streets.

I went back to Buffalo for a while. When I got there I dressed myself in a disguise and went to the Perry Projects, just to walk around for a while. I realized I was there to get back to the streets. I needed to feel the essence of the ghetto and the projects again. I needed "Street Songs."

Chapter Forty-three
Super Freak

It was a revelation. I put the entire band on a plane and flew to Sausalito. It was time for my fifth album and I knew exactly what I wanted—a street album, an album that talked about ghettoes, pimps, hoes, dope, police, passion, and love. Before I even started recording I knew the name of the album: *Street Songs*. The Record Plant made me a room to sleep in and I would lock myself in it with my guitar, bass and a drum machine. In there I'd write from dawn to sunset. I wanted something different, something powerful. I wanted to make some kind of statement with this album, something people would never forget.

Before the *Fire It Up* tour, the band went through some personnel changes. Tom McDermott was now on guitar, Erskine Williams on piano, Greg Livias was on synthesizers. Danny Lemelle was on sax, Lamorris Payne on trumpet, Cliff Irving on trumpet, and John Irving on trombone. Val Young and Sheila Horn sang backgrounds. Levi was still on synthesizers. Lanise was still on drums, Oscar still on bass, and Nate on percussion.

When I'd cut *Garden of Love* I wasn't excited, but with *Street Songs* the passion and the desire to record had returned with a vengeance. *Street Songs* would either be my biggest album or my worst. I didn't believe in in-between.

People often ask me what tunes on *Street Songs* I like the best. I can only say all of them except "Super Freak." When I wrote "Super Freak," the album was all but finished and I was satisfied. One day I was sitting in the studio playing my bass and I started singing with this funny voice: "She's a very kinky girl…" While singing, I played this punk-type bass line. The band started to laugh, and one of the cats said "Cut it, Rick."

When we had started recording the album, I had said that I wanted to put something on it for white folk, just as a joke, something that they could dance to. "Super Freak" was that song.

One of my favorite songs on the album was "Fire and Desire." After hearing how great and funky the track came out, I said, "This would be great for a chick to sing on." I didn't ask Teena to sing on it. In fact I had found a local girl with an amazing voice who was going to record the female vocals. Teena was in Sausalito at the time, sick with a fever of one hundred and eight degrees. But when she heard I was going to use somebody else she immediately got out of her sick bed to sing on the track. Needless to say, that's how it came out.

"Ghetto Life" was an autobiographical piece that summed up my life in four minutes and fifty seconds.

Narada Michael Walden had been hanging around. I have always considered him one of the greatest drummers in the world. I asked him to play on "Make Love to Me" and he said he'd be happy to. Janet Dubois from the TV series *Good Times* made those sexy moaning sounds on the track.

"Give It to Me Baby" was inspired by getting too fucked up to fuck, something that anyone who drinks and snorts coke can relate to.

"Mr. Policeman" was a true account of a friend of mine in Buffalo who was shot by the police. Stevie Wonder played harmonica on that track, along with vocals by Teena Marie. I loved the reggae feel to it.

"Fire and Desire" was a ballad about breaking women's hearts and changing. At the time I wrote it I had met this Ethiopian Princess in Paris, Zimma, who made me change my attitude toward women. We had spent an amazing time together in a hotel on Champs Elysses and though she didn't approve of my lifestyle, I really cared for her. She was the first woman in my life to really rebel against my drug use and she finally left me because of it. She changed me with her love and sensitivity.

"Call Me Up" was a fun tune. Girls were always getting my number from God knows where. They would call me up and say with a sexy voice, "Hello, can I speak to Slick Rick?" So I thought I'd write about the experience.

"Blow the Funk" was another autobiographical tune about Buffalo that I used to close the album, along with this African chant.

The lyrics to "Super Freak" were nasty, to say the least—too nasty for radio. Alonzo Miller, a friend of mine, was hanging out with me during the vocals. He was a DJ and a Program Director at KACE, a LA radio station. After hearing the lyrics, he just shook his head and said "Rick, they'll never play it on radio." I asked him why. He just said, "Radio won't play it." Then he told me he'd always thought I was slicker than that with my lyrics and that's what separated me from Prince. I agreed and sat down with him to change the lyrics. After we came up with lyrics he wasn't offended by, I gave him ten percent of "Super Freak" for helping me see the light.

Later, when Alonzo showcased the album on his show, he got all these calls about "Super Freak," from old ladies who complained about the lyrics. Alonzo caved in and stopped playing it. I was pissed! I confronted him head on, telling him how I had changed the record for him and asking him where was his integrity? Why was he letting those few calls sway him from playing the record? Finally, he agreed he was being weak, and put the song back in heavy rotation. The minute the first single, "Give It to Me Baby," hit the air it was an instant hit on both Black and white stations. The album was released four weeks afterwards and became an instant radio success. My whole life changed drastically after *Street Songs*. I was no longer a Black artist, I had officially crossed over.

Famous and Fabulous

Rick at the American Music Awards

Stevie Wonder, Chaka Khan, Rick

Rick on Tour

Rick and Friends

*Rick having a won-
derful time*

Rick having a wonderful time

Sharing Some Great Moments

With Isaac Hayes

With Michael Narada Walden

Rick with special friends

Rick loved the girls

Rick with his mom, Betty

Rick with Bernadette Peters

Rick with Friends

I'll drink to that

Rick with Morgan Fairchild

Chapter Forty-four
Beginning a New Era

With "Super Freak," "Give It to Me Baby," "Fire and Desire" and "Ghetto Life" blasting the airways, there wasn't a station you could turn to, Black or white, that wasn't playing something off that album.

I had changed management. My new pimp was named Jerry Wientraub. Jerry handled such notables as Sylvester Stallone, The Pointer Sisters and Frank Sinatra. At that time I was writing scripts and wanted to do a movie and Jerry's main focus was on acting and movies. He had a producer named Mark Johnson working for him who grew fond of me. Marc always felt I needed to do a film and my desire to do so was the main reason I signed with Jerry. But Jerry and I disagreed on everything as far as movies were concerned. The only consolation was that he loved my scripts.

Jerry hadn't produced a successful film when I signed with him but as far as his acts were concerned, he was a good manager. Jerry was less effective for me because I was already a star when I hired him and he didn't have to go out there and hustle for me, but anybody was better than Shep Gordon.

When *Street Songs* hit, everybody wanted to be my friend. Suddenly I had white fans as well as the Blacks who had always loved me. Before I would sell out twenty thousand seats to Blacks, now we were playing to stadiums three times that size to mixed audiences. Now we were going to the top of all the charts, Pop and R&B. People were really freaking, but I clung to my philosophy of maintaining the funk, and not selling my soul for a dollar. I could easily have given up the funk and just played Rock & Roll for white folks, but I had seen what happened to people like Ray Parker, who copped out and lost their Black audience. I always wanted a black base and I always kept the funk in my shit.

At that time I was hanging out in New York with Mark Fleischmann, the owner of Studio 54. Mark was an older man who had as much energy as I did. Our birthdays are on the same day, February 1 and we became really close. He introduced me to the cream of the crop in the entertainment industry. Janice Dickinson, who was the Number One model in the world and we were dating. I had a wide group of friends: Iman, a beautiful Somalian model, Tanya Tucker, the Country & Western singer who is as soulful as you can get. Peter Max, an artist who offered to do lithographs of me; Grace Jones, a friend who I still consider a sister; Rick and Kathy Hilton. I sang "Happy Birthday" to Kathy at their Hotel in New York and they gave me Baccarat Crystal for my own birthday. The Studio 54 crowd was the most exciting group of people I'd ever met. I was always there, partying and getting high in the upstairs office. Mark would throw everybody out if I needed a quiet spot to chill.

One day Mark came downstairs and told me there was a friend of mine in the office I should go see. I found a crowd of people, and one of them was the son of a prominent political family. Everyone was getting high. Jr. asked me if I knew the keyboard player for Earth, Wind & Fire. I said I did and he introduced me to this Black dude who was posing as Larry Dunn.

I asked the dude "Who the Fuck are you? Don't you think I know who Larry Dunn is, Motherfucker? Who the fuck am I?"

He said "Rick James."

I said, "That's right, motherfucker, and you ain't no Larry Dunn."

I called my security. But by the time they got there his ass was gone. I told Jr. he should be more careful who he lets hang around.

Politics are something I take seriously. They involve my life, your life, everyone's life. If more people made it a top priority this country might be different.

Anyway, there was never a dull moment at the Studio.

Street Songs was reaching the top of the charts and it was time to go on the road. All the promoters wanted to do the tour, but I had no idea of how much to offer them. Louis Grey had been a West Coast promoter, doing well with Earth, Wind & Fire. One day he came to my hotel suite in LA and told me he really wanted the whole *Street Songs* tour. He had an offer of forty million to do the tour, with a deposit of a million to me. He had two hundred and fifty thousand dollars advance on the million and I gave him ten days to come up with the rest. He never did, so I gave him back the money and thought nothing more of it. I found out later that this asshole Louis Grey had gone to some rich dudes in Arizona and borrowed the money, telling them he could get the Rick James tour. Louis never gave the money back and his investors would hound me throughout my tour thinking I had their money.

I had a brand new stage made along with my new costumes. We rehearsed for a month and got tight. We were ready for the largest–grossing Black tour in history and though we didn't know it yet, *Street Songs* was on its way to being the second-biggest selling Black album of all time.

Teena Marie and I had just released her third album, *It Must Be Magic*. My sister Penny was handling her management, so I hired Teena to open. We hired some other cats to come on before Teena—groups like Cameo, SOS Band, Grand Master Flash, Luther Vandross, Ray Parker, New Edition, Gap Band and more.

Before the *Street Songs* tour began, George Clinton asked me if we wanted to do his Funk Festival. The Funk Fest would put me into stadiums of eighty thousand plus—the biggest crowds we had faced to date. He had done Funk Fests before with such bands as the Isley Brothers, Maze, Barkays, Con Funktion, Bootsy, Brides of Funkenstein, and Parliament. George would use these Funk Fests as a way to showcase his groups, basically with a take it to the stage concept. They were like the championships of Funk.

Anyway, George wanted to kick my ass on stage. I didn't mind. But if I was going to be funked out, it would be for a good price, so I told him I wanted seventy five thousand dollars a show—and I got it. We would do three stadiums: The Coliseum in LA, the Houston Astrodome, and the Motordome in Detroit. We sold out all three. George let me pick the slot I wanted to come on. So I picked about nine PM, right before Bootsy. It was great. I'd always known I'd get a chance to pay George back for those earlier years. Now was payback time.

The group and I did about an hour show. By the time we finished people were hoarse from singing along. When we left the stage most people left the stadium. It was my greatest moment. George never asked me to do another Funk Festival. I had made it clear after that Funk Fest that I was not fucking around. Punk Funk was here to stay.

The Street Songs tour began with a bang. Every twenty thousand seater in every major city was sold out—not once, but twice. We played the Philadelphia Spectrum for two nights, then went back and sold out the stadium. We broke Elvis Presley's record in Memphis selling out the Memphis Coliseum, three shows.

When I first arrived in Memphis there were fifteen Black plainclothes policemen there to protect me. It seems some white racists were planning to kill me in Memphis. They had fire bombed a couple of record stores that had my albums and pictures in the windows. They didn't want that longhaired, pot-smoking nigger in their town. I was nervous, because Memphis is where they got Martin Luther King. But the Black police weren't going to take any chances. They all volunteered to protect me. It was a trip.

I went to Elvis's home in Memphis and was asked to leave. They said we were causing too much commotion for the tourists. I wasn't doing shit, just looking, and all these white folks came up to me for autographs. The thing about Memphis is they just don't believe The King is dead. I mean, Elvis is everywhere: gift shops, shirts, cars, posters, I mean everywhere.

When I walked on stage at a packed coliseum, I had the rebel flag in my hand. I tore it up. Then I yelled at the crowd, "I went to Elvis's house today." The crowd said "Yeah!" I replied, "And the motherfucker wasn't home." They loved it. It was no slur on Elvis. I thought he was cool. But come on, the motherfucker is dead!

Everywhere was sold out. One night in Detroit the SWAT team showed up looking for Rick James. They asked me if I knew where Rick James was. I said I didn't and they moved on.

Another time in Dallas, SWAT surrounded the coliseum. They had warrants out on me to collect the money Louis Grey had stolen from his investors in Arizona. They followed me everywhere on the tour. It was funny. After a while we'd find ways to sneak past them. It became a game for us. Once in a city down south, the police surrounded the auditorium. This time a big fat cop with a cigar in the corner of his mouth and about ten other cops were standing at the steps where I would walk up. The fat pig was determined to serve me. He also told me if I smoked weed on stage he would take me to jail. Well, I smoked weed at every concert. During "Mary Jane," I had these twenty-foot joints made out of paper-mache, which had smoke that would come out from the top. During "Mary Jane," I'd go through this classical trip with the band, conducting while I was smoking a joint. I did it at every concert.

Well, when that part came, I brought the music down to where it was almost silent, then I told the audience the police wanted to take me to jail that night. The crowd booed. Then I said "Y'all gonna let them come up here and take me away?" The crowd yelled "Hell no!" Then I said, "Fuck 'em then." That ended any attempt to take me away.

Things got even crazier in Dallas. We had sold out the Dallas Coliseum, and played a great show. One of my roadies came onstage and told me the place was surrounded with SWAT. When the last song was done, all of my roadies came on stage and circled me while the audience screamed for an encore. Meanwhile, I was hurriedly changing clothes. I dressed up in a funky mechanic's outfit that belonged to one of the guys. I stuffed my braids under this Rasta hat, and along with my security Big Moe, quietly slipped out of the auditorium, into a cab and split. I had beaten the SWAT again.

So there Moe and I were, walking around downtown Dallas without knowing where the fuck we were going. It was late at night, Sunday, and no cabs were to be found. We went into this dark bar to have a drink but some kids came in and recognized me. I couldn't believe it. I thought I looked inconspicuous dressed as raggedy as I was. We finally found another cab and went to Denny's to get some food. The restaurant was packed with kids who had gone to the concert and they were all talking about it, calling over the booths to their friends and causing a hubbub. I turned around and asked some of the kids behind me how the concert was. They said it was the bomb. When the waitress came with the bill, she stared and said, "If I didn't know any better, I'd swear you were Rick James." I said, "I wish!"

As I went to pay the tab I could hear the restaurant begin to get uneasy. All the kids were whispering and pointing at us. Even the cooks were poking their heads out of the kitchen to stare. As we walked out to the cab I looked around and everyone's noses were pressed up against the window of the restaurant. So I thought, "What the hell," took off my hat, shook my braids at them and gave them the funk sign. They went wild running out of the restaurant. The cab driver was gone, shouting: "I knew you were Rick James, I knew it!" as we drove down the street, the kids running behind us.

The driver took us to the Coliseum. Thank God the tour busses were still there. When I walked up to my bus, Security was standing there.

My own brother Carmen didn't even recognize me and asked where I thought I was going. Then, recognizing me, they all laughed.

Somewhere down South SWAT confiscated two hundred and fifty thousand dollars worth of my equipment. We missed a week of gigs because of it. My attorneys got a writ for them to release it. That chase was over.

We had been on the road for three months, with three more months to go. After Chicago, I decided to go to Maui, Hawaii for a two-week vacation. I took thirty-seven people with me, including the band, crew, roadies, security and valets. It was great. The roadies said they had worked for a lot of people—Elton, Stones- and no one had ever done something like that for them. I felt they had worked hard and deserved a vacation. When the tour started up again, everyone was rested and ready for another three months work.

Street Songs was Number One R&B for over twenty-one weeks across the board. Teena's album stayed under *Street Songs* at Number Two. The first time we made love was during the tour in Pittsburgh. She wrote a song about it called "Portuguese Love." She told me later that I was the first one to ever give her an orgasm. I mean we made love sundown to sunup. She came like the pouring rain. But we were never boyfriend and girlfriend. I always would tell her that I prided myself on maintaining my freedom. Sometimes if she was angry about other women she'd cuss me under her breath when we sang "Fire and Desire."

Once during the tour I was headlining a stadium date, in Atlanta, I think. Teena wasn't billed on this date. Two weeks before it I had told her it would be good for her album sales to sing "Fire and Desire" with me on this gig. There would be eighty thousand people there. She said she would do it. Come time for the date, she comes to my dressing room with my sister Penny. I asked her if she was still going to sing. She said not unless I paid her something like ten thousand dollars. I got so fucking mad I raised my hand at my sister. Penny said, "Just do it motherfucker. You'll hear from our attorneys." I was so hurt. My own sister was stabbing me in the back. Teena I could see, but not my own blood.

I was on stage and Teena was sitting near Ashford and Simpson on the sidelines. The show was going well. But I wished Teena had said yes. During "Fire and Desire" I was facing the crowd and I heard this loud uproar. I looked around and it was Teena on stage. I was still pissed but I played off it. She sang great. But after the show I didn't want to see her face, especially after I found out that my brother Roy, who was not working with me on tour, paid Teena her money. In my heart I knew that it was reasonable to pay Teena more for her appearances. Her album was very big at the time, but I never wanted to admit that she was a big draw on the tour. In retrospect, I admire her for standing up to me like that.

Chicago was my downfall as far as drugs were concerned. I had never freebased. A matter of fact, whenever someone pulled out all that base shit, I would either leave or have them removed. That time in Chicago it was different. After playing two nights, I returned to my hotel with my personal security guy, Richard, or "Daddy Big Bucks" as we called him. Richard went into his room and I was in mine with a couple of freaks. Eventually, I decided to leave the girls and look for Richard. When I found him he was in his suite with these guys called the Black Stone Rangers, a political gang in Chicago, that were becoming known for keeping the drug dealers and pimps and hoes out of the ghetto. They had even been on the cover of *Time* Magazine for their work on the Chicago streets.

So there I was with the Rangers. They thought I smoked, and had come to turn me onto base. However, when I told the head of the Rangers I didn't smoke, he immediately closed up the case, which contained the rocks and paraphernalia. He said if I didn't do it, they were not going to be the first to turn me out.

I just laughed and said I was just kidding. Big Moe was there with us, and he also lied about smoking it. The Ranger prepared a pipe and asked who wanted to go first. I told Moses to; cuz I wanted to see what it did before I tried it. Moe then took this big hit and fell down. He just toppled over like a felled tree. I was next. I had seen people bass, so I knew how to hit it. I took a much smaller hit than Moe. When I held the smoke in, I got this incredible rush, but afterwards I couldn't tell if it was a high or not. I think I might have hit it again, but I can't remember. It would be weeks before I freebased coke again, and when I did, it would turn out to be an ongoing thing.

I never got high before a gig. I might drink some cognac, or smoke a joint, but I never did coke before a show. The one time I did, I found it fucked up my voice and my timing. I was determined never to let that happen again. I didn't want to disappoint my audience by not hitting my falsetto notes. But never say "never."

The night before our Dallas show I was visited by Duane Thomas, a former Running Back for the Dallas Cowboys, and some of his white dealer friends. Duane would always come to our shows along with other athletes: Sugar Ray Leonard, Tommy Hearns, Patrick Ewing, Darryl Dawkins and many others. The group that came with Duane had a brown shopping bag of cocaine. I got high from the day before the show till show time. It was s stupid thing to do, and till this day I don't know why I did it—but I did.

Come show time, I was feeling like shit, physically. When the show began I felt kind of dizzy. By the time we got into "Fire and Desire" I collapsed on stage. I was carried off and put in a hospital in Dallas for observation. The Press had been kept in the dark about my drug habit, so nothing ever leaked as far as drugs were concerned. They just said I was exhausted and needed rest.

I returned to LA where I stayed at one of Jerry Weintraub's homes in Beverly Hills and recuperated. Two weeks later we were back on the road finishing a grueling six-month tour schedule. I was glad it was over. I had a temperature of one hundred and eight degrees and I was hoarse and tired. When we did *Saturday Night Live*, it was basically our last show. The whole band was tired and we didn't have enough dressing rooms for everybody in my band. There was this young, Black comedian who just started his first year with the show. The Producer let us use his dressing room, and the comic, Eddie Murphy, changed somewhere else.

After sound check I got pissed, mostly because I was scared, sick and tired. I took it out on the band. I started shouting at them for not playing something right. Levi, my best friend and keyboard player was tired and sick too. He told me to kiss his ass, so I fired him. He went back to Buffalo and didn't do the show. One of the trumpet players played his part on "Give It to Me Baby." I missed Levi, and apologized to him in Buffalo. He returned to the band

Chapter Forty-five
Throwin' Down

After the tour, I got rid of Jerry Wientraub. We just didn't see eye to eye. I decided to spend more time in Buffalo and built a recording studio in my home. I spent about half a million dollars building a twenty-four-track state of the art recording studio that my engineer, Tom Flye, designed. I called it Joint Recording Studios.

One day my valet California came to me and showed me an interview with Linda Blair in *Oui Magazine*. The interviewer had asked her who she thought the sexiest man in the world was and whom she would choose to be with if she could pick anyone. She said, "Rick James." I read the interview then told California to send her some roses. Shortly afterwards Linda wrote me a letter telling me how to find her and said that she wanted to meet me. After seeing her layout, I couldn't wait to meet her! She had really grown up since *The Exorcist* and now was this voluptuous woman.

Linda flew to New York and we kicked it off immediately. She is one of the sweetest ladies I've ever known. We went to see Mark Fleishman at a hotel he owned on Lexington Avenue. He stayed in the Penthouse. He asked me and Linda to pose for a picture and we both took off our tops. The picture showed up everywhere. We didn't mind. It was a great picture. Linda and I still love each other and have stayed close friends.

The only argument we've ever had was on the first night we went out. We were up in the office at Studio 54. Steven Tyler was there, Ron Wood of the Stones and Janice Dickenson. Linda was busy talking to Steve. I was downstairs getting high with Janice and her sister Debbie.

When we got back to the hotel we were both high. Linda stood in the middle of the room, just giving me this cold stare. I said, "What's the matter?" She screamed how I disrespected her by leaving her and talking to Janice. She was pissed. I told her I didn't think I was disrespecting her, I just thought since she was talking to Tyler and Woody, I'd talk to Janice. We started yelling and next thing I knew I told her to get the fuck out. She packed her bags and slammed the door as she left. However, while she was downstairs waiting on her brother to pick her up, I apologized and she came back. That was our one and only argument in years of knowing each other.

Linda, Mark Fleishman and I flew down to the Islands where we spent two beautiful weeks sailing and having fun. Mark owned a hotel and another Studio 54, so we had a blast. Linda and I continued to see each other on and off and we are still close friends.

When I got back from the Islands I went home to spend some time with my family. It was good to see Mom. I took her out to dinner and we'd dance for hours. She had more energy than I did. I'm sure she could have danced all night long. I bought her a huge house that at one time belonged to the richest family in Buffalo, the Albrights.

By now I was making a couple of million dollars every year, easy, and my drug habit was accelerating since I had started freebasing regularly. I went from spending a couple hundred thousand dollars on dope to almost a half a million a year. Between private planes, shopping and partying, I was having the time of my life.

On my arrival back in LA there was no doubt about who was the King of Funk. Everyone wanted to hang out with me. Everyone wanted to be my friend. But I kept my people from Buffalo closest. My bungalow became the hangout spot for a lot of Hollywood stars. After the clubs closed, we'd get high and have a good time. Rod Stewart, Eddie Murphy, Timothy Hutton (who was my running buddy at the time). Denny Terrio, Ben Vereen, Jim Brown. TK Carter, Stoney Jackson, Miguel Nunez.

Christopher Atkins, Frankie Crocker, Ola Ray. Penny Baker, Robin Williams, Jerry Buss, Harry Nillson, Chico Ross, Helen Shavers were just a few of the people who hung out at the bungalow parties.

While staying at the Chateau Marmont I met this young actress. Her name was Elisabeth Shue. She was one of the hippest young girls I'd ever met. She had just done a film, *The Karate Kid*, and was doing a weekly television show. We would jump in my Rolls, throw down some blankets in the back, buy some wine, and take a bag of cocaine. We'd just sit on the beach at night listening to music, snorting and talking. We'd talk about life, love and spiritual shit. She was well educated in everything. She ended up going back East and I haven't seen her since.

Timothy Hutton and I hung tight in those days. One night in Carlos and Charlie's the manager came over and told me that Timothy Hutton wanted to meet me. I said, "Who the fuck is Timothy Hutton?" He said he had just won an Oscar for a movie called *Ordinary People*. But I'd never seen the movie, in fact, I was thinking, "Who the fuck would want to see a film about '*Ordinary* People'?"

Timothy came over and I found him to be a very down-to-earth cat. Whenever we would hang out, we got into shit together. One night we went to a party for the GoGo's. After the party, a couple of GoGo's came with me and Timothy to Carlos and Charlie's. We stayed for a while and then decided to go to my place. As we waited for the valet, I saw Tim arguing with some Iranian dude. I went over and the Iranian's friend got out of this car. Punches flew and I jumped in. It was a real brawl. The Iranians jumped in their car while me and Timothy threw punches through their window. My brand new, one hundred and fifty thousand-dollar Rolls Royce pulled up. When the Iranians saw it was my car they backed up and rammed it three times and split.

I was invited to do the American Music Awards and the Grammies for the third straight year. *Street Songs* was nominated in a bunch of categories and I was going to play live at both.

Timothy and I went to see the producers of the Grammies. They showed me the previous year's show and told me they wanted me to have more room to work at this year's show.

I performed "Super Freak" at the American Music Awards. Before I went on stage the Grammies actually called the American Music Awards and told me not to perform "Super Freak" on Dick's show. I couldn't believe it. They told me to play sick or something—but not to do it. I said, "Fuck you." I would never fuck Dick over in that way.

I won the best R&B Album of the Year on Dick's show then did the Grammies. I knew they were mad at me, but I didn't know how much until the show. I performed "Give It to Me Baby" on the Grammies. When I played my Clavinet keyboard at sound check, everything was fine. But during the actual performance, the keyboard collapsed as I played the first note. I was shocked, but I balanced it with one leg and kept my cool and we finished the song. I didn't get one award. (I was told before the show it was because of my politics.) I was sabotaged.

A few weeks after that Dan Akroyd asked me and my friend T.K. Carter to have dinner with him and the director of his newly made film, *Dr. Detroit*. We ate sushi and talked about the film. It seemed interesting, but when we all went to the director's house and watched the film it was not funny. I made up some excuse not to do the sound-track, but for one scene they used "Super Freak." They gave me thirty thousand dollars for that.

I went back to New York to hang out with Mark Fleishman. One night I went to see Etta James. I had loved her since childhood. She was appearing at The Red Parrot, and after her show, I was escorted to meet her. There was a bunch of well-wishers in her dressing room getting high and hanging out. Mick Jagger was one of them. I had only met Mick a couple of times and most of our meetings were in darkened offices at some nightspot. He greeted me with an especially warm welcome and told me how proud he was of me. Then he mentioned the Grammies. He said that they tried to sabotage me but I kept it together. He was smiling like a little kid. He was so happy that I didn't blow it and loose my cool. Then he went on to say how me and Prince were his favorites and how much he loved my music. We later went to the Studio and parties. We both got so fucked up my Security man, Arron had to take Mick to his hotel. Mick was all by himself and too high to get home. I couldn't believe it. I always have security; you never know. Just ask John Lennon.

I stayed in New York, caught a couple of plays and bought a bunch of coke, then went home to Buffalo. I was starting to miss my daughter Ty. I hadn't seen her for years. I had heard I had a son by Ty's mother, Seville, but I had not seen him yet, nor did I know if he was really mine. Every Christmas I rented a Learjet and flew to New York, bought gifts for all my family, then flew home. I was starting to wonder where my kid was and how she was doing. I'd wake up at night sometimes, soaking wet from dreams—bad dreams. As time went on I felt more and more guilty that my own kids where poor and struggling. I had all this money and success but no family of my own. All I knew is they were out there somewhere. But I didn't know where.

Once in LA, Seville had come to see me. She said she needed money for Ty and we ended up sleeping together once. She took the money, about ten thousand dollars. A week or so later she came back for more. I knew it wasn't her fault that she was here, it was her mother who told her to do it, and I never could stomach her mother. I was so mad I told her if she thought she was going to milk me, she was crazy; and I'd do everything I could to take Ty from her. She and Ty disappeared, changing her name and everything. I tried everything to find her—police, private investigators, everything—to no avail.

After Christmas I flew back to LA. Petey, my drug-dealer, met me at the airport and we went to the bungalow at the Marmont. I had a bunch of TV shows to do; *Midnight Special, Merv Griffin, Dinah Shore, Toni Tennille Show, Entertainment Tonight, Lifestyles of the Rich and Famous,* Don Kirshner's *Rock Concert* and Dick Clark's *New Year's Show.* I taped so many shows I thought I was going crazy. I wanted to get them all out of the way before I started work on my next album. *Street Songs* was still on the charts, and kicking ass. I could have waited five years before I released a new album. But Barry Gordy talked me into it. He made me a deal: if I did another album for him, he'd give back all my video rights and publishing—a deal he never kept.

Petey and I were still close; getting high and fucking chicks. Petey was never that good at drinking alcohol. He could blow coke, but when it came to liquor, his ass was through. Once we took a private plane to Vegas to see Diana Ross at Caesar's Palace. When we got on the plane I told Petey to take it easy because I didn't want him getting too drunk. I wanted him to see the show and meet Diana. Soon as he gets on the plane, vodka straight with ice. I knew he was fucked up when I saw his shit-eating grin while walking through Caesar's. We went in and took our seats. Diana came out. Soon as she sang "I'm Coming Up," Petey vomited all over the fucking table. It was disgusting. He was wearing this beautiful white silk suit. He went up to the suite and missed the whole show.

Diana stopped the show and told the audience the King of Punk Funk was in the house and introduced me. It was a great evening. I went backstage and met her for the first time. Barry and I joked around. I always loved to joke with Barry Gordy. He had a great sense of humor.

I had to fly to Europe on a promotional tour. It was the first time I wasn't with the band. I took California and Richard, my Security. When I arrived in England there were hundreds of photographers and reporters at the airport waiting, taking pictures and asking questions. Most of the questions were about me and Linda Blair. There was a white Bentley waiting with two American dressed motorcycle police on bikes. There were even groupies waiting. It was a trip. All these people, mostly white, wearing braids with signs saying "Welcome Rick." On the ride into London the motorcycle police got pulled over and busted for imitating police. I attended a lot of press parties and met a lot of beautiful English women. All any of them wanted to know was, what is a Super Freak—before I left England, I'd show a few of them.

We based ourselves in London, and visited Paris, Rome, Amsterdam and Milan. It was a great promo tour. In London, it was arranged that I would do a one-hour radio show on the biggest radio station in England, the BBC. The night before they had a big party for me at the embassy. Some cat there had this pure coke from Peru and I bought some. These two fine English babes and I went to my hotel and I got high and fucked all night. I was so high I missed the most important radio interview of my life. Instead, I stayed in bed all that day recuperating from my night of partying. I even conducted my interview with the London newspapers from my bed. I told them I was really sick and my doctor had ordered me to rest, but I don't think they believed me.

The following night I took two girls out on the town and the next day the papers all ran stories about how I overcame my illness rather suddenly and was seen at Stringfellows in the arms of two women. I just laughed. A few days later the *Evening Standard* ran a list of England's ten most terrible people. I was voted number three, right under Idi Amin.

I returned to the States and prepared the band for a festival date in Jamaica called The Jamaican World Music Fest. It was the first and last of its kind—three days of music with the biggest artists in the world: Beach Boys, Gladys Knight, Peter Tosh, Aretha Franklin, The Clash, Ziggy Marley, Black Uhuru, Jimmy Buffet, just to name a few. These three-day concerts were put on to bring American tourists back to Jamaica. There was this big fenced-off area where the concerts were held and for a few hundred dollars you could see all three nights. The only problem was that there was no way your basic Jamaican could afford such prices. Had it been held openly, like in a field or something, they would have gotten half a million people. This way they only got forty thousand people and they were all tourists. The Jamaican people were pissed. When I arrived, I was welcomed by Jimmy Cliff, Sly and Robbie, Black Uhuru and Peter Tosh. They would come to my room and bring all different kinds of weed, or ganja as they called it. They knew I loved the Mary Jane.

There was a full moon the night we headlined. The side of the stage was crowded with acts watching and cheering us on. When we did "Mary Jane," Black Uhuru came on stage and brought me a huge spliff. I passed it around to the band. They got so high they said they were hallucinating. The people putting on the Fest let me fly down thirty-seven people in my entourage. Mark Fleischmann and Senator Daniel Moynahan's daughter Moorah were just two of the people who flew down with me and my band.

Chapter Forty-six
Germany

I was glad to see my band when I returned to the US from Europe. They were all curious about my reception over there. I told them Europe couldn't wait for us to get there.

Rock Palast is a TV show from Essen, Germany that is broadcast every year. It goes out to one hundred and fifty million people and all over Europe fans get together to watch the hottest bands play. The show consists of three world-renowned groups playing a live concert and in between the sets they show videos, like MTV. It's a huge affair. I was invited to perform there along with The Kinks and Van Morrison. Before the flight over I stood at the door of the airplane and gave every one of my band members a Quaalude as they walked on. I just put it in their mouths like candy. They all wanted one cuz the trip was such a long one and most of my guys were afraid of flying, including me.

The auditorium in Essen held ten thousand people. We were more nervous doing that gig than any other gig we'd ever done, because we had no idea what to expect. I didn't even know if the Germans knew my music.

The show went great; even better than great. Here are all these Germans with their hands in the air giving up the Funk Sign—too much. They knew and sang every song. It was a trip. They couldn't all speak English, but every one of them sang along to my tunes like a motherfucker. It was great. I met this serious German babe there and she showed me that sex is an international language, whether you speak the same verbal language or not. They gave us three encores, and the next day we sold out of our albums all across Europe.

207

The band and I flew back to the US to begin work on my sixth album, which was called *Throwin' Down*, a term I coined for freebasing. At that time I was seeing a lot of Roy Ayers, considered by many to be the best vibe player in the world, and the Tower of Power horn section, who I used on my albums before as guest artists, along with the beautiful vocals of Jean Carne. I wrote this piece called "Standing on the Top," which featured The Temptations. It was a tune about being Number One and going down—something The Temps knew all about. The tune featured all of them: David Ruffin, Melvin Franklin, Richard Street, Dennis Edwards, Eddie Kendricks and Otis, all the originals.

The first day they were all in the studio together, Levi looked at me with this glow in his eyes and said: "Look at this Bro. Here we are recording The Temptations." I couldn't help but think back to when I was a kid in Buffalo singing their songs on a street corner. Now here I was showing David, Eddie, Dennis, Melvin and Otis what I wanted them to sing and how. It was amazing.

The Studio was filled with friends: Jim Brown, Timothy Hutton, Motown president, Barry Gordy—the entire control room was packed. I didn't mind. It was a great reunion, and a great day. "Standing on The Top" is the only song with all—I mean *all*—seven of The Temptations singing. On "Super Freak" there were only four of them. Even their Reunion album didn't have all of them. But they were all on this one.

Throwin' Down is a great album. I had a lot of fun recording it. My favorite tunes on that album were "Dance with Me," "Money Talks," "Throw Down" and "My Love." Teena and I united again on a tune called "Happy." This was the last time I'd use The Record Plant studios. My studio, "The Joint," was all but finished. From here on in I'd be cutting in my own studio. I couldn't wait.

The *Throwin' Down* tour was the first tour where we stopped wearing costumes and wore outfits that were comfortable but hip. We did a three-month cross-country tour. Again, we sold out twenty thousand seaters. The tour was another huge success. That year I was voted *People Magazine's* Best Dressed. I always wanted to look good in public—so they couldn't see how empty I was starting to feel inside.

Rick with Marvin Gaye, Gladys Knight and friends

Rick and his boys

209

Jerry played a crazy bass—Rick loved him

Rick in the studio in Sausalito

Rick always gave mega percussionist Stever Ferrone a hard time

Jan Gay was Marvin's wife, and she was one of the most beautiful Black women I'd ever met. Jan and I were starting to get very close, though we didn't become lovers until after they divorced. I loved Jan, and she's still very dear to me. Our relationship was just starting to get deep during the *Throwin' Down* days. Our story was one that changed my life.

I was getting high every day freebasing three thousand to four thousand dollars every week. It was the first time I started to notice it getting out of control.

Petey had accidentally found out where my kids were. One day he told me he had a son by this girl in the ghetto. His son went to this ghetto school where, he said, some boy went there claiming to be Rick James' son. I sent a detective to take pictures of him. I wanted to know for myself. When I saw the pictures I was positive he was mine. Then I sent Roy, who was now a lawyer working with me, to see Seville and make some kind of financial arrangement with her so I could see my children. She was given enough money to move out of the jungle to the valley, where she got a new place, and sent my kids to Buffalo to see me. The day they arrived I went to the airport and waited for them, I was nervous, and not sure how they were going to react to me. I saw this young girl and little boy holding hands and rushed up and hugged them. They weren't my kids. Ty and Ricky came out a few minutes later and it was great to see them. They stayed for three weeks and at first they were calling me "Mr. James" and were a little timid and overwhelmed. At first I tried to buy their love but they said no to the presents. They were well-raised kids. Seville had done a good job.

My son Rick is the spitting image of his dad. He's a Taurus and a very strong, well-mannered child. He's also a helluv' an artist. It's funny cuz art is something I always loved, but was never great at.

While in LA I did the video with The Temptations. I also put the long version of "Standing on the Top" on their Reunion album, which enabled them to go on a successful tour.

It was 1982 when *Throwin' Down* came out. Jan Gaye and I were freebasing together regularly. I took her to Maui, Hawaii, where we had a great vacation. Although they were divorced, Marvin was putting her and the kids under a lot of stress. He cut her and the kids off financially, so I gave Jan a job as one of my secretaries in my LA office. The only condition of employment was that she had to show up on time. She only lasted a few months. Marvin had started basing and was out of control. He'd call her up on the phone at the office and say all this perverted shit.

Once when Marvin was in Belgium, Jan flew to Buffalo to take care of me because I was bedridden with a high temperature. I could hardly even talk. She gave me tender loving care, made medicines and helped nurture me back to health. Marvin called me while she was there. I told Marv that Jan was there and I was too sick to talk to him. While Jan was talking to him he was saying shit like she wasn't shit, calling her a whore, saying shit about her and the kids. But as soon as I got on the phone he'd talk sweet as pie. That's when I realized Marvin was a seriously sick motherfucker. I still loved him. We've all got a little sickness in us, don't we?

When Marvin won his first Grammy for "Sexual Healing," I gave it to him. Grace Jones and I were on stage together and presented two awards, one to Diana, and the other to Marvin. When Marvin came on stage, my fists were clenched. Jan had told me Marvin wanted a piece of me and I was ready for him to start some shit on national TV, if that was what he wanted. I was never the type of motherfucker to back down. I was ready for his ass. When he came on stage he embraced me and whispered, "She gave me the best years of my life," and left the stage.

Once while getting high with Jan I told her I had a dream that Marvin didn't have but a year to live. She cried but within a year, Marvin was dead. I miss him. Even though we sometimes disagreed he was still my friend.

People think that Marvin's father did it. I always heard it was his brother Frankie. In any case, he's gone. The night he died I was home freebasing. All of a sudden I got this terrible headache, like none I've had before. Jan called me on the phone crying hysterically. I knew something was terribly wrong. She said, "Rick, Marvin's dead." I threw the pipe down and cried myself to sleep.

Chapter Forty-seven
MTV and Me

Street Songs came out in 1981. After winning the American Music Award for Best Album, I took some pictures backstage with Grace Jones. Grace and I were clowning with the photographers. A newsman asked Grace why she wasn't on MTV. She replied, "Cuz MTV has no taste." She said that's why she and I weren't on it. I said something similar, but using slightly stronger language.

Dick threw this great party after the American Music Awards. There was incredible food and plenty of drink at the after party. My Mom was there with me, proud as punch. Prince was there. He hadn't come to the award show, but he brought his little ass to the after party. My mother asked him for an autograph—and he actually ran away! After I heard about that, I went off. I was going to kick his little ass.

When I found him, I started to get in his ass. His manager, Steve Farnoli, asked what was wrong. I told him the little motherfucker had insulted my mother. Steve brought Prince over to apologize like the little bitch he is. He said, "I'm sorry" to my mother and tried to apologize to me. But I didn't want to hear it. Someone snapped a picture of him trying to apologize to me. My expression said it all.

The MTV thing started to catch fire. It seems whatever the fuck I said that day with Grace moved a lot of people. Everyone wanted to talk to me about MTV, the racist TV station. At the time I came out and called MTV racist, there were one hundred and fifty videos on it. Out of those only three were Black: Musical Youth, Eddie Grant and someone else I can't recall—that was it. Two out of three were Jamaican groups. MTV was supposed to play Top Forty groups. That means anybody in the Billboard Top Forty should be on MTV. Their policy was to play Urban Contemporary, Top Forty stuff. This being true, where was Teddy Pendergrass, Rick James, Diana Ross, Donna Summer and a few other Blacks that were crossing over big time? They were not being played.

In the Fifties that was called "Jim Crow programming." Radio DJ's at White stations were not allowed to play Blacks. It was considered "Devil Music." That's why Elvis, Buddy Holly, Pat Boone and other white singers became so successful covering Black tunes—and getting hit records out of them. Imagine Pat Boone getting a hit off Little Richard's "Lucille." It was fucked up. Then Alan Freed, a white DJ, opened the doors for Black artists. MTV was the same shit, fifty years later.

I had spent thousands of dollars making some great videos only to have MTV say "No way." MTV even refused to play the classic video "Standing on the Top," which featured me with all the Temptations—the only video they are all in. Linda Ronstadt could sing "Ooh Baby Baby" but when it came to Smokey Robinson, MTV said "No Go." I had had enough and was going to bring MTV into the light, no matter what the cost—and believe me, it cost me plenty.

Bob Pittman, the Program Director for MTV, was a well-known racist in telecommunications. He was brought into jobs to hire and fire Blacks. He programmed MTV, which was owned by Gulf and American Express, big ass companies. They started MTV as a big fucking tax write-off, a tax shelter with just one law: KEEP BLACKS OFF. I did an informal survey to find out what was going on. I even talked to Jay Johnson, one of the DJs on MTV, a British Black. We got drunk together one night in New York and I got a lot of shit out of him.

Newsweek called my efforts "gallant" in my fight to have Blacks aired on MTV. I even talked to Bruce Springsteen about it. He told me he didn't want to get involved cuz MTV had just aired a video of his called "Atlantic City" that he wasn't even in. I freaked. Can you dig that shit? I was pissed off like a motherfucker.

Bob Pittman came out in *Rolling Stone* magazine and said certain Blacks did not make the kind of music he thought appropriate for his station. If that wasn't a racist remark, nothing was. Sammy Davis, Jr.

and Hall & Oates even appeared on TV and said I was right. I was told that when Bob Pittman found out about my feud with Prince he immediately put Prince into hot rotation with this record called "Little Red Corvette." The record had died on the charts—I mean died. As soon as MTV started playing the video, the record was re-released and became a smash. That's the power of MTV. I could have sold thirty or forty million more albums had MTV played my videos.

My efforts did not go in vain. Little by little MTV added more Blacks to their play list. Now they even have an alternative MTV, VH-1, just for Blacks. The first video of mine they ever played was a record that wasn't even mine. It was a tune I composed for Eddie Murphy called "Party All the Time." Eddie and I did a video together for it. It was a Number One record and the first time MTV ever put Rick James on screen.

Chapter Forty-eight
A Family Affair

After *Throwin' Down*, I decided I wanted to put together a girl vocal group, which had been a lifelong dream. I had been casually looking for years to find the right combination: four girls who could all click and work together. I was now ready to do some serious auditions. I asked around Buffalo for a girl with a good voice. My keyboard player told me about a girl named Joanne McDuffie who worked at a record shop called Record Theater. I went to meet her. She wasn't attractive, but not ugly either. I felt with some work, hair and teeth etc, she could work. She came to my house and sang. After that I had no doubt she could blow.

While in LA I held auditions and meetings. My concept was four girls: one with a Valley Girl image, one with a Classy Vamp image, one with a Leather Queen image, and one with a Rick James Bitch image. I also wanted the group to be mixed. My original concept was called "The Colored Girls." I showed the concept to Prince's manager: three girls in negligees. Next thing I know, here's Vanity Six. That taught me not to show my cards too quickly. This time I wanted four girls and I would make sure they'd be able to kick Vanity's asses.

After Joanne McDuffie, I hired Candice Ghant, a tall and attractive brown-skinned girl with a sweet disposition who had been dancing at an exotic bar and working an office job. The third girl was Sharri Wells, a very pretty mixed race girl who was an aspiring singer and was perfect for my Valley Girl. Finally I wanted to find a white chick but couldn't find one that danced her ass off. Candy told me about this girl from Pittsburgh who danced with her, saying the girl had a Black attitude. When Kim walked into the studio in Sausalito and started dancing I knew she was the one.

Joanne was called Jojo. Candice I called Candy. Kim I called Maxi. And Sherri stayed Sherri. All four of them needed a lot of work: clothes, hair, skin, teeth, the whole nine yards. I even sent them to Seth Riggs, a well-known vocal teacher in Hollywood. Jojo sang lead and background on their first album, basically cuz I had to find out what they all could do vocally. Maxi was the weakest. She always needed extra help on the vocal side. The only Mary-Jane girl I ever had sexual involvement with was Maxi. We'd do dope and fuck our brains out. I was actually very fond of her.

Maxi was a strong girl and very sensitive. All the other girls got terribly jealous over our affair. It started out hot and heavy, but later slowed down, mostly to take the pressure off her from the other girls. They couldn't stand the fact that I was with her and not with them. They always needed my attention as confirmation of their talents and the other girls took it badly that I was paying that extra attention to Maxi. I had confrontations with each one except Candy over Maxi. Their first single was called "Candy Man," a bouncy little tune. Their second single was "All Night Long," a Jazz Funk groove. Jojo sang the shit out of it. After their first album went gold, they were gaining a reputation as Rick's girls. TV was begging to interview them.

I shot two videos in Buffalo: "Candy Man" and a funky tune called "Boys." When my mother came to the set and met the girls, she thought I had done a pretty good job grooming them and making them look hot. She had met Jojo before in Buffalo and always thought she was the plainest of them all, so she was especially impressed at the job I had done on her.

Jojo was really into the Bible and at the time didn't drink or smoke. She was the most intelligent of the girls, but I thought she was the nicest one, and the least likely to ever back-stab me. Mom said I was wrong and unfortunately, Mom turned out to be right.

During the *Throwin' Down* tour, I let them open the show. The Girls went over extremely well, and I was like a proud father as I saw the fans enthusiastic reaction every night. I always thought I treated the girls very well. Even though they were my concept, I gave them points on the record, which is something that isn't done with concept acts. I bought all of their clothes and paid for their hair and dental care. Jojo and Candy had had terrible teeth when they joined and I spent thousands improving the appearance of their smiles. I also gave them a good salary. They had nothing to complain about. I was like their father and mentor. On tour I had Security watch them like hawks. I did not want just any schmuck getting hold of my girls, I wanted them to have the best and I made sure they did. Guys like Sugar Ray Leonard, Malcolm Jamal from the *Cosby Show*, football stars and basketball stars were chasing the girls down. Unless a dude was really on his job and had his shit together, he got no Mary Jane action. The girls would bitch and moan, but that was the way it was.

Val Young was a lady I wrote and produced two albums for. I met her in Memphis during the *Bustin' Out* tour. She came backstage with this other chick. At that time the Gap Band was opening up for me. Their lead singer, Charlie Wilson, was hanging out with me. We both met Val at the same time. When I asked Val what she wanted, she said "You." She was a beautiful black thing, I mean she had it all—tits, ass, lips, everything. While looking at her I said, "You're a Gemini, aren't you?" She said, "Yes." After that I just told Charlie "You got her." I did not want to fuck with another Gemini, Seville was one and so was Kelly. I could always feel a Gemini. Charlie was an Aquarius, like me, and a wild motherfucker.

Val used to sing background and shit with George Clinton. She also sang background with me during the *Street Songs* tour, till one day she got tired of taking the Stone City Band's shit and she quit. I always liked the way she sounded. She had this sexy-ass rasp to her voice. It was magic when she sang. The first album I cut with her was called *Seduction*. After her first single, Seduction was one off the longest standing dance records on New York City's Dance Chart. She was a Diva in New York. They loved her.

Her second album was called *Private Conversation* with a hit dance tune of the same name. Although she didn't get a huge hit like the Girls or myself, I always loved recording her. She was a joy to work with.

Sometimes getting a performance out of Val was like pulling teeth, but the outcome was always worth it. Val looked like a Black Marilyn Monroe, so I had her hair done blond and dressed her in sexy clothes from the thirties and forties. She pulled it off well. She was one of the most down-to-earth ladies I've ever known, simple and straight.

Val and I used to smoke base together and just have wonderful sex. Then one day after leaving the tour, she said, "No more freebasing!" I've never known her to take another hit off the pipe since. She'll smoke weed—she loves her weed—or maybe a Co-co puff (cocaine in a cigarette), but no pipe. I always was impressed with her ability to give it up.

When the Grammies were over, Diana Ross asked Val, the Mary Jane Girls and me, plus some other people, back to her house. Diana had just broken up with Gene Simmons and was heartbroken. She asked me "Who is that girl, Val Young?" At first I thought, "Uh-oh, what has Val done now?" But Diana said "Rick, don't you ever loose her." I said "What?" Then Diana went on to tell me how she and Val were both from Detroit, and how they talked about recipes and growing up in the Brewster Projects. I think Val brought Diana down to earth for a moment. Diana wasn't Diana anymore, just a poor, struggling girl from Detroit's Brewster Projects.

Bobby Militelo is one of the best tenor sax players living today. He's from Buffalo, like Jay Beckenstein of Spyro Gyra who, by the way, can't touch Bobby Militelo. I would go see Bobby whenever I could. He played at his brother's club in Buffalo, a place called Mulligan's. Mike Militelo was one of my best friends at the time. After hearing Bobby, I wanted to do all I could to help his career. The first thing I did was tell Motown about him. Then I had Bobby and his band fly down to LA to showcase. I booked an exclusive restaurant in Beverly Hills, then invited all my friends: Robin Williams, Stevie Wonder and OJ Simpson were just a few of the stars who turned out to a packed house to see my latest discovery.

Bobby blew the whole house away. He looks like and reminds you of Cannonball Adderly. But to hear him blow—he's in a class all his own. Even Danny Lemelle, my sax player (who is great), started practicing again after he heard Bobby.

Motown agreed to sign him. I was too busy at the time to produce him, plus I wanted a real jazzy motherfucker to do him. So I got Lenny White, drummer extraordinaire from Return to Forever. Bobby blew Lenny away. Bobby's album was called *Rick James Presents Bobby M. "Blow."* His single was the al Green remake of "Let's Stay Together." The music press agreed that Bobby's album was one of the best Jazz albums of the year.

Chapter Forty-nine
Process and the Doo Rags

The Stone City Family now consisted of the Mary Jane Girls, Stone City Band, Val Young, Bobby M and Kenny Hawkins. I had everything I wanted in my musical family except a male singing group, so I decided to create one. I came up with the idea for a smooth sounding and soulful yet funky take on an old Doo-wop band.

I held auditions in Buffalo and out of the hundreds of guys who came I selected five of the best singers in the country. Bunty, Stacey, Gumps, Shorty and Smooth. I named the band Process and the Doo Rags, which itself was named after a hairstyle called The Process, a slick, wavy hairdo that was popular with Blacks in the Thirties and the Forties. As soon as I had found my singers I took them to the hairdressers and gave them all a Process as well. We dressed them in vintage Zoot suits and Stetson shoes to complete the cool retro vibe. William "Bunty" Hawkins had sung background with me for years, and his voice was higher than Philip Bailey of Earth, Wind & Fire. He was a Gemini who could sing his Black ass off and had always wanted to build a group around him. After I completed *Cold Blooded*, I finally had time.

Columbia bought the band immediately and quickly released their first album, *Stomp and Shout*. I showcased Process at the Cotton Club in Buffalo and backed them up with members of the Stone City Band and some new cats I had found. I flew Charlie Atkins, a wonderful old choreographer, to Buffalo to teach the Doo-Rags how to move. Charlie had taught The Temptations, Gladys Knight, The Jackson Five, Smokey Robinson and the Miracles and Marvin Gaye. He was the best in the country. Over sixty, Charlie could still dance his ass off and by the time Charlie had finished with the Doo-Rags, they were stepping like the young Temptations. They were tight.

For their Cotton Club showcase, Eddie Murphy flew in with Jan Gaye. Eddie liked the Doo-Rags so much that when he sold out the twenty-thousand-seater in Buffalo, he asked the Doo-Rags to open for him. Jan was blown away by their version of Marvin's "The Bells" and said she thought it was better than the original. Although I was getting high a lot in those days, I always managed to stop and make records, especially when it came to the various members of the Stone City Family.

After we signed at the Columbia office in LA I took them out on the town in Hollywood. We went to Spago's for dinner. Everyone was staring at them with looks of "Who the fuck are they?" James Woods, the actor, came over to the table and complimented them on their looks then asked them if they would like to sing. I told the boys to do some of the a cappella tunes they did on the album. They did "Daddy's Home," "What's Your Name?" and "Thin Line." By the time they finished, everyone in Spago's was on their feet applauding.

After the *Throwin' Down* tour, I was invited to do a record called "Slow Dancin'" with Chaka Kahn. I loved Chaka and had always wanted to work with her. Unfortunately, her record company didn't release our duet as a single; it would have been hot. Instead, they released a tune called "Tearing it Up."

Chaka and I spent some time together when she was playing Buffalo. After the show, we all went back to my house, and Chaka and I went to my bedroom. However, there was already a crowd hanging in my room so we went into my bathroom and hung out for about six hours, just talking. Chaka's very spiritual and intelligent. We talked for hours about love, our careers, books, you name it.

I brought this Mafioso friend of mine who had never heard of Chaka Kahn to meet her, I figured they would get a kick out of each other. At one point my Mafioso friend tried to join in our conversation, but Chaka pointed her finger in his face and told him to shut the fuck up. The funny thing about it was that he did what she said. He would later tell me he had never met a woman that fearsome in his entire life.

There were a lot of people waiting for me in my house that night, including Beverly Johnson, the model and a whole bunch of hot girls lounging in the sitting room. I kept telling Chaka to leave because she was on tour and needed to rest before her next show, but she wouldn't go. She said she liked talking to me too much.

Chaka always had a pretty wicked sense of humor. Before she finally left she took off all her clothes, covered herself up with this military coat of mine and made her way to my indoor pool. While walking to the pool, she stopped to talk to all the girls waiting, Beverly being one of them. She screamed "How many of you bitches masturbate?" No one spoke. She said, "That's why Rick's got no time for none of y'all. You're all lying bitches." Then she went and jumped in the pool, coat and all.

After doing the record with Chaka, I hung around New York visiting friends. One night I ran into some friends at this club called The Limelight. While we were walking upstairs to the VIP room, Catherine Bach from the *Dukes of Hazard* brushed past me while walking downstairs. I grabbed her arm and said, "No, you're not." She came back up with me and we sat down and started talking. I had met her before in LA when we'd done the *Dinah Shore* show together. I'd found her very attractive. We got on the subject of movies. I asked her if she saw *Purple Rain*. She said she had. I asked her what she thought of it. She said she thought it was good. I yelled "Good! How the fuck can you call that shit good?" She said I was pissed because Prince beat me to the punch and made a movie first.

I got up. I was furious. I wanted to snort some coke. She said, "Sit down and listen. You don't need coke. Don't you know Prince knows you're always fucked up on coke? That's why he's beating you these days. You're too fucked up."

I had my limousine take her home, but Cat stayed in my mind. Her words had cut deep with truth, no one had ever dared talk to me like that before, and as angry as it made me feel I knew I needed to hear it. I wanted to see Cat again. She'd given me her number and told me to call when I hit LA. I was already anticipating our next meeting.

Robert Palmer and I went to his hotel that night with some cuties, but all I could think about was Catherine's strong words, and her beautiful face.

After the *Throwin' Down* tour I had some time on my hands. I flew to Paris and hung out with some actors I met when I was there the last time. From Paris I flew to London where I spent my time with this mother and daughter team, Marianna and Monique. They were both ballet dancers and very liberal towards sex. I was never into a lot of S&M- it always freaked me out how people could dig pain. But these two loved it: cat o' nine tails and everything. Our sex was very kinky and very wild, but I didn't draw blood out of either of them. There were many orgasms, and both mother and daughter taught me a few hot tricks about pleasuring women. Both women were pretty strange and I guess I was getting that way too, seeing as I was the star of this sexual extravaganza. After leaving Marianna and Monique I went back to the States, stopping off in New York.

I had to see my good friend Kay Santiago, a beautiful Puerto Rican woman who weighed close to three hundred pounds—but she was all lover, and all gay. (And if you don' like it, fuck you!) I loved her attitude. She would cook for me and stay in my ass about being too nice to people. I would buy a big bag of coke and go to Kay's where I'd cry my eyes out as I endured the emotional highs and lows of the drug. Kay was a real friend, a big, loving woman and she was always there for me.

I went to see another old friend of mine, Dizzy Gillespie who played The Blue Note. Dizzy was like a father to me. I had met him years before in LA and I'd call him sometimes and ask him questions about life and music. Dizzy would just belt out his raspy laugh and say I was getting too serious at my young age. He told me not to look at life so black and white. Then he'd tell me stories about Charlie Parker and say I reminded him of Bird. He said I seemed to have the same death wish.

Dizzy used to get high a long time ago but had stopped. He used to watch me and say, "Boy, I remember when——" I miss Dizzy. When he died, I lost a good friend.

Chapter Fifty
Cold Blooded

My twenty-four-track-recording studio in my house in Buffalo had just been completed and I couldn't wait to start work on my seventh album. At the Grammies the year before I had the pleasure of talking with Quincy Jones, who told me that it was time to change my sound and that everyone was hip to my shit. I listened carefully to his words, and they stuck in my mind while I prepared for my next album. I decided that the way to move forward musically was to give my music more space, more room, and to use different instrumentation and textures. Having my own studio really helped in this process of experimentation, because whenever I felt like creating, I just had to take a few steps and there I was, sitting behind a twenty-four console. It was great and really helped me in finding new sounds for *Cold Blooded*.

Linda Blair had come to Buffalo to see me around then and I was very happy as always to see her. A few months before her visit she had called me to say that she had had an abortion, and that it had been my child. She said she was in the middle of shooting a movie and was starting to show, and she didn't think I would care anyway. She was wrong. I did care deeply. I loved Linda and it hurt me that she would choose to abort our child without even wanting to talk to me about it first. I still look back on her choice with sadness and wonder about our baby, and how having the child might have changed my life.

One night during her visit, I took her into the studio and we sat down at one of my synthesizers. I was showing Linda how to write a song on keyboards and I started playing. I told her that in composition your ok as long as you keep playing. It's when your fingers stop moving that you're in trouble. The next thing I knew I was composing a tune about her called "Cold

Blooded," which became the title track to the album. I used this extraordinary young guitar player named Kenny Hawkins, the younger brother of Bunty, the lead singer in The Doo Rags. Between me, Kenny and my new keyboard player, Treadwell, we completed *Cold Blooded* in a matter of months. Tom McDermott and Danny Lemelle were also featured heavily on it.

I took a track called "Pimp the Simp" and flew to New York to have Grand Master Flash's Mele Mel, Scorpio and Rahiem come in and lay down a rap. The Flash are very down to earth brothers and it was good to see them again. "Pimp the Simp" was the first rap I had ever written, and it was also the first record of its kind with Rap and vocals. It went:

> *You pimp, you simp*
> *You're on the street*
> *Runnin' yo game*
> *On all the girls you meet*
> *Fake diamonds on your fingers*
> *And your Cadillac cars*
> *Tryin' to catch a girl in the local bar and you school her*
> *And you teach her the game.*
> *And next thing you know the girl is gone insane*
> *Now she lost at the cost of a trick she's turned*
> *She's just another hoe whose just been burned*

Rick and Billy Dee Williams

Soon after they left, Billy Dee Williams came in and laid down this romantic rap on a ballad called "Tell Me What U Want." It had a beautiful, cosmic intro and when I composed it I knew it would be perfect for Billy. We were already friends and we had talked about him doing an album, something romantic where all he had to do was speak. I had always wanted to do *The Prophet* by Kahlil Gibran. I told Billy about it and found out that he also loved that particular work. Billy's a very learned man with a good disposition and we share a lot of the same interests, like Classical music, food and art.

Smokey Robinson and I had been talking for years about doing something together. Now was a perfect time. After finishing Billy, I flew to LA to do vocals with Smokey on a ballad called "Ebony Eyes." I felt like a kid when Smokey walked into the studio to do his vocal. I was nervous instructing him on how and what to sing. After he finished, he asked if there were any mistakes. I told him I was completely satisfied, but in fact I had heard him do something in the second verse that I wasn't sure I liked. I told Smokey that I'd listen to the track overnight and I'd let him know.

The next day while in the studio, I talked to Smokey over the phone. He asked whether or not he should come down and I told him I still wasn't sure. The fact was, I had heard something that wasn't right, but was afraid to say "Smokey, do it again." To my surprise, Smokey showed up at the studio and said, "Okay Rick, I know by your voice there's something that you don't like." I said "Well..." He said, "Show me." I played the second verse and he heard it too. He said: "Oh, no, you can't let that go like that. I'll do it again." He immediately ran into the studio and sang the part beautifully. Linda Blair was there. She loved Smokey and they had both wanted to meet each other. We took pictures together and Linda was in heaven. So was I; the album was officially done.

As I wrapped *Cold Blooded,* The Mary Jane girls underwent a minor change. Cherri Wells left the group to pursue a solo career. I had always known she would leave. Her Mama was a complete stage mother and thought the group should revolve more around Cherri. Cherri never was and never will be a solo performer. She is a great group performer but she's just not strong enough to stand alone.

The girl who took Cherri's place was a beautiful woman named Yvette Brooks. I called her "Corvette," and she was the finest of the four. I had dated her mother in the earlier part of my career. Corvette was never that strong a singer, but she had lots of charisma. The Mary Jane Girls album was called *Only Four You*. The single, "My House," was a song I originally wrote for Val Young but I ended up giving it to the girls. "My House" went Number One worldwide and gave the girls their first platinum album.

I was working on the cover concept for *Cold Blooded*. Usually every album I did came with a strong concept and I took great care to make sure that the inside of the album coincided with the outside, and that there was a strong coherent message. One night I had my whole concept for *Cold Blooded* appear to me in a dream. Having ideas come to me in a dream was not unusual. In fact, all my ideas for my various albums first appeared to me as visions. But this time the dream was very strange, and stronger and more vivid, and more prophetic than I had experienced before. I dreamt I saw a circle with a pyramid inside. When I awoke, I had my concept.

The circle meant the planet Earth. The pyramid meant black and white living together on the planet with perfect harmony. It was great, I thought, and original. I even wrote a song, "Unity," that ended the album. I said to myself "Wow! What a great concept!" I found out years later when I went into drug rehab for the first time that the circle with the pyramid inside was the symbol for alcohol and drug addiction. God was talking to me, even then.

The *Cold Blooded* tour was one of the most successful yet. I hired two dancers to dance behind two triangle scrims—a brother named Bobby Sepheus and a beautiful sister named T. Bobby and T. danced throughout the show, and were especially wonderful during "Pimp and Simp" and Fire and Desire."

The Mary Jane Girls rose above my expectations. The crowd loved them, especially when they broke into "My House." The girls had a great show, especially the choreography, which was tight. I would watch them driving the crowd crazy and feel proud of their achievements.

During the tour we did a couple of nights at the Universal Amphitheater. Everybody in Hollywood was trying to get tickets. The second night of the show Rod Stewart and his wife Alana, and Frank Sinatra's daughter Tina and her boyfriend Bob, came to the show. I decided they'd all sit together in front-row seats—the seats that belonged to Prince. Rod came backstage then walked me to the stage. When we got to the backstage Prince came down. When he saw us he jumped over the stairs and fled. Rod looked at me and said "I hate that little prick." I agreed. I had heard that during the Mary Jane Girls' performance Prince had his bodyguard carry him around during the middle of the Girls' show, just trying to get attention. I was pissed. That little bitch. Had Prince not jumped over the stairs and ran, I swear I would have kicked his little ass.

While on stage I saw Prince's bodyguard attempt to throw Rod, Tina and my personal guest out of their seats. I think I might have said something while on stage. Rod's wife Alana has a lot of balls and after the show she told me that she had told Prince to kiss her ass. I just laughed. I heard later that Prince went to Michael Jackson's concert trying to disrupt shit. When Michael found out he was there, he came out badder than ever and Prince left the show. I always thought of Prince as a great player and a very innovative person. But as far as himself as a person, he could use a good ghetto ass kickin'.

When the *Cold Blooded* tour ended, I was happy. I had been getting high all the time and spending more and more time alone on tour and I really needed a rest. Occasionally, I would see Catherine Bach. She told me she once had a problem with coke, but no more and I knew that to be true cuz she never got high when I was around and that was fine with me. I never got high when I was around Catherine. She had this way of making me feel like I didn't need it. We'd eat home-cooked meals, rent movies and make popcorn. It was a nice, easy time when I was with Cat, but I made sure I didn't spend a whole lot of time around her because I didn't want to hurt her, and I knew I could.

One day while cruising down La Cienega in Hollywood, this chick was driving next to me, smiling and signaling me to pull over. I did, we talked, then I had the guy I was with drive her car and she came with me. She was a Gemini and very sweet. We went to my hotel and snorted coke, fucked and sucked our brains out all night till morning.

In the morning she said she had to go to work—she starred in a soap opera. I told her I hated soap opera, but I'd watch hers. Her name was Robin Bernard. I haven't seen or heard from her since that wonderful night.

It was my luck in those days to meet and date soap opera stars. Shannon Tweed was another one who I dated for a while. Shannon didn't get high and we never had sex. We would come real close, though. I always felt I wanted to marry Shannon, but she was in love with Gene Simmons, this ego'd out motherfucker with the group Kiss. I saw Shannon while Gene was in New York. To catch Shannon, I had to use her sister Tracy Tweed, who was married to a good friend of mine, Chico Ross, Diana's brother.

Tracy told me if I wanted Shannon I'd have to fight for her. I always loved a good fight. Gene was away in New York and Shannon had been living with Tracey for months. I used this time to woo Shannon with her favorite flowers and chocolates from her favorite store in Beverly Hills. Tracey helped me pick out the things that would please her sister the most. I even had dinner with her and her family. The last time I saw her was that night. I dropped her off at home and Gene was walking up the street with his luggage. I never saw her again. I heard they are married now with children. I think Shannon is a wonderful person and deserves the best.

After tripping around LA for a while, I went back to Buffalo.

Moving in the Fast Lane

No Holds Barred

Keepin' it Real…

Rick and the Mike Were As One

Rick with Jermaine Jackson having fun

"Process and the Doo Rags": Stacy, Eddie Murphy and Rick, James Bunty Hawkins, and Shorty

Lyle Alzado with Rick and afriend after a show

Rick with friends

Rick being honored in his hometown of Buffalo, New York

Val Young and Rick at photo shoot for her CD which he produced

Rick is Adored

241

Rick with Gladys Knight and the Pips, Stevie Wonder, Leslie Uggams and Dionne Warwick

Rick Chillin'

Mary Jane Girls

Mary Jane Girls

Rick and his best friend

Rick celebrating his birthday

Chapter Fifty-one
Reflections

I was making a million dollars an album—I wouldn't settle for a penny less. My drug habit had gotten out of control. I'd stay in my room for days and days just getting high. I found it impossible to quit; I seemed to be in a hopeless pit where there was no way out but to die. I can't tell you how many nights I sat alone, or sometimes in the company of others, women usually, when I hoped the next hit would bring instant death. I had OD'd a couple of times in LA, but it had been kept secret. Usually, my security or a nearby doctor I had on the payroll would bring me back. My life on the inside was lonely and dark, while on the outside I always made it look like I was together. The truth was I felt like I was the loneliest person in the world. No one understood, not friends, not my mother, no one. When I would try to explain my pain to friends, they would just laugh, saying: "You're Rick James. It will be all right." But I wasn't all right.

I OD'd in Buffalo and was rushed to the hospital where the doctors quickly brought me back to life. I was kept there for observation, till one day I just got up and left. My Mom had come to the hospital to stop me from leaving. When she saw me getting dressed to leave we got into a yelling match. I pushed my Mom to the floor just to get her out of my way. As I looked down and saw my beautiful little mother on the floor, I knew my life was terribly, terribly wrong. I never forgave myself for that moment.

I went straight home and got high again. I bought an ounce of cocaine and began to freebase it, alone. I didn't stop for two days straight. Finally, after most of it was gone except maybe an eight, I lay down on my bathroom floor and called on all the Powers That Be to kill me.

I'd be alone with a bottle of bourbon, Valiums and a big bag of coke, continuing till I either passed out or just finished it. Then I'd get some more. The feeling I used to get after the first hit had vanished. Now I just found myself smoking and smoking, trying desperately to get that same ol' high I used to get when I first started. It was in vain.

When I wasn't getting high, my life was a constant struggle between wanting it and not wanting it. Wanting it usually always won out. I'd pray. I'd meditate. I'd do anything to get rid of the pain I felt on a daily basis. The physical and emotional pain was so bad that I felt I was always walking the thin line between life and death. There seemed to be no way out, no way at all. I felt I was cursed with what some might call a blessing. In my heart my life was not a blessing. How could it be when all it consisted of was "sucking the Devil's dick?"

It got to the point where I hardly slept. I lost my desire to write music. When it was time for my eighth album I had nothing in my head. It seemed my creativity was gone, lost in a realm were smoke was I all I could create and rock coke was the only music I understood.

Jay Lasker was now the President of Motown. One day he called me into his office. Also present was Skip Miller, Head of Promotion. When I walked in I knew they wanted to talk about my new album—an album that I didn't have. I told Jay the album wasn't ready and I thought it was time for a greatest hits release. The only problem was, I wanted my regular million dollars. I also told him I'd put three new songs on the album. Well, after hearing that, Jay just cracked up with this big cigar in his mouth. He said by contract "We could release a Greatest Hits on you and not give you a cent." I immediately got crazy. I said, "Do it, motherfucker, and I'll find a new record company quick!" I had meant it. Had Motown not given into my demands, I would have left. After, I slowly walked back to my office. My security guy with me said, "Rick, are you crazy/?" I told him not to worry they'd call my office. No sooner than I'd sat down, the phone rang. It was Skip. They had talked it over and said okay to the million for three songs.

I had a lot of tracks in the can, but nothing I wanted to use on this new album. Even if it was only three songs, I wanted those three to be special.

I went to New York to cool out and think. One night some friends and I went out to Studio 54. We ran into five models, got high with them, had a few drinks, then asked them to come to my hotel. I was interested in one in particular, a white chick, six foot one, long brown hair and very mature. She was only seventeen years old. We got into a deep discussion in the club and took it back to my hotel. I had about an ounce of coke. We got high, snorting for a couple of days. She was from the south and had won a beauty contest which brought her to New York at her young age—only to find it wasn't what she wanted.

While talking to her in the peace of my bedroom, all desires to get into bed with her vanished and I found myself engulfed in her conversation. I wondered how such a young girl with so much going on could be so confused about life. I mean, she had it all: looks, charisma, brains and spirituality and she didn't even care. She reminded me of myself, a lost soul.

After two days of getting high with her, we finally went to bed and made love, which was something that I didn't expect. I got out of bed suddenly and she asked me what was wrong. I told her she was too inexperienced. She began to cry. I wasn't putting her down, just stating a fact. You see, in those days, I had developed this thing in me that wanted to be totally for real with people, even if it hurt, which sometimes it would. The girl's name was Lisa Keeter.

251

After drying her tears I began to tell her how she should leave New York and travel; go to Europe, see the world and decide what she really wanted to do in life. I had a strange feeling about this girl—not bad, but a feeling she would have a monumental effect on my life. How right I would be.

The following day I told her I had to go to Buffalo to begin work on my new album. She said I'd probably forget all about her and this experience. I assured her there was no way I'd forget her, she could be sure. I told her I would write a song about this experience.

While flying back to Buffalo, all I could thing of was this tall, voluptuous seventeen-year-old who had made such an impression on my mind and heart. When I arrived at Buffalo, I immediately went into my studio and began to write. I was instantly inspired. The first song I wrote was a tune called "Seventeen and Sexy," about a girl I had met in a club. The second song was a Latin Funk tune inspired by my good friend Kay Santiago, my lovely Puerto Rican friend. The third was a ballad called. "Oh What a Night." The Greatest Hits album was finished. I called it *Reflections*.

I flew to LA and had my photographer Ron Slenzak take pictures. I shaved my mustache, took out my braids and curled my hair to look fifteen years younger. The concept was Rick as a teenager. I thought it was pretty hip. I guess people were ready for a greatest hits album after all, because *Reflections* went platinum almost immediately. Even Motown was happy.

After *Reflections*, I finished Val's second album and Process's second album on Columbia. I was spending more and more time in my room and spending up to six thousand dollars a week on coke. My life was getting completely out of hand.

I decided I didn't want to tour anymore. Near the end of the *Cold Blooded* tour, something had happened while playing the New Orleans Astrodome. I looked out at the audience and saw these little young girls sticking their tongues out like snakes. I froze. A chill came over me. This feeling of dead guilt, guilt that I was wrong, that what I was doing on stage was wrong. These girls, young enough to be my children, were pulling down their tops to show me their small breasts, sticking out their tongues and trying to be sexual. It was all too overwhelming. After that gig I decided I would never tour again.

This sudden revelation was strange. I had never felt that what I was doing to young minds was wrong or right. I just never thought much about it. Now like a smack in the face, here I was, looking at mortality like a doctor looking through a microscope. I was confused, to say the least.

I began to spend a lot more time in New York. I ran into Steve Tyler. Aerosmith had broken up and he was as strung out as I was; not smoking, but shooting everything he could get his hands on. He looked bad living in this huge apartment in Manhattan with some blond guitar player. Steve was trying to do Aerosmith without Joe Perry and it wasn't working. I can remember the both of us sitting in his bedroom wondering what our lives were all about and how the fuck had we come to this, while trying to get high off anything we could find.

I was staying at The Plaza Hotel and throwing so many parties that they asked me to leave. I checked into The Parker Meridian, a very classy French hotel. All I did for three months was get high, fuck chicks and party. That was my life.

I ran into Lisa again. She had changed. She had taken my advice and gone to Europe where she met Mick Jagger and Herbie Hancock. She and her girlfriend, Debbie Falkner, another model, stayed with Mick. And from the way she had matured sexually it had done a lot of good. She had become a bona fide freak. I guess Mick and Herbie had the time to school her.

Debbie and Lisa were running buddies. Where you found one you found the other. The three of us had the time of our lives in New York. We'd stay in my room getting high as a motherfucker and ride in limousines all over New York.

Debbie Allen was a dear friend of mine. She wasn't a party girl and we never had sex, in fact she was more like an older sister, and a very strong lady. She was doing a show on Broadway, which had sold out. I told her I wanted to come to the show and she said she'd love to have me come. She said she would buy tickets with her own money just to make sure I would. I sent her a bunch of roses and told her when I'd be there. Come time for me to go, I couldn't get out of bed. Debbie, Lisa and I were lying in each other's arms, totally out of it. My phone rang and Lisa answered it. I was so tired I told her to tell whomever it was to call back. Lisa said: "Rick, I think you better talk. It's Debbie Allen and she's mad." I took the phone and all I could hear was Debbie saying: "Rick, get your ass up and bring your ass to the theater. I'm not playin.'" I tried to give a million excuses, but she just said: "Fuck that. You'd better be here."

So I dragged myself out of bed, called a limo, and Lisa, Debbie and I went. We ended up sitting in the light booth where they lit the stage. I found a couch in the corner, lay down and never did see the show. After the show, we went backstage and Debbie dragged me into her dressing room and slammed the door. She threw me into a seat and sat on top of me so I couldn't move. She told me I was killing myself and throwing my life away. She spoke to me in a way no one ever had. I'd always liked Debbie, but feared her too. That's probably why I never pursued her when she was free, before Norm. She reminded me of that too. I just looked at her, knowing she was completely right. Maybe if someone like Debbie was in my life I would not be doing what I was doing. But for some reason, I doubt it.

I stayed in New York for a few more months, spending most of my time with Lisa and Debbie, eating out, seeing plays, dancing and getting as high as we could get. Lisa and I would talk for hours into the night about her family. She was from West Virginia and most of her life had been spent around Black people. Her mother was a devout Christian and her father a devout redneck. I told her I couldn't wait to meet her family. She said her father and I would never in a hundred years get along. I told her, being my cocky self in those days, that when her father met me, he would not only invite me into his home but would give me a hug and make me some coffee.

Lisa said I was dreaming. Little did I know then, but God was getting ready to do some serious work on me.

Chapter Fifty-two
Eddie and Me

Eddie Murphy had two movies under his belt and was quickly becoming America's Golden Boy. I had heard he wanted to get into singing and I read a *Rolling Stone* interview with Prince where Prince said Eddie wanted him to produce his record. I thought "Uh-oh, too bad for Eddie." The last thing he needed was to end up sounding like a sterile Prince clone.

Eddie and I had spoken a couple of times by phone and I'd found him extremely pleasant. His success had not gone to his head, which was the first thing I checked out. He still maintained his roots by surrounding himself with his family and loved ones, kind of like me and my band.

One day Eddie called me and asked me to produce him. I immediately asked what had happened to Prince. Eddie told me he'd met with Prince in LA and thought Prince was a faggot. I laughed and asked him what he meant by that. He said Prince sat across from him at this meeting staring into his eyes, and a couple of times during the meeting he gave the impression he might be gay. I asked Eddie why it mattered. Eddie said he didn't want a faggot producing his record. He said once Prince quietly stared at him while putting his fingers in his drink and then licking them. Eddie said when he saw that, he said, "Fuck it."

That was the first time I heard of Eddie's phobia toward gays.

Eddie's record deal was on the same label as his comedy deal, Columbia. I was in the middle of completing work on the Girls' and the Doo Rags'. I told Eddie I wasn't sure I had the time to do another album and he asked if I could at least arrange one cut. I said I probably could, but any more would be impossible. During my next conversation with

Eddie everything was settled. Columbia's legal department met with my attorneys and we were ready to go.

Eddie had just finished his last and final taping for *Saturday Night Live* when I picked him up from the airport. He was even wearing the clothes from his last skit. I asked him if he was going to do any more *Saturday Night Live* segments. He said, "Fuck, no." He told me how there was a lot of bitterness and animosity between him and the cast. He felt extremely hurt about the way they treated him on his last day. I didn't push the issue of *Saturday Night Live*, I could see in his face that he felt really bad about it.

I had my whole entourage with me at the airport, including all six of my cars. Eddie and I rode in my Rolls Royce while the rest of my crew followed close behind. We talked like two old women. He was really interested in how I felt performing in front of so many people. I tried to explain then asked him why he wanted to sing. While he explained, I suddenly heard him scream "Rick!" I had barely missed this car coming from the other direction. Matter of fact, I did graze it a bit. The car swerved around. At first I thought the passengers were hurt, then I saw they weren't. A Jeep pulled up beside me and Joe Jackson, one of my guys, told me and Eddie to sneak out of the Rolls and into the Jeep. Joe put on this cowboy hat I had been wearing and Eddie and I drove to my house. It was a close call to say the least. We arrived at my house safe, but I was still in a little shock. I said to Eddie: "What if I would have killed us both. Then what?" Eddie replied, "Then there would have been two less niggahs in the world to deal with."

That winter in Buffalo was one of our worst ever. We were stranded in my house for two weeks, which was good cuz that gave us a lot of time to work. The tune was called "Party All the Time." It was about a girl Eddie was seeing in New York. Eddie bought her all kinds of shit—cars, diamonds, everything—only to find out she was partying her ass off without him. She fucked him up, although he tried to play it off.

I was on my best behavior while Eddie was staying at my house. I don't think I got high once while he was there—maybe smoked pot, but that was it. I didn't want to expose him to freebasing, especially when he didn't smoke or drink anything; never did. In the future my attitude changed. But at the time, that was how I wanted it. Besides, we were just becoming good friends. Why spoil it on account of a fucking drug? Yes, I would wait before I exposed him to it. The first time he ever rolled a joint was in my office. He didn't smoke it, but he was like a proud kid showing everyone in the house how he had rolled a joint all by himself.

When the record was finished, Eddie and his boys flew to LA where Stevie Wonder completed the rest of the album. Eddie was a joy to work with. He caught on quick to singing in the confines of a studio. The only problem I had was finding his true sound. He could emulate so many vocalists, including me, Al Green and Michael Jackson. Once I found out what Eddie sounded like, the rest was easy.

After Steve finished the album, Columbia threw a huge listening party in a luxurious beach house in Malibu to select the single. I wasn't there and was positive the guests would select one of Stevie's tunes. Eddie called me from the party to tell me what happened. He said the whole album was played over a huge sound system and as soon as "Party All the Time" came on the crowd were on their feet dancing. I had beat out Stevie and I was happy for both me and Eddie. But I had mixed emotions about Stevie. After I hung up the telephone, I went back to the solitude of my pipe.

Eddie's record was Number One around the world. It was unfortunate that nothing else hit as a single, but that's the record biz. Anyway, with "Party All the Time," Eddie was an instant recording star. He decided to do his video in New York City at Jimi Hendrix's recording studio, Electric Ladyland. People said that I stole the show away from Eddie in the video, but to me we just looked like two friends having fun.

The "Party all the Time" video was the first one featuring me to ever play on MTV. I was surprised to finally get air time, but it was Eddie's video, and Eddie was hosting the MTV awards, so I looked at it as another political move on MTV's part. MTV also aired the Mary Jane Girls' video "In My House" and the Doo Rags' "Stomp and Shout," so I felt I was making a little headway with MTV, even though they still weren't playing my videos.

After finishing "Party All the Time," I found myself more and more isolated. If I wasn't locked in my room (where my housekeeper would leave food by my bedroom door), I was flying here and there in private planes getting high in the clouds. I was slowly but steadily losing control. I had turned into a nocturnal monster who existed solely on the smoke from a freebase pipe. I'd wake in the night and begin. It got so bad I had my staff put aluminum foil on all my windows so no sunlight could get in. I'd just sit and get high, usually with the company of a female or two. When that was done, I'd take Valiums to go to sleep. This went on and on.

The first time Eddie saw me get high was in LA. He came to my room after I had spent days locked inside, jumped on my bed and began asking all these questions about how we felt and what the drugs were like. Rod Stewart and his girlfriend Kelly were there snorting coke, and Eddie's questions made them feel so uncomfortable that they got up and left. Eddie sat there for hours and hours asking stupid questions like "Are you high, or not?" I told him: "Yes, I'm high, motherfucker. Stop asking those silly-ass questions." He just continued to sit and observe my every motion. By the time he left my room, I'm sure he had picked up a serious contact high. Eddie was just like that: he wanted to know everything about the drug, knowing he wasn't going to do it. I never understood that about him. I used to think it was just his curiosity getting the best of him.

A little while after that in New York, I decided to go on one of my serious drug binges. I had run into Lisa and Debbie, and, as usual, the three of us decided to have some fun. We checked into a suite at The Parker Meridian. Debbie was a diabetic, which always kept me alarmed. She needed her insulin shots at certain times every day. Surprisingly enough, it never fucked with her ability to get high—at least not yet.

It was almost Christmas and New York was beautiful. Debbie had met Billy Idol and brought him over to my hotel to meet me. I told Debbie I had never heard his music, but had heard he was almost as crazy as me. Billy was this shy, blond-haired dude who I liked right away. We tripped down to his place in the Village and hung out. He was trying to stop smoking dope at the time, so all we did was smoke grass and snort. Eventually I decided to go back to the hotel and Lisa came along with me. Soon as we got inside the room, we ripped off our clothes and fucked and sucked ourselves into a coma. Debbie came and joined us later.

It would be Christmas in a few days and Debbie and Lisa both went home to see their families. I was left alone. I didn't want to see anyone, except my Mom, but I was afraid to call her because I was so high. I bought a bunch more dope and just sat feeling sorry for myself. Chico Ross, Diana's brother, and his wife, Tracey came to see me. They were on their way to Diana's for Christmas and asked if I wanted to join them, but I refused. They knew something was wrong, but didn't speak on it. Eddie also called and invited me for Christmas dinner with his family and I refused that invitation as well. I finally did talk to my mother and she could tell by my voice that something was extremely wrong. I hung up with tears streaming down my face.

Then I started to smoke as much as I could. The loneliness set in and I became more and more depressed. I had always heard that Christmas was a lonely time for the lonely. Now I could tell why. After every hit of coke, I felt myself falling deeper into this black hole of self-despair until my only way out was to do the final act—suicide. I slowly took off all my jewelry, which in those days was quite a bit. I laid my wallet, my jewelry and the dope on the hotel nightstand with a suicide note. I then threw on an old Army jacket and stuffed my hair under a Rasta hat, then walked into the cold of New York. Looking and wondering where a lonely Funk n' Roll singer might take his life.

The night air was freezing cold. I didn't even want a cab. I just walked. My mind was going in ever direction. I didn't know what was happening. I just knew I didn't want to live in this skin any more. I had had enough.

Before I knew it I was in the Village. I went into a corner bar and began to drink one bourbon after another. I drank so many back-to-back the bartender cut me off and told me to leave. Before I walked out the door, I used my last sip of bourbon to wash down a bunch of Valiums. As I staggered down the dark and icy street, I heard someone yelling my name. I was so well disguised it seemed impossible anybody could have recognized me.

I turned my head and saw Scorpio and Mele Mel from Grandmaster Flash, yelling at me "Hey Rick, where you going?" They were trying to talk to me, but I just dug my chin down into the collar of my coat and pushed by them. I could no longer hear what they were trying to say. All I saw were their mouths moving. I stumbled away as quickly as I could, and somehow lost them.

I remember little else of what happened that evening. At some point that night I found myself being awakened. I was lying down on the street being shaken by this girl. She got me to my feet and took me to her flat, a small apartment in Midtown Manhattan. The girl told me she had met me in LA and that I was welcome to stay because she and her boyfriend had just broken up. She had jet-black hair and a pretty face. She made me a pot of black coffee and sobered me up.

I felt much better after dozing for a while and drinking the hot coffee. When she went to take a bath, I quietly left and walked back to the hotel. I didn't know why, but I had to leave her apartment. Just as I was going in through the hotel doors, I saw the van. It was Joe and my mother.

I was never so happy to see my Mom in my life. I asked her what she was doing in New York. She said when she heard my voice on the phone she immediately had Joe drive her down from Buffalo. I said "What about the family?" She said the family could take care of itself, at least for one Christmas. I hugged and kissed her. I was overwhelmed. I felt my life had been saved.

The next morning I got up bright and early and Mom, Joe and I went shopping. I bought some clothes for Eddie and some edible underwear for Diana and her new husband. First we went to see Eddie and had a great time shooting pool and having dinner with his family. Then we drove to Connecticut to see Chico and Diana. They had already finished dinner, which was cool, cuz I wasn't even hungry.

Mom loved talking and meeting Diana and Diana loved Mom. I think Diana saw a lot of her own mother in Mom. She held Mom's hand gently and told me at one point I had an angel for a mother. Diana had some bowling alleys in her house, so we all went down to the lanes and bowled. I met her new husband, Arni, who was a total gentleman and made Diana very happy. I also met a beautiful lady who was a real princess—Princess Elizabeth Von Oxenberg, the Princess of Yugoslavia. She was very charming and I could tell she liked me a lot. Her daughter was Catherine Oxenberg, the actress. I was not that impressed by Catherine, but her mother and I kicked it off. My mother and I had a great Christmas. We hadn't spent one together in a long time. I never told her of my suicide attempt.

Princess Elizabeth and I talked by phone many times and I was always amazed at how down-to-earth she was. Not only was she smart and witty, but her body was in excellent condition, and she had a beautifully toned, exquisite facial structure—like a little girl.

One of Princess Elizabeth's youngest daughters wrote a book about New York City cabs. There was a huge party to launch the book at Stringfellow's. I met Peter Stringfellow in London and he is one of the nicest men I know, and a good friend. He has always shown me love and respect. At the party, the Princess had me sit right next to her for dinner. Even the Prince, an older debonair gentleman, had a look of disbelief on his face. But Elizabeth didn't mind. We had fun whenever we were together. She hated the fact that I did drugs, and was constantly telling me I should be like her and work out. I took her to see Eddie Murphy live. At first I was bashful to ask her cuz I knew how vulgar Eddie's show was. Then in my hotel suite before the show she asked me "Rick, do you know why a dog sucks his own dick?" I said no. She said "Cuz he can." I busted up laughing. I knew then she was ready to see Murphy. After the show, *Jet* magazine released a picture of the two of us together that got us a lot of notoriety and attention.

We had a great time at the concert. I took her, her son and daughter. We all got along great. We continued talking to each other but fear made me stop. I just didn't want to hurt Elizabeth. She didn't need a loser like me in her life.

After going back to Buffalo, I never spoke to the Princess again.

Chapter Fifty-three
Straight and Sober

It was now time for my ninth album with Motown and my life hadn't changed. I would lock myself in my room for a week or two, then record for a week or two. The only good thing about my addiction at this point was my ability to stop long enough to write music. I hadn't lost my zeal for writing. I would always manage to stay straight enough to make music. I found it very difficult, if not impossible, to write while doing base. My songs came out dark—dark and lonely. So I made it a point not to write while freebasing.

I decided on this album I would go back and cut like a live band again. I needed that live feeling and it gave my boys a chance to work close with me again. It was exciting sitting in the studio with all of them again. The close contact gave me a high in itself.

I hired Steve Ferroen to play drums. Steve was famous for his funky drums with The Average White Band, Eric Clapton, Chaka and numerous others. He was a Black cat from England with this big smile—I mean this cat had teeth. Soon as Steve hit town he had the girls. They loved him and he loved them. He stayed about two weeks cutting tracks. I was never happier. When Steve was around, I seemed to regain something that had been missing. It's hard to explain magic.

The album had a beautiful live feeling. I called the album *Glow*. Its concept was a boy in search of the *Glow*. I wrote this little fable or story about the little boy's trip into the dark forest. I guess you could say the boy in the Glow fable was me; although I didn't know it then.

Before my album was mixed, my attorneys, Irv Shuman and Les Greebaum, and my accountant Dick Romaler came to my house for an unexpected visit. They told me my addiction was out of control and I needed professional help. They said they'd look for a good rehab and set it up for me to go. I felt strange about it, even scared. I never thought other people could see I had a problem, least of all my straight–faced attorneys. The way I was spending my money, though, I couldn't hide it.

Irv soon got back to me to say that he'd found a hospital outside Boston called McLean's, a drug rehabilitation clinic. I was quickly booked in for the next available twenty eight-day session, however, when it came time for me to go, I almost didn't. I used all the excuses, "maybe I don't really need it," and "I can probably quit on my own," and every other excuse I could conjure up. But somewhere in my heart I knew it was now-or-never and I finally broke down and went.

I had this luxury van at the time that I used for longer rides and as I sat in comfort I couldn't help dwelling on my life and wondering how things had come to this. With such heavy contemplations the drive went quickly, and before I knew it, I had reached Boston, and McLean's Hospital. For the entire length of the drive I had been smoking and getting high. When the van door was finally opened at the clinic, I stepped out in a huge puff of smoke.

McLean's was huge, with beautiful buildings and magnificent grounds surrounding them. The landscapes and rolling hills were peaceful and serene, and I felt a little sense of the calm I needed to find within myself. In the back there was a small building called East House for drug addicts.

East House Two was a twenty-eight day lock-down clinic. If you decided to leave, you had to give a three-day notice. The program included group sessions, sports, meditation classes and a twelve-step program involving addicts and alcoholics.

The first familiar face I saw was Steve Tyler's. I was happy to see him. He looked good and healthy. I went through the program not really wanting to be there. I was a rebel from beginning to end. But I was at least straight and sober, which was a miracle in itself.

Once while attending a NA meeting, I heard this guy speak. He seemed to have suffered the same pain I had. I felt like he was inside of me. When he finished speaking, I immediately asked him to be my sponsor. A sponsor is someone who has at least two or three years sobriety, someone you call to talk to when you want to get high, or even if you don't. A sponsor is a special friend in need. The speaker's name was Chuck Toomey. I liked him immediately. He was a real straight shooter, and from his testimony I could tell he had been through this thing called addiction to the point where we could really relate to each other.

Chuck agreed to be my sponsor and when I had been sober for a month, he gave me a coin as a symbol of my success. The coin was circular with a triangle inside it— just like the symbol in the dream I had while creating the *Cold Blooded* album—the exact one. It was uncanny and for the first time I felt God was intervening in my life, telling me to get it together.

After completing the twenty-eight day rehab, I hung out in Boston for a while, going to meetings with Chuck and enjoying this new feeling of sobriety. It was definitely a feeling I was not used to. I couldn't remember the last time I had been straight. Even as a child I would have something; wine, weed, anything. The feelings I was having were wonderful and strange at the same time.

When I returned to Buffalo after the treatment, I was happy to see all my friends and family. They even gave me a sober party—no alcohol or drugs. The aluminum foil had been taken down off my bedroom windows, and everyone commented on how healthy I looked. Even I could see the change. But keeping that feeling wasn't easy. I had to attend a lot of NA meetings where I had to sit and listen to addicts tell their horror stories of addiction. That was the hardest part, the constant reminder that addiction was an incurable disease that I would have to live with all the days of my life.

After spending time at home I headed out to LA to finish the *Glow* album. While in LA I went to meetings every day and was inspired by NA to make the *Glow* video, which was like a mini-movie about me kicking the bottle. When I had shot the "Ebony Eyes" video with Smokey Robinson both of us had stayed high sunup to sundown. For

Glow, I was totally straight, I even had to act like I was drunk in the video and fall on stage. I pulled it off with no problem. Everything seemed easier when I was straight.

I even did the *Johnny Carson Show* and played piano on "Happy" from the *Throwin' Down* album. Joan Rivers was the host, and she made me feel real comfortable on the show. We talked a lot about addiction. Joan is and will always hold a special place in my heart. She had always said I was her favorite.

I stayed straight for almost five months. Then I stopped calling Chuck, stopped going to meetings, and finally I got fucked up. But this time my high was different. I just couldn't—no matter how hard I tried—get that same high again.

The night of my slip, Carrie Fisher and I threw a party. We had become friends, going to NA meetings together, movie premieres, just basically enjoying sobriety. She decided to throw a party and invite all our actor friends and try to encourage them to twelve –step out of their drug addictions. The party was held at her Hollywood Hills home and everyone came. Harrison Ford, Jack Nicholson, Timothy Leary, Mo Ostin and his wife, and Anthony Michael Hall were just a few who attended. Every one of them wanted to see if me and Carrie were really straight—and we were.

I caught some of my friends snorting coke in the bathroom. They pulled me in and asked me how the hell I did it. I just laughed and got the hell out of the room. The temptation was too great.

Catherine Bach and I were a Hollywood item and she loved the fact that I was straight. As we left the party, I ran into Susan, an actress friend of mine, who had just been dumped by Mo Osten's son, Kenny. Susan asked me and Catherine to drive her home. When we got there, we went inside and she pulled out a bag of coke. She asked me if I wanted some and at first I refused. But then, seeing Catherine wasn't around, I suc-cumbed. Catherine came back in the room and saw I had gotten high. She asked me if I wanted to stay and keep Susan company. I said I did. Catherine kissed me goodbye with a deep look of concern in her eyes. I told her I'd be all right.

As soon as Catherine left, Susan and I got fucked up and made love. This was just the beginning of my new bout with addiction and I was ready to smoke my ass off.

It's funny how sobriety can affect your life. It's like you turn into this nice person, which is not what I was known for, to say the least. But with sobriety came this contentment that I had always longed for, that feeling of going to sleep at night and waking up in the morning to hear the birds sing and watch you children grow. All those wonderful things that make up a normal living human being, which after that first hit, you lose completely.

One of my best friends at that time was Jim Brown. Jim was probably the best running back that football ever produced. We'd spend hours talking philosophy, politics and life in general. Jim always talked from the hip, straight at you. And if someone didn't like it—tough. He viewed life as he viewed football: hard and without mercy. He's a brilliant and sensitive man. He's not into drugs at all. Matter of fact, he almost looks at them with a deep resentment. I guess cuz he's seen it destroy so many of his friends, including me. He used to just look at me and say, "Rick, when are you going to get it right?" He was always concerned with my welfare. Once he even got minister Louis Farrakan to talk to me. I deeply respect the minister and I became close to his son Wallace.

The minister talked to me about my belief in Allah, who could heal all wounds. I would listen to the Minster up at Jim's house—and as soon as I left, get high. I couldn't understand it, and neither could Jim. But if ever God made a patient man, it was Jim Brown. I thank Allah for putting him in my life. I love Jim Brown. Had I just listened to him from the beginning of all this shit I might have been able to stop it. But at that time it seemed too late. It seemed I was getting worse than I was before. I even stopped seeing Jim, for Jim would surely see how I was sinking into a state of dark depravity.

My sister Penny and Teena would try to see me, but I would have my security either tell them I wasn't to be disturbed or have an extra hotel suite I could hide in when family or friends tried to find me. Teena and Penny were the last two people I wanted to see. Penny was my little sister and I didn't want her to know that I was getting high. I had started Penny on her career in music when I persuaded our mother to let her go to California at fifteen with Teena. There was so much joy in Penny's face when Mom let her go and I felt a lot of responsibility to keep her away from the drugs and the insanity. No matter how hard I tried to hide the truth from her, Penny always knew when I was fucked up. She and Teena were good like that and eventually they would find me, no matter how many hotel rooms I had.

Penny and Teena were having problems of their own as they tried to leave Motown, which was suing and threatening them. Had they listened to me about how to deal with Motown, all that shit wouldn't have happened. They were not two of my favorite people—Teena with all these fucking love songs about me, "Cassanova Brown" and "Square Biz," "Portuguese Love" and so on. I just couldn't think how she could love someone as crazy as me.

While in LA I was asked to star in an *A-Team* episode. I hadn't appeared in a TV series yet, and *A-Team* was at the top of the ratings. I said "Yes," to shooting one episode with Isaac Hayes as my co-star. When I saw the script, I was surprised by how much dialogue my character had. I decided that I would study the script the evening before the shoot and get an early night, so I'd be well rested and ready for my 6:00 A.M. pick-up. But the night of the show I met this girl and we got high and had sex. She was incredibly kinky, asking me to asphyxiate her, and wanting to try every position in the Karma Sutra. It was the kinkiest sex I ever had, and I never even got to bed, let alone read the script. By the time I was in makeup, I didn't know one word of dialogue, and I was still high from the excitement of the night before. I had the director write the words on big cue cards so I could read them while the camera rolled. George Peppard got so upset with me that he walked off the set. Mr. T told me not to worry, that this was my show and if I didn't feel comfortable with my lines, I should change them or do it again. Mr. T made me feel at home. He knew I hadn't slept.

Isaac and I got along great. The day before we were in the studio cutting a tune for the show, a Blues number written by James Taylor called "Steamroller Blues." We performed it together during the show and it sounded great. I told Isaac what a big fan of his I was. I can't remember much about performing. All I knew was it felt great.

I always felt I let myself down with my *A-Team* experience. But rehab taught me not to feel like that when I made a mistake because of my addiction. I should have gone to bed and read my script. I made a vow that the next time I had an opportunity to do nationwide TV, I'd try to be more careful. That next time came real soon. I was offered a part on *One Life to Live*, a soap opera. Normally I would have refused, but *One Life to Live* was my mother's favorite soap, and when she heard I had the chance to be on it, she insisted I do it. She wanted to have the inside scoop on what was going to happen the next day. The money was good and the producers used a lot of my music on the show. I also felt like I needed to redeem myself for my *A-Team* fuck up, so I accepted the offer.

This time I got the script a few days ahead of time and learned it easily. When I got to the set I was treated like a king. The stars of the other soaps on the lot came over just to meet me. I was ready. I had even gotten a good night's sleep. It was a long day, with lots of lines and a performance, but I dug it. I had hated soaps up till then, but after appearing in one I realized how hard the actors actually worked. The producers even had my brother William and my security man Squeaky in one scene because they needed more Blacks. The boys got paid and I proved to myself I could do the right thing every once in a while.

I started to get more TV offers but I turned them down. The only show I really wanted to do was *Miami Vice*. But every time they sent me a script, I sent it right back. I didn't like the way they wrote my character and the way they focused on drugs and sex.

After my TV experiences in LA, I returned to Buffalo and just hung out, going into my studio and recording when I got the urge. Jan Gay was often at the house. She would come and stay for two or three weeks, then go back to see her kids Nona and Frankie. Mostly Jan and I would get high and have kinky sex. We were very close and once I even asked her to marry me. But by the time we got serious about it, we were both high or laughing too hard to do it.

I had this little poodle dog named Jimmy-Eddie that I'd bought for my assistant, Linda. He was named after me and Eddie Murphy because we were both considered dogs. I used to watch him participate in sex acts with girls; Jimmy would sneak under the covers of the bed when I was fucking a few girls, and start licking them. After the initial surprise, the girls loved him, because Jimmy was the very best at giving head. When I tried to kick him out of bed Jimmy would growl and try to bite me. Eventually Jimmy was kidnapped. The people who took him left me a note saying, "We are saving this dog from your abuse!" Jimmy would stay in my room while I was getting high, his white coat slowly turning brown from the smoke, and when I'd kick him out he'd stagger like a drunk from the contact high. I'd actually hear him knocking on the door trying to get back in. Jimmy's Jones was as bad as mine. When I went away on tour, it would take a week for him to de-tox and he would just stay by the door going cold turkey.

Once more my life was slowly going out of control. My bedroom windows had been darkened again and I'd have sex with three or four women at a time while getting high, then lay and watch them. That was all my life seemed to consist of. The only time that I felt released from my addiction was when I went down to the Island of St. Marten, rented a yacht, and just sailed and smoked grass. Something about the sun and the peacefulness of the yacht would almost cause me to lose my desire to do cocaine. As soon as I was back in Buffalo or LA the monster would return.

It had been over a year since I was clean. I needed to get straight again, so I checked myself back into McLean's Hospital for another twenty-eight days. I felt that maybe this time I might hear something I needed to hear, something I missed the first time. After all, I'd stayed clean for five months after my first visit. Maybe this time it would be longer.

As soon as I had settled down in my room at the hospital I was startled by someone jumping on top of me, kissing me and laughing hysterically. It was my old friend Steven Tyler. It turned out he had relapsed around the same time I had. It was good seeing him again.

Chuck was still my sponsor and he was very understanding of how difficult staying straight could be. At our first meeting Chuck had a story he was eager to tell me. He said he had been at a Political Dinner in Boston where a clairvoyant woman known as the Boston Witch had come up and started talking to him. The Witch was well known in Boston for using her clairvoyant powers to help police in catching violent criminals. She'd touch pieces of evidence and from the impressions she saw would be able to tell the police where the killer was. She told Chuck that he knew someone with the initials RJ and that she needed to talk to that person. Chuck was startled and promised to bring me to her soon.

I had heard stories like his before, of witches and fortune-tellers, and had often sought out people like these in my younger days, but had never really found one who was true. A couple of times I got close, only to find that they did not have any real power. In the days of my youth, damn near every girl I met claimed to be a witch, carrying Tarot cards or I Ching coins. But this was different. I didn't go looking for her—she found me. From what I heard about her she was respected in Boston, even by the politicians and lawmen. It was difficult even to see this mysterious woman. But eventually I was able to contact her and arrange to meet. I was going to meet The Boston Witch.

I had revolted against my Catholic upbringing since my youth and had turned to other religions and the occult in my search for some meaning in life. I have always had a longing to know about myths, theology and ancient cults. Egyptians are one of favorite studies: Osiris and Isis, Rameses, the Druids, the Secret scrolls, the Cheops and the Pyramids, the Egyptian Book of the Dead, the queens of Egypt, Rasputin, Allister Crowley. My desire to meet this woman was very strong. I had to find out if she could tell me the future and the past. I would meet her and test her. I just prayed she would pass.

The drive through Boston was beautiful and my mind drifted back to the first time I played in the old, historical city, when I'd seen police beating up on Black people outside the Orpheum. For a long time afterwards I had blamed myself for the violence, but eventually I had realized that Boston was inherently racist. Whenever I am in Boston I am reminded of a photograph I once saw on the cover of Life Magazine. The picture showed a Black man being beaten by a crowd of men who encircled the victim with smiles on their white faces. The rage I felt when I first saw that image comes very close to the surface whenever I am in Boston. I'll never forget those Brothers and Sisters being whipped because they had wanted to go out, see my show and have some fun.

We reached Old Boston with its cobblestone streets and beautiful ol' gaslights. She lived next to where the Boston Tea Party was held, across from Paul Revere's house. The old fashioned setting seemed an appropriate place to find a Witch.

We parked and walked to the door, which was covered in garlic and strange symbols. I imagined they were some sort of protection from evil. The witch came to the door and let us in. She was a big Italian woman with jet-black hair. Every part of her clothing was black. She said she was glad I had come and that we should go upstairs and wait for her. When she spoke I could tell she had a sweet nature. Her laugh was loud and heavy, and though I was still too nervous to think one way or the other, I wasn't afraid. I knew she was safe and not crazy like some people would believe. She had two sons who were fat little guys around eight and ten years old. They were watching a Black dance show and they knew who I was. They asked me all kinds of questions about music.

I walked around the small apartment looking at everything. In her kitchen she had a fascinating table. Under the glass top were all sorts of pictures, designs, writings and scriptures. As I ran my eyes over the display I saw that right on the corner of the table she had the *Glow* fable. I was shocked. She had cut it out of the album insert and placed it under the glass like it was a sacred piece of paper. I felt a chill as I looked at it. I had forgotten that what I wrote was so profound. It was like I had forgotten what I had created.

She came back into the house and in her hand was a small object wrapped in velvet. I knew what it was. We went into the living room and began to talk. I asked how she had found me and she explained that her spirit had told her to go to Chuck. I was surprised by her sense of honesty, but when I looked in her soft eyes they gave nothing but truth, as gentle as a mother's eyes give. I believed her story. No one at that party had known Chuck sponsored me and he had never met this woman before.

My belief sharpened my curiosity. I asked her where she got her power from and she let out a loud, healthy laugh and said she knew I would ask that. She told me a story of how her first husband had passed away. He had been into a lot of criminal type things, and when he passed, he left her and the family broke. She cursed him for it. How could he have done this to the family after taking such good care of them while he was alive?

One day while she cursed his dead soul for leaving them broke she heard his voice. The voice told her to break open her favorite lamp and look inside. She got up, took the lamp and broke it open. There was over eighty thousand dollars inside. After that she could call on this spirit whenever she had to know anything.

I smiled at the story. It was cute. Just from knowing her that short while I knew she deserved the money.

I could tell she wanted to be alone with me and she asked Chuck to leave and come back in an hour. As soon as Chuck had gone I asked her if the velvet package in her hand was a set of Tarot cards. She said they were and I asked her where she kept them. The witch said she kept them buried in a quiet place outside.

She passed the first test. Tarot cards can't be read properly if you keep them inside your home—too confusing. They need Mother Earth to lie in.

She had tied the cards with three knots, which meant she passed the second test. Tarot cards have to be tied in a certain way and wrapped in velvet.

The Witch told me to come into the kitchen, where I asked her about the *Glow* fable. She said she just happened on it and thought it was nice so she decided to put it in her table.

The card reading was spellbinding. She knew everything. The simple things I can tell, and the deep, dark, secrets I can reveal to no one. She knew my mother's name and the number of members in my family. She told me of an evil in and around our family, a person who has caused our family lots of bad. Before the reading I had been eager to hear the future, but suddenly I was afraid to know. She was so on it and sharp, I feared that what she saw for me might be too much to bear.

After my reading, she gave me the most beautiful crystal I'd ever seen wrapped in a velvet bag. She said it had incredible healing powers. She gave me her number and told me I was free to call whenever I wanted. When I asked her how much my reading would cost she said, "Whatever you think it is worth." I gave her some money and quietly left, my mind spinning. I believed in God and in the Evil One—but this was something different. Chuck pulled up just as I walked outside.

I went back to Buffalo and continued on my road to sobriety. I missed Catherine terribly, so after a short stay at home I went to visit her in California. I attended lots of NA meetings in LA. They take sobriety seriously out there and I needed that. I stayed clean for almost a year.

Then one day, while hanging out at Tramps, a well-known Hollywood club, I slipped and got high. This time I felt this sudden twinge of impending doom, this loneliness that I never felt before, this violent rage. I felt like lashing out at God and Satan for letting me go through this hell. I chose Satan as my master and Hell as my future home.

Chapter Fifty-four
The End of Motown

It was time for my ninth and final album with Motown. I felt it had been long enough and I needed a change. Motown and I had so many disputes over the years that it no longer felt like the family organization I had joined a decade ago. Usually, when an artist makes a last album for a company, the company gets schlock. But I would never do that to Motown or to anyone else. I prided myself on my music, if nothing else. If I was leaving, I was going to give them the best album I had in me.

I had been experimenting with sounds. I hadn't been listening to the radio, which was probably bad. I'd always listened before, just to be up on the latest sounds. But I rarely listened anymore.

I called the album *The Flag* and I came up with a great concept for it. At that time I was reading a lot about nuclear waste and missiles. I was horrified to find that there were fifteen thousand missiles in the US alone. I was totally blown away, so I wrote this little piece of music expressing my feelings about it called "Silly Little Men," about Gorbachev and Reagan, the assholes with the power of the button. I also wrote a song about my addiction called "Free to Be Me." The album had a great feeling to it, I thought.

Motown disagreed. They wanted some bubble gum shit like "Party All the Time." But I felt a need to express my views, even if it put my career at stake. I needed to compose for me, not for Motown.

The album took almost a year to make. After recording the tracks I had smoked so much dope that I couldn't sing. My lungs were fucked up. I flew to New York to a lung specialist who took pictures of my lungs and showed me a grey spot on them. The doctor said that if I continued to smoke coke, I would never sing again. That scared me to death. I had no degree. I hadn't even finished high school. If I couldn't sing what would I do?

The doctor told me I should go somewhere warm and relax; and not to smoke anything, not even cigarettes. So I went to Saint Marten, rented a one hundred and fifty-foot yacht called *Monkey Business* and sailed around the Antilles. I played my guitar and lay on the deck thinking and enjoying the scenery. The boat was the same one Barbara Walters had her honeymoon on. It was truly a magnificent yacht and, for a couple of weeks, I and a group of intimate friends sailed the balmy Caribbean on her.

When we docked in St. Marten I was pleased to find a friend of mine playing there named Jimmy Cliff. I hung out with Jimmy for a while, still not smoking anything. I could feel my voice growing stronger and stronger. Before I left for the islands I couldn't even get a full note out of my mouth. Now I was singing like my old self. It felt good and I was relieved that I had not lost my voice after all.

The *Monkey Business* trip cost me close to one hundred thousand dollars—thirty thousand for gas alone. But despite the cost I felt it was a small price to pay for a moment of peace and tranquility.

I flew back to Buffalo and immediately began singing my vocals on *The Flag*. I shot the cover in Buffalo, and turned over my last album to Motown. It was the end of an era, but only too soon I found out that Motown would not let me go that easily.

Motown served me with a lawsuit stating I owed them one more album. Even more upsetting, The Mary Jane Girls went behind my back to Motown saying all these lies about me. Joanne McDuffie, the ugly duckling, was the biggest liar of the bunch. She said the cruelest things about me to the press, things that just weren't true. My mother always said she'd be the Judas and I was really hurt and saddened by her behavior.

Joanne had married this neighborhood Buffalo trick named Robert Thunderbird who was always hanging around trying to get his slimy hands on any of the girls. Joanne, being the homeliest, was weak for him. The day they got married, I could see he was after the fame and the money. Jojo's Maid of Honor was Anita Baker. Anita, who is one of the most stuck-up bitches I'd ever met, was nasty to everyone at the wedding except Jojo. I tend to think they were lovers. They certainly acted like bitches in love.

Jojo started to change after *My House* was released. She started to get stuck up like that bitch Anita.

A quick story about Jojo and her Don Juan Jerk–off husband. Ted Dansen and Howie Mandel made a movie called *It's a Fine Mess*. I was invited by Blake Edwards, the director, to do a song for it. Well, I thought performing on the soundtrack would be a great break for the Girls. Blake wanted me to record a funky version of "Walk Like a Man," a song that was originally done by The Four Seasons. Blake even said he would pay for a video. It was a perfect opportunity for the girls to shine.

I got a copy of the song and did a hip arrangement, then put the Mary Jane Girls on it. Blake loved it, but when the time came to shoot the video, Jojo refused. I fucking went crazy. How could anyone in their right fucking mind refuse a video with Ted Dansen and Howie Mandel in it? I begged and pleaded with Jojo, telling her it would be great for her career. Her husband was by her side through all the meetings, which was something that hadn't been allowed before. Then and there I knew he was up to something.

Jojo kept saying she wanted thirty thousand dollars to do the video. I screamed, "What? No one—not me, not Prince, not no one—gets paid to do videos! We just do them to help our careers!" I finally threw up my hands and told Roy, my brother, to deal with the stupid bitch. I think he gave her fifteen thousand dollars or something. After that, I was through with Jojo. She embarrassed me, herself and everyone by trying to come across like a fucking superstar. And I had made that silly hoe! After that episode I realized Jojo was not what I'd thought.

Anyway, Motown sued me. I counter sued for Motown stealing millions of dollars of my royalties and for trying to steal the Mary Jane Girls.

I had begun to cut another album on the Girls, but after six or seven tracks I said: "Fuck it! They aren't worth it." The Mary Jane Girls were finished and I was glad. I had made them and now I would break them. It gave me joy when the lawsuits began. Now I'd see if they were strong enough to make it. But they weren't. None of them ever made a record on their own. Jojo ended up singing background behind Anita Baker. Corvette sued and lost a judgment against Paula Abdul. Candy went back to a nine-to-five job singing back up behind rappers like Ice-Cube. Maxi got married and she is still making demos. What a shame, I thought. They had the world, but instead of singing and making money and thanking God for their break, they got ugly and thought they had no need of me. And after all their lies and accusations, I deserted them.

The Motown lawsuits weighed heavily on me. I knew it would take years for the outcome and that Motown was hoping I would not survive. I wasn't sure I would either. I also knew I couldn't record for another company till the suits were over. All I could do was watch the money I spent and try to hang in there till the suits were over. I knew it was going to be hard, at least a five-year wait. But what would I do for five years? I'd just play it by ear.

Around this time, Willie Nelson was organizing a fund-raiser called Farm Aid. He phoned me one night while I was in the middle of one of my binges and asked me if I would appear. I was so high I didn't believe it was Willie. I'd always had a deep respect for him although we'd never met. He told me he liked my music, especially "Silly Little Man," from *The Flag* album. I thanked him and asked him if the Farm Aid had anything to do with Black people. He said it did and that's why he was calling me. He said Black farmers were suffering too and my performing at a concert would help make more Black people aware of the farmer's difficulties. I told him I would love to help. He told me how many people I could bring and said we'd work the rest out. I hung up thinking maybe this was just a dream. Willie Nelson didn't just call me, did he?

The next few days I rehearsed with three of my guys. I even wrote a song on the piano called "Farmers in Need" which I was going to perform live. The day I was to leave for Texas, Lisa and I got so high I almost didn't make it. We started having kinky sex and I barely made it into the shower with enough time to catch the plane. I took Tom

McDermott, Kenny Hawkins and Leno Reyes with me, plus security. When we arrived Willie picked us up and took us to his ranch. It was a huge spread with a gold course, forty-eight-track studio and his own cowboy town in the back. We even attended a real wedding in the cowboy town chapel. Willie was friendly and congenial and much nicer than I'd thought he'd be.

Before the show Willie threw a huge barbeque with a Country band and half cows cooked on the spit. It was loud and fun and a good warm up for the concert. Willie made us feel right at home and I appreciated his kindness and concern for our well-being.

The day of the concert I saw a lot of cats I hadn't seen in years; Taj Mahal, Neil Young, and my old friend Dennis Hopper. Even Catherine Bach was there—but we didn't speak to each other. The last time I'd seen her was in Buffalo when I took her to see The Temptations and The Four Tops. She got so drunk she fell all over the van, with me and The Tempts looking on. When we got home she was obnoxious and wouldn't give me room to breathe. I ended up locking my bedroom door and jumping out the window. I stayed the night with a girlfriend just to get away. Catherine left the next day and I hadn't spoken to her since. How funny the whole thing was with us. All and all, Catherine is a sweet lady and I still think of her and the fun we had.

The concert was a success and the crowd loved us. You should have seen all these rednecks with the Funk sign high in the air. It was a trip. We did short arrangements of "Give It to Me Baby," "You and I," "Super Freak'" and "Seventeen and Sexy." I called President Reagan an asshole during the show and some people came down on me for it. I didn't give a fuck. Reagan was an asshole.

After the concert we drove into Austin and partied at a nightclub called "Alley Oop's." Joe Walsh, Bon Jovi and a bunch of us had a great jam that lasted into the morning. I met the owner of the club, Mark Hannah. In Mark's office he had hung all these pictures of an older man with the Kennedys and Nixon. I asked who this heavyweight was and Mark said it was his father. I asked what his story was. Mark said his father had created *The Flintstones*. I told him I loved *The Flintstones* and Mark said, sadly, that everyone did. I let the subject drop, feeling I had touched on a sensitive topic.

Mark had an ol' lady named Ashley who I also grew fond of. The three of us built a strong friendship, which stands to this day.

After the concert I flew to LA. I hung out, going to new clubs and partying. One evening, I went to see Robin Williams live, I had heard he was trying to get sober and I wanted to see for myself. Robin was as funny as ever. After the show, I hung out with Christopher Atkins and Christopher Reeve, snorting coke. Christopher Reeves snorted up the little coke I had. I think he was taking his Superman role too seriously that night. Christopher Atkins and I, along with his girlfriend, went back to my place and I stayed up for a couple of days. Chris went to work and a lady from my hometown named Penny Baker came over. She was a centerfold for *Playboy* and we got high and fucked all night. Penny became a good friend after that and one of my best buddies.

I flew to New York to see my friend Joey Cinque, a short, sharply dressed Italian whose godfather was the great George Raft. Joey and I would hang out everywhere in New York. He had a beautiful apartment on Park Avenue, and from there we would go out all over the town. Most people were afraid of him because of his Mafia ties, but I would just laugh whenever we were together. We got our biggest laughs going to young, white preppie clubs like Monkey Bar and Surf Club. We'd walk in like we owned the joint, order the best champagne, take all of their women and then leave. God, those times with Joey are some of my fondest memories.

One day when Joey and I were in LA he called Chasen's, one of the most exclusive restaurants in Hollywood, and arranged for us to sit at Frank Sinatra's table. Meanwhile, sitting right next to us were Ronald and Nancy Reagan, Kirk Douglas and lot of others. Trent, a brother and good friend from Buffalo, was my security man at the time. He sat with his head almost touching the ex-Presidents head. Joe and I were fucked up, laughing hysterically, eating Chasen's world-renowned chili. I mean we even out-clouted the President by taking the table right next to him, which he had wanted for his security men.

When they got up to leave, Joey called to him: "Ronnie! Ronnie! Come here!" Reagan walks right over to us and Joey says, "Say hello to the King of Funk." Reagan put out his hand and we shook. Then I said, "You might know my cousin, Congressman Louis Stokes?" Reagan looked right at me. I thought he was going to answer but all he said was "Thank you very much." I almost fell on the floor laughing. I couldn't believe this man actually had run the country. Scary.

Joey is something out of a *Good Fella* movie. I could write a book on him alone. Once he gave me a vase from the Ming Dynasty. It even had it's own seat on the ride from New York to Buffalo. Joe, a guy who worked for me, brought this boxed-up vase out of the plane. It was a magnificent piece. Even the pilots and stewardesses were amazed by it. Just as Joe got close to me the vase fell out of the box and shattered on the ground. I almost broke down and cried. I told Joey and eventually we were able to laugh about it. I did manage to find a guy in Buffalo to put it back together, but it was never the same.

Hanging out with Joey was an experience, to say the least. There was never a dull moment. I hung with Joey during the lawsuit years when I had nothing to do but pass the time and wait.

Chapter Fifty-five
The Lawsuit Years

Nothing seemed important during the lawsuit years. I was comfortable financially and my addiction was always taken care of. I spent most of my time in LA and Buffalo with trips every now and then to New York.

In LA I continued to live in hotels. I always felt safe in them getting high. I'd pay the doorman extra money in case he saw something strange, like narcotic cops. I always had this sense of paranoia because of the police. I knew they couldn't wait to bust me. I had heard they wanted me in a bad way.

Once while in a Hollywood hotel I was visited by Ola Ray. Ola and I had been friends long before she ever did Michael Jackson's "Thriller" video. We'd started our relationship as lovers and slowly ended up being good friends. Ola was a smoker, like myself, and we enjoyed each other's company immensely. Once while visiting me we ran out of drugs. She decided she wanted me to come with her to cop some more. We went to a friend of hers named Billy Thornton. I had met Billy, known to every one as BT, in my earlier years in LA and I had never really cared much for him. I always felt he thought he was God's gift to everybody. He would attempt to sell me drugs. But by the time we finished, I wouldn't buy anything and would send him on his way. Billy was a handsome fellow whom women were attracted to. He had been married to a beautiful lady named Jenny, but they had divorced. I don't think she approved of his dope selling or his using. She got tired of all the women, dope and shit and left.

When Ola and I arrived at his apartment he was more friendly to me than before and we got along great. I ended up never leaving, and we became the best of friends. He was moving into a nice apartment with the help of two beautiful girls. I ended up moving in with him. He gave me my own private room.

Billy had always been one of the more successful drug dealers in Hollywood. He was *high-profile*. He loved expensive clothes and beautiful women—I mean lots at one time—expensive restaurants and expensive cars—not the usual taste for a young Black male in Hollywood dealing dope to celebrities. He loved to surround himself with the best Hollywood had to offer. His personality was basically quiet, until he threw down a few vodka Stoli's straight. Then this quiet mannered person put a smile on his face that Satan alone could chuckle at. After that he was good to go. I mean after he'd drunk a few, he'd stick his dick in a bag of liver. He had no shame. He was a funny guy and we hung everywhere together. Billy was from Ohio, and his mother and father were beautiful people. There was never a time—I mean never—when there wasn't a living room filled with beautiful women. I used to think it was because of Billy's and my beautiful personalities, but looking back I tend to think the drugs also had a little bit to do with it. Cocaine dealers get more pussy than rock or movie stars. It's a fact.

Billy and I would go to a club and the next thing you know half the club would want to follow us. Seems everyone had heard about our wild parties. I was buying coke from Billy most of the time but he was always apprehensive about it. I smoked coke, but he didn't. He seemed to frown on the fact that I smoked it the way I did even though he made double the money of a snorter, even triple the money. I always hated it when people who snort look down on people who smoke. It doesn't matter whether you shoot it, snort it, or stick it up your ass, the intake of cocaine is the intake of cocaine. You dig?

One day after watching me binge he refused to sell me any more dope, saying he "Didn't want to see me die." I was pissed. Sometimes while he was asleep I'd go to his stash and take some. He was taking so many sleeping pills at the time that he never noticed. If he did, he just never spoke on it. He was that type of guy.

I stayed with Billy off and on for about a year. After that I was cut off. I moved out to the beach with Mark Hannah. Mark was another guy who didn't smoke coke. We shared a beautiful place that sat directly on the beach. I'd get fucked up and just watch the ocean. One time I was doing one of these trips where I'd stay in my room and never leave. This English girl named Nikki and I were together during one of these escapes. We were getting high and having a great time when all of a sudden someone started beating on the door. It sounded like thunder. We almost had heart attacks. I asked who it was. A voice answered "Jim." I asked "Jim who?" The voice said "Jim Brown." I almost lost it. What was Jim doing way out here? He kept saying he wouldn't leave till he saw me. After continuous knocking, I finally went out. Billy had brought Jim to get me out of my room and it worked. I never knew quite how to refuse Jim Brown. Richard Pryor was a good friend of Jim's, and I think Jim didn't want to see what happened to Richard happen to me. After talking to me and seeing I was okay, he left.

I was booked to do the *Arsenio Hall Show,* but I was so high I didn't go. I gave his producer excuses like I had a sore tooth. Every time she called I told her my tooth was being fixed. Finally she just gave up on me. For a week all I heard was friends calling and telling me how Arsenio used me as a topic for one of his sketches, saying that Rick James was supposed to be on the show, but due to a toothache, he can't make it. The rib went on for two weeks. Even I laughed.

In those days I had the right intentions, but I just couldn't quite get it together. I really meant no harm. Teena and Penny even forced me, after being up for five or six days, to go to my son Ricky's graduation ceremony. I felt so bad after hearing Teena and Penny get in my ass that I got a limousine and went. When I got there, Ricky wasn't in the graduation ceremony because something had gone down between him and his gym teacher. I was never so mad at Teena and Penny in my life. I was dressed to kill, somewhere in the fucking Valley, attending a graduation ceremony that my son wasn't even in.

I stayed with Mark a while longer. I even managed to do a couple of tunes with Teena on her album: one up-tempo Funk tune called "Call Me" and a beautiful ballad Teena wrote called "Once and Future Dream." It was good to be in the studio working again.

After that stint in the studio, I got the jones to record again. But how? The Motown suit had been going on for almost two years and there still was no sign of a settlement. How long would it go on?

I moved back to Billy's but it was the same mundane groove: women, drugs and expensive restaurants. My frustrated desire to work was making me angry. I became short tempered. I even found that I had a violent side of me that scared me.

Once while my friend K, who I'll allow to remain anonymous was visiting us. I exploded. K's father, let's call him M, is one of the biggest record moguls in the world and K has been spoiled by coming from extreme wealth. K is the type of guy who, whether high or not, feels the world owes him. When it came to me, he was all wrong. I had been getting high with a very cool lady named Avery, who happens to be especially well endowed with beautiful, very large breasts. We were all high and all night K kept making comments about wanting to see Avery's tits. At first it was humorous, almost childlike, but gradually it became a fucking drag. I made the mistake of leaving K alone with Avery and my drugs.

Rick and Mike Tyson

When I came back into the room I found my drugs missing and Avery trembling in fear. Seems K had smoked my shit and fucked around with Avery. I became enraged. He and his date—some blonde who worked as Burt Sugarman's secretary—had gone into my bedroom and lay down on my bed. I grabbed a long, sharp knife and ran in after them. I put it against K's neck, threatening to kill him if he moved a muscle. I had the knife so hard on his neck I could see blood. I told K that if he ever put his hands on anyone in my presence or laid his hands on my drugs, I'd cut his fucking heart out—and I meant it. Seeing his fear gave me a sense of power I had not experienced before. I had seen him do shit to other people and I figured it was time to let K know I didn't gave a shit who his ol' man was. Don't fuck with me.

After releasing the knife from his throat, I told him to get the fuck out. He did, quickly, and I never had any trouble out of him after that. K loved women and good drugs, especially coke and downers. When he wasn't being an asshole he was an extremely likable cat. Eventually we became friends. I guess with K fear was better than respect.

K asked me to write a song and produce a record for Jeffrey Moore, this twenty–one year old kid he was hanging out with. Jeffrey was a tall, good-looking kid who wanted to sing. His father, Roger Moore, was the star of the James Bond films and Jeffrey had come from his home in England to spend some time in their LA home, a beautiful, private estate in Coldwater Canyon. When I first met Jeffrey it was at a party in the estate. He spent most of the evening in the bathroom wearing a golfer's hat, sitting down and looking in the mirror while smoking co-co puffs—that's cocaine mixed with a cigarette. I call it "baby basin'." He was a bit of an egocentric motherfucker. I mean, I don't know many motherfuckers who look at themselves in the mirror while getting high. But the funniest shit was, there'd be a room full of bad bitches waiting just to see his ass. It was amazing. K would bring them in one at a time, but he'd just stay in the bathroom smoking co-co puffs. My initial impression of Jeffrey was not positive.

When I asked Jeffrey to sing he broke out with a selection of Frank Sinatra songs. I laughed my ass off. He was totally in love with Frank. However, I did at least find out that at least he could carry a note. I thought of Tina, Frank's daughter and wished she was there to hear Jeffrey. I know she would have laughed at this tall, lanky, good-looking British kid with a strong British accent singing Frank Sinatra songs.

Anyway, I told K, who was acting as his manager, to record him. Jeffrey had undeniable magnetism and the uncanny ability to attract women like flies to shit. I thought if he had charisma like this now, think of what a hit record could do. I wanted to be there.

K sold Warner Bros on the idea and they immediately started to budget a record. By the conditions of my contract I could record anyone but myself, so why not cut whoever I wanted? At least I could keep my recording chops up and make some money while at it.

Jeffrey asked me to move up to the guesthouse in the canyon, which was nicer than most peoples' homes, complete with two-car garage. I started to hang out with Jeffrey a lot, because I needed to know him in order to compose just the right tune for his character. That was always important to me as far as writing was concerned. Once I felt like I really knew a person, the music and lyrics would just flow.

Jeffrey was a strange character. He'd been brought up in the best of Europe's private schools and was a very sophisticated and smooth cat. He was also in total fear of his ol' man. I mean, Roger had a fear inbred in his son that was spooky. Whenever his mom or dad called, he cut off all the music in the house and told everyone to remain perfectly quiet. Then he'd change rooms and talk almost in a whisper—not the kind of thing a grown man does in his own home.

Jeffrey had this huge ego too. Not with me but with other people like K and Billy. Once while we were sitting by his pool he decided he wanted to challenge K to a race. I quickly pushed K to take the challenge. Now, K never exercised at all, but somehow I knew he could beat young Jeffrey. They raced and K won. I was glad to see the young boy put in his place. Then he challenged Billy to tennis saying he had been the captain of his tennis team in school. Billy ended up kicking his ass on the court.

Jeffrey always felt the need to show off his manhood with the wrong people. Once he was seeing Farrah Fawcett, without Ryan's knowledge. I walked in a couple of times while they were fucking around. Ryan ended up catching Jeffrey out somewhere and almost kicked the kid's ass. He stayed at home weeks after that incident. I always thought young Jeffrey had a lot of growing to do.

I wrote a tune for Jeffrey called "Down All Over You," a sexy, funky, British-type groove, if you can imagine that. My guitarist Kenny flew in from Buffalo to play on it. It was a serious tune. The only problem I had in recording it was the vocals and getting Jeffrey to stay in the studio. He was constantly running out to the bathroom and smoking co-co puffs against my wishes. I told him over and over they'd fuck up his vocals. So he'd sneak around thinking I didn't know.

Teena Marie came in and heard the tune. While Jeffrey was in the studio, she and Penny said it was a hit and that I should keep it for myself and fuck Jeffrey. They never liked him and thought he was a phony and didn't deserve it or me. Teena sang some great vocals on the tune, regardless of how she felt.

K took the tune to Warners after it was finished and they loved it. Jeffrey played it for everyone up at his house, even over the phone for his mother and father, whom he said also liked it. I looked at it like a mission accomplished.

The Moore home was the party spot. I mean we fucking partied from sunup to sundown. There was never a time we didn't go out to Helena's, Jack Nicholson's club, or Tramps, and come home with the best Hollywood had to offer.

I met a very beautiful blond girl named Marrett Van Camp at Jeffrey's. She was European and very snobbish. Marrett was a model who had been chosen out of thousands to be Princess Daisy in a television movie. The movie had a cast full of big names and she was the star. We got into a huge fight at Jeffrey's when she started to shout at me saying, didn't I know who she was. I immediately slammed back at her with "Fuck who you are. Do you know who I am?" She just stood in the middle of Jeffrey's living room, crying. After that, I must have changed something in her cuz she chased me like no other woman had, from Paris to New York.

Like I said, life was a continual party up at Jeffrey's. There was a record out by The System that I loved called "Don't Disturb This Groove." It became a theme song for us. Everywhere we went it seemed to be playing. There was a nightspot called Helena's run by this old friend of mine named Helena. She was from New York, but it was financed and supported by Jack Nicholson. All the beautiful people of Hollywood frequented it on the weekends and we were no different.

Once while in Helena's I saw this beautiful angel sitting with Jack Nicholson. They obviously knew each other very well. I told K I just had to have her. After she left Jack's table I moved in. She was very sweet, and I could tell she liked me too. She was an actress and her name was Lana Clarkson, I found her stunning, and very intelligent. I invited her and a bunch of other women up to Jeffrey's. As usual, when we arrived, there were women everywhere. I took Lana and a makeup friend of hers, along with four or five other women, to the guesthouse. Lana and I ended up sitting and snorting coke in one of the rooms, away from the other guests. We talked and got high for hours until she had to leave. We promised to see each other again and I was in heaven. I didn't even care about the other women in the house waiting for me.

When I rejoined the main party in the house, I noticed this one particular white girl who was wearing a hat and acting as if she wanted to be hip and Black. She was sitting in a chair with no underwear, showing me her pubic area, talking about how she was a Super Freak. I disliked her immediately, although she was fine, I hate bitches who talk shit like that. Leave that shit to a man. I was more into having women who were less forward. Her name was Rhonda.

Rhonda was accompanied by a beautiful, brown-haired girl, who wasn't loud and crazy like her friend. Something very strange attracted me to her. Her dark eyes looked right through me and I felt like she was young, yet also old and wise. She had a tenderness that I needed. I invited her to come to my bedroom. She hesitated then finally came. I went straight to the bathroom where I had my pipe stashed and I closed the door and began to smoke. She came in while I was smoking. I asked if she'd ever smoked before and she said she hadn't. I didn't know whether to believe her or not but something in her eyes said she was telling the truth.

After a few hours of smoking and talking, I did something I'd never done before—I put away my pipe and told her to sit and talk to me. She did. I mean I never pushed her into smoking. I never blew smoke in her mouth or her pussy, like I normally would do. I simply put down the pipe. As badly as I would have liked her to get high, something inside told me to spare her. I can't explain it. So I followed my feelings.

The girl's name was Tanya Hijazi. She was only seventeen years old.

She stayed with me for a few hours. We just sat on my bed and talked. It seemed the more we talked, the more beautiful Tanya got. I used to thrive on always being a good judge of character. But finding myself wrong so many times I changed that to every now and then. In Tanya I felt I had found someone who wasn't jaded by Hollywood yet and I wanted to keep it that way. We talked for hours. Then she told me she lived with her mother and she had to go home. I asked her to please come back. The next day she did.

By coming back she showed me she could keep her word and I was impressed. We hadn't gone to bed yet, and I was happy about that. I wanted it like that—almost to preserve her innocence. Oh, I knew she wasn't a virgin, but still there were special qualities about her I wanted to keep precious. We talked by phone a few more times then I just kind of stopped communicating.

I was becoming restless. I was starting to feel the Motown suit would go on forever. I had never had such a long spell of just doing nothing. All I basically did was hang out and get high. Finally, I was little more than a recluse within my home. I had never stayed in Buffalo for such a long period of time, mostly staying in my room, getting high, smoking day in and day out. When I wasn't smoking, I'd fly to LA and see Billy. We'd hang out at Richard Perry's house, who was a producer friend of mine. Richard had the most beautiful girls in Hollywood stumbling in and out. It was outrageous. Plus he's a beautiful cat. If I wasn't with Richard, I'd be getting fucked up with K. It was the same old thing. My accountants were on my back about money, telling me I was going into tax problems with all the money I was spending, especially on dope. But I couldn't help it—I was hooked, with no way out.

The Mary Jane Girls were gone. Process and the Doo Rags split up. Val Young was now with Bobby Brown and most of my band had gone with her. I was glad they had left. I couldn't support them any longer, because I was too busy getting high. My world was crumbling right in front of me—and I didn't give a fuck. I was even angry with God. I felt he had deserted me. I used to cuss him out, especially when I got stoned. I talked to him like an entity that played games with people for his own pleasure. If not, then why was this blessing such a curse? And why when I was so low wasn't he there to help me up? I had so many questions—so many unanswered questions—I felt there was no hope, only death.

So all my time was spent getting high and waiting on death, or the end of the Motown lawsuit, either one.

Tanya surprised me by coming to see me in Buffalo during these difficult days. She told her mother some strange story and flew to see me. I was glad to see her. I was very lonely then and she was very young with a lot of energy. I still hadn't exposed her to freebasing, not since she had seen me doing it in the bathroom at Jeffrey Moore's.

I introduced Tanya to my Mom and family, even to my daughter Ty, who was the same age. That was a trip. Ty handled it well and they got along well. We went out to dinner and smoked lots of weed—the good shit, Indica bud. One night we attempted to make love. I say "attempted" cuz that's what it was. She was not very experienced in the art. I could sense her innocence immediately and I was not into teaching anyone at that time. Tanya knew something wasn't right. We talked about it a little, but there usually was no need for talk. I made up my mind I didn't need a young girl like that in my life. So after a couple of days, I sent Tanya home. She left with no hard feelings, but I knew she was sad.

I thought about Tanya a lot after our Buffalo experience. I can't really explain why. Maybe it was because she still appeared to me to be honest and sweet as opposed to having that fake Hollywood groove. I welcomed the change, especially because of the other girls I had met in Hollywood. Most of them were one-night stands. Occasionally I'd meet a girl and develop a long relationship with her. That's something I loved to do. I'm still close to a few of the girls I met in those days.

I saw Tanya out at clubs and could see she was changing drastically. Her clothes, hair and mannerisms were becoming Hollywood—pretentious and fake. It hurt me to see that happen. I knew deep down she wasn't at all like that.

Sometimes I'd invite her and some of her girlfriends to my hotel. She'd come in with this street attitude, which had always made me sick. I'd just get high—not with her—then ask her to leave. She was changing right before my eyes and there was nothing I could do about it.

Then one day while I was home working in my studio I got a call from Billy, my good friend in LA. He said Tanya was working in Vegas. I almost flipped out, especially after predicting it up at Jeffrey Moore's house. I just hung up the phone and got high, trying to forget what I had just heard. Tanya would always stay in my mind and I couldn't— no matter where she was or what she was doing—get her out. The spell had been cast.

Marrett Van Camp was an internationally known model and a good one. She constantly called me at my home in Buffalo. We usually just talked small talk. We even rendezvoused in New York once, but nothing happened. She was a spoiled bitch and whenever I saw that side of her I was turned off, especially when I knew how sweet she could be. She was living in Paris and Hollywood with Jean Claude, her rich, French old man.

She called me one day and asked me to have dinner with her and Jean Claude. I found him friendly, even charming. He was wealthy beyond compare, living in a fifteen million dollar home and having retreats in Paris and Spain. He was one of Europe's international playboys until he met Marrett. After he chased her down he was determined not to ever let her go. They had this freaky kind of romance, sharing their lovers and shit. Well, I was not going to partake of that shit, and I let him know in so many ways. I liked Jean Claude and he liked me. I know he believed me when I told him me and Marrett were just friends, and I could see he was a bit relieved.

Jean offered me fifty thousand dollars to write and produce three songs for Marrett. If she had any talent at all I could cut her, no problem. Besides, I could use the fifty grand.

I was given a tape of some stuff she had already recorded. I thought it wasn't bad. I mean, she was no Teena Marie, but she had a raw Rock and Roll vibe—kind of like a female Mick Jagger—that was enticing. With the right Rock and Roll song, she could do well.

So I went back to Buffalo to begin work on Marrett's shit. I wrote the three songs. One was a Rock dance song called "Animal." Another was a duet for her and me called "Rainbow," which was about an integrated romance." Marrett and Jean Claude flew to Buffalo and upon hearing the tracks they were ecstatic. They loved all of them. Jean and I had a long talk upstairs in the guestroom. He wanted to make sure that Marrett would be okay. I assured him not to worry. I had no desire to fuck her. He said he had to leave to take care of business in Paris and he would call to see how things were going. We embraced and he left for the airport. Before he got into his waiting car, he reached down into his bag and pulled out half a pound of coke and gave it to me as a gift. I laughed and threw it back to him explaining, "If you leave this here I'll never finish." I was proud of myself for turning the drugs down.

Well, here I am with one of the most beautiful women in the world whose main aim in life was to fuck the shit out of me. I was nervous. I really liked Jean Claude and I wasn't one of those dudes who fucks his best friend's girl—I never got into that. I also stayed away from married chicks, although some people might find that hard to believe. I practiced that art with a lot of fortitude; maybe because of my Catholic upbringing, maybe because my Dad cheated on my mom. No matter what was going down in my life and no matter how crazy things got, there were some moral standards I set for myself that I clung to. I stayed away from married ladies and I didn't sleep with friends' girls.

Sometimes I'd meet a chick and we'd get high for hours. Soon as she said she was married, something inside me said "NO!" The night I met Vanity at the awards I also met Robert De Niro's wife Barbara. She came on so strong that I was freaking. As soon as I found out she was Bobby's wife, I left her alone, and that's the truth. Oh, there were times earlier in my life when I didn't care, but those times were few. I kept to my standards (although I broke this law often, mainly because I found out they weren't my best friends, in most cases they weren't friends at all); the third law was—stay straight, no dudes. I would hear rumors about me being gay and shit. The band and I would laugh our asses off. We'd say, "Yeah, if Rick is gay, bring yo Mama on in to find out." That was a funny rumor.

I love gay people, especially the one's who don't throw their shit in your face. I have found some men handsome and even attractive—on a man level—that's honesty. But never have I wanted a man to suck my dick or me to suck his. Come on! Think about it!

One thing more I've always hated was anyone living in the closet. That goes for sexuality, drugs or whatever. I've always waved my freak flag high. If the day came where I ever became gay, I wouldn't hide it; that's for damn sure. I could give a fuck about what people say. I've always felt that way. People who don't like what I say and do can kiss my ass. That's my attitude. I'd rather make love than war. But most people are so opinionated it makes me sick. They sit on their asses and point their fingers at everybody and say "See?" Well, fuck that. If all you can do is talk and not do anything to change it, whatever it is, then fuck you! And I believe that.

In Buffalo I fed thirty thousand to forty thousand poor people. This went on for a couple of years. I could afford it. I felt I was making so much that I should give some back. Of course, I heard all the talk about me doing it for publicity or a tax write-off. That hurt. How come the fuckers didn't say "Wow, Rick's doin' a good thing?" No, they talk bullshit. I never even advertised that I was feeding people. It was news in Buffalo, but that's it.

But fuck it. People will be people, and people love to talk.

Anyway, I got off track here—oh yeah, Marrett.

So she's staying with me in Buffalo working on her music. One night we went to a local bar and got drunk. Not completely drunk but enough that I should have known better. Next thing I know Marrett is all over my shit, aggressive as a motherfucker. I tried to resist for as long as I could.

Then it happened in my living room, rolling around on the floor. I thought I was an animal. Shit, that girl is on another level. All I could think of was how much fun I'd missed by not fucking around with her sooner. Marrett was a "Super Freak." After freaking, smoking, drinking and everything else, the worst thing happened: I was overcome by a feeling of guilt. I hated that feeling. All I could think about was how I had betrayed Jean Claude.

Marrett had finished her vocals and that morning was supposed to go to LA to begin work on a film. Well, here we are feeling good and bad about what had gone down. She didn't want to go to LA. I pleaded with her to go. I called Jean Claude to explain what had happened. He said he knew how she was and thanked me for my honesty. The last thing he said to me was "Rick, make sure my baby gets to LA." Marrett spoke to Jean Claude, got herself together and left.

I found I had deep feelings for Marrett. She was in a lot of pain, just like me. Here's this beautiful girl with everything she could want—money, prestige, looks, talent and a good man—yet she was as lonely as could be. I was right about her: she and I were duplicates, soul mates in pain.

I finished Marrett's record and flew back to LA. I longed to see her again. She was happy to see me when I arrived.

Marrett had one bad habit that I didn't like—she loved her heroin and that scared me. One night she was snorting heroin and I was smoking coke. I decided to do some scag with her. I almost OD'd. My worst fears were coming true. When you're around something you like, eventually you wind up doing it.

After getting over that OD shit, I decided to cool it with Marrett for a while. The China Club had opened in LA and I had become good friends with Danny Freed, the owner. There'd be jam sessions every Monday. I mean great jams with cats like John Entwistle from The Who, Elton John, Chris Squire from Yes, Nick Rogers, Tower of Power Horns. The whole place would be packed with people just digging each other. The vibe was beautiful. I'd go every Monday to play. It was something I looked forward to. We'd rock the house for hours.

One day Danny asked me to play some of my stuff at the club for a benefit for burned children. I loved Danny so there was not much I wouldn't do for him. Danny had some great people performing: The Doors with Eric Burdon singing lead, and Donny Osmond, who was a good friend of mine. Donny used to come to Buffalo and see me. We were at one time talking about me doing his album. It never materialized but we stayed friends.

Danny had a bunch of people playing this benefit but the focus was on me. Well, I rehearsed with the band, and it went well. I was looking forward to performing again. Come show time, I ran into my good buddy Herbie Hancock. We began to get fucked up on tequila. By the time I went on stage I was blitzed. I told Herbie he should come up and play. All was well for a minute. I was excited about playing with him on stage. I was looking at him behind the Clavinet when all of a sudden I was out cold. I had fallen through this hole on the stage. The next thing I remember is this incredible pain in my ribs. I could hardly breath. I was pulled out and carried across the stage to the back. Outside, they laid me down. I couldn't believe the pain. Looking up all I saw were the faces of anxious people, including Lawrence Hilton Jacobs, from *Welcome Back Kotter.* A few years back I had lent Lawrence thirty thousand dollars and he had never repaid me—the stinking motherfucker. I was groaning with agony but when I saw his face I wanted to jump up and smack the motherfucker. He still hasn't repaid me.

The ambulance came and took me to Cedar Sinai Hospital where they told me I had four broken ribs. I was put in a luxurious private room on the Entertainment Floor. When I opened the fridge I found bottles of the best champagne and the best food. I even smoked dope in my room. Why not? It was all private. Visitors could come and stay till morning and bitches would be coming in and out of my room all day. My dope dealer would even make deliveries. And to top it off, I got morphine shots pretty well on the hour. It was heaven.

Mom even came to see me. She was so upset because she knew I was drunk when I'd fallen. She stayed for a few days and then left.

I stayed in the hospital for three weeks. Most people thought I would sue the China Club, but Danny and I were too close. I couldn't find it in my heart to sue him—but the thought did cross my mind once or twice.

After leaving the hospital I went to Palm Springs to recuperate. I stayed at a friend's and basically did nothing but lie by the pool and get tanned. After I was feeling better, I needed to see my mother and try to get myself together again.

Chapter Fifty-six
Love Thy Brother

Roy had been working with me now for a few years and as I returned from the hospital I found he was going through a difficult time himself. He had met his wife Brenda while he was attending college at Georgetown University. They married, and just a few years later Brenda died. Roy stayed by her side every day of her illness and he was devastated when she passed. After her death he came to work for me.

I never really saw Roy much when we were on tour. I mean, I'd see him backstage, but usually we kept to our separate worlds, unlike when we were kids. Roy dealt with my merchandising and usually was there at the end of a concert totaling up the money. Although Roy was very Washington DC, a bit bourgeois, and a bit GQ, I trusted him, he was my brother.

Mom moved into a little apartment inside a house of a friend of hers named Mimi Loved. I had bought her a big house, but just like at Coldwater Canyon, Mom said she never felt comfortable there. It was just too big for her. Roy moved into the big house.

After I came out of drug rehab the second time, I gave Roy my Power of Attorney so I couldn't spend all my money on drugs. The idea seemed good at the time—I mean, if you can't trust your own brother, who can you trust? Well, Roy had the Power of Attorney, which meant he had power over my money: royalty checks, publishing checks, writers checks, producer checks, TV checks, mechanical checks—Roy had it all, the power of the pen. He even set up his own company called Leroy & Associates. He was tight with my money like it was his, but I understood where he was coming from. He knew that any money he let me have would be spent on drugs, so he watched ever dime. As long as I had my drugs and enough food and shit, I didn't care.

The Motown suit was now in its fifth year and Roy was telling me I was broke. I was lost and alone. I didn't even have my own family to turn to. Penny was now managing Teena Marie. But Penny was just a smaller version of Roy, tighter than a motherfucker. Once while out in LA staying at a Hollywood hotel I called Roy for money, but to no avail. I was flat broke. I called Teena and she came down with a credit card and paid the bill. She never let me live that down.

The lyrics in Billie Holiday's "God Bless the Child" were ringing through my ears. "God bless the child whose got his own, his very own." I was starting to see who my real friends were. I hadn't had to hustle in a long time, but now I was having to.

I still had a car in LA and a few friends left. But my world was collapsing around me and I was scared. I was staying in the Cezanne, a French hotel in Hollywood and I was hanging out with Marrett Van Camp, who fed me and usually kept me as high as I needed. I was only getting so much a week to eat and live on, but at least my drug use was slowing down due to a lack of cash. After a few weeks, I moved up to Marrett's hillside mansion while Jean Claude was away in Europe. I had my own room with maids and a butler, and Marrett made sure all my needs were met. She knew it would just be a matter of time before I was on my feet.

I was jamming a lot at the China Club. Danny, the owner, even helped me financially sometimes. I didn't want too many people to know I was hurting for bread. My lawyers in Buffalo would ask me to sell one of my six cars for money. I ended up selling my Rolls and my Excalibur.

Every night at Marrett's was a party. We'd have her friends and mine come up and we'd party, usually into the next day. I was hanging out with an actor friend named Dale Metcalf. I met Dale at the China Club. Right after he did Elvis and Priscilla, we would hang out ever night snorting coke and fucking chicks. Dale was good dude, a bit weird, but aren't most of us? He helped me during those times. His friendship gave me strength.

Dale and I would be at Marrett's running around naked with a house full of women. I never freebased around Dale. I thought I'd spare him that, but we'd snort our brains out. I finally had to cut Dale loose for his own good. We were hanging out tough and people in Hollywood began to talk. His career was just starting to take off and the last thing he needed was to be linked to a dope fiend like myself. Dale was always there when I needed him, and I'll never forget that.

Once I was hanging out at the China Club, drinking with Danny Freed, Julian Lennon, Nile Rogers and some more music buddies, when I happened to see this, gorgeous, very sophisticated woman. Mary, my gay girlfriend, made a bet with me: Who would get her? The blond woman kept walking back and forth, eyeing either Mary or me. I didn't know who, being in Hollywood and shit. She ended up coming over and inviting us to her home. She knew Danny Freed, so we all went. The home was incredible, spacious and classy. She told me she lived there with her husband, who she was divorcing soon. Her name was Norma Jean.

Chapter Fifty-seven
Me and Norma Jean

Like I said, these were trying times for me. I was living each day for the moment. Roy was still not letting me at my money, so I was in a desperate way financially speaking. Norma was around my age, maybe a little older. She was a classy sophisticated woman who knew where she was going.

Mama used to tell me "You'll never know who your real friends are till you're in need." Well, I found out how true that statement really was.

Everyone had left Norma's house except one of her girlfriends, me and Danny. Danny and I would sing every Fifties song we knew when we were together. At Norma's it was no different. I could tell he wanted to be with her. But so did I. Time prevailed and I won out. Norma and I clicked immediately. We liked the same music, same art and same food. She even knew how to cook soul food and everything else. Man, Norma could cook! She ended up coming to my hotel suite because her husband—who she'd found out was gay, which is why she was divorcing him—was still living in the house.

Norma and I had snorted so much coke I had what in general terms is known as a "cocaine dick." You get it from snorting too much. Anyway, we began to mess around. Usually, I wouldn't be able to function sexually (snorting coke did that to me), but this time it was totally different. I was into her something fierce. It was unbelievable. My shit would not go down and all I wanted to do was make love over and over again. It was one of the most passionate sexual experiences I've had under cocaine. We made love all day long. When we were finally through, she told me she had to go. I asked if I would see her again and she said she would call. I thought this was a really incredible one-night stand. All day I waited for her to call. She finally did, inviting me out for dinner.

Norma's company was the best. I loved her humor and even the dimple in her chin. We began to develop a strong relationship, seeing each other every day. And every day we made love more passionately than before.

Norma had her own business and did very well at it. She had a two-seater Benz and two beautiful daughters, sixteen and twenty-one years old. She was even a grandmother by her twenty-one year old.

Norma filed for divorce and got a good settlement where she got a nice little house where her and the kids stayed. By now we were a Hollywood item. Everybody was talking about me and Norma Jean. We loved it.

Norma knew I was hurting for money and she did all she could to keep me living the way I was accustomed: expensive dinners, clothes and trips to Palm Springs. It didn't matter as long as I was happy. We had nicknames for each other: she'd call me "Dad" and I'd call her "Ma." I was never into taking money from a chick—never. I've always been my own man. At Motown I had pimped and played, but deep down inside I felt bad about it, because it was distracting me from what I should be doing, music. With Norma it was more like she was investing in me. That's what she said, anyway. I used to feel bad and I'd show it and she'd just say, "Shut up, Dad. You'll pay me back soon as soon as you're on your feet."

We spent a lot of time in my hotel suite getting high, mostly snorting. Then one day she began to smoke with me. I told her she could never afford the groove, but she insisted. She loved to smoke. It even made our sex kinkier and more intense. Sometimes we'd run out, jump in her car and drive to the ghetto where I'd tell her to stay in the car while I'd go cop. Usually she would jump out and come with me. She was never afraid of shit.

Norma would try anything. After we'd cop, we'd go back to the hotel suite and sit in my closet—yes, closet. There it was always dark. I mean no sun, just me, Norma, our cassette player and some candles. It was like our "get high" room—no phone, no one to bother us. We'd fuck, talk, everything, and never know if it was day or night.

Norma supported me in those days and for that I'm eternally grateful. Norma ended up losing her business because of all the time she was spending with me. She didn't care. She'd just say, "I'll find another gig." And she did. She somehow conned her way into a billion-dollar company as a vice president or something. Man, that woman could get you to buy snow in Alaska. She was a true hustler.

One time when I went up to Marrett's, Penny came in. I asked Marrett to throw her out, because she was interrupting our time together and Marrett refused. I was furious and I ended up pushing Penny down on the floor and leaving. As angry as I was, I still felt intensely guilty for pushing my sister, but when you are stoned, shit happens.

Seems Penny got very acquainted with most of the ladies I knew: Teena, Marrett, even Norma. All these girls I had been intimate with now knew Penny. It was like the Roy Syndrome of jealousy or something. My attitude was "Fuck Penny and Roy" and whoever else would try to take anything from me again.

I flew back to Buffalo, hurt and broke. I still had my home, still had had my cook, Mildred, still had Linda Hunt—my best friend and housekeeper and, most importantly, still had me. No one was going to take that away. Back in Buffalo I spent most of my time writing songs, riding horses and just relaxing. I'd call LA from time to time to see what was going on. Petey had been busted for coke and had spent the last couple of years in jail. Petey and I had fallen out over a girl I fell in love with named Linda Slice. I wanted to marry Linda, but Petey fucked it up by telling her shit and playing with her head. I got so mad at Petey that I stopped talking to him altogether. Then he got busted. Marrett and Jean Claude were still together. Penny and Teena Marie were still working together. Norma was waiting for my return.

It was now the winter of 1990—four days before Christmas. I was wondering how I'd spend Christmas broke. As I sat in my living room pondering this, I received a phone call from Irv Shuman, one of my attorneys. He told me I had just received a huge check and that finally the Motown suit was at an end. I had won!

I hung up the phone in shock. It had been almost five years and now the fight was over. I'd beaten Barry Gordy. Now I could get a record deal, pay off my debts and, most importantly, get out of my brother Roy's clutches.

The first thing I did was take Mama to dinner, just me and her. It was a wonderful Christmas....

Remembering the Good Times

JoJo, Rick and his daughter Tyenza

Rick with Keith Sweat

Rick and a fan

Tanya, Rick and Danny Lemelle at a concert

Rick and Friends

Family and Friends

Chapter Fifty-eight
Warner Bros. Records

I settled my business with my attorneys' fees. They had worked extremely hard over the last five years and their bill came to around five hundred thousand dollars. I made sure before anybody got a penny they severed my Power of Attorney with Roy. After taking care of business, I flew to Miami for a well-needed vacation. I love Miami, especially The Coconut Grove. It's a beautiful area filled with boutiques and sidewalk artists. It kind of reminded me of early Yorkville, but sunnier. The Mutiny was one of my favorite hotels in the Grove.

After years of housing the top dope dealers, musicians and actors, The Mutiny was about to close down and I was the hotel's last guest. Even when they closed it down they let me stay. I was there all alone when I flew Norma Jean down. I especially wanted to pay her back. I had a huge suite with a Jacuzzi in the bedroom. When Norma Jean arrived it made my stay complete. We actually made love for three full days straight. It was wonderful. I had all the dope I wanted a suite overlooking the ocean and my favorite girl. What more could a man want?

After a few weeks in Miami I flew back to LA. My friend Billy had been busted for coke and was in jail along with some other friends of mine. But basically, everything else was normal. Marrett and Jean Claude were in Europe. Penny and Teena weren't speaking to me, which was fine with me. I spent most of my time going out to the China Club and jamming. I was ready to look for a new label because I was hot to start recording again. My drug use picked up where it had left off. I was smoking ounces every week, nonstop.

My addiction began taking on another dimension around then. I began to feel suicidal—not to the point where I wanted to shoot myself or anything, just a feeling of total hopelessness. I went back to Buffalo and attempted to smoke an ounce of coke by myself. I had no one with me. Oh, I could have called a lot of people, but I just didn't want to. I felt if I smoked an ounce alone, I'd surely die. This was reason enough, so I smoked. It was just my luck that nothing happened, except a severe headache. I was coming to my last days and I could feel it.

My attorneys came to see me to tell me there were a lot of record companies interested in me, regardless of my addiction. I was pleased to hear that, especially when my drugs were telling me I was washed up. So I flew to New York to meet with record executives. The first was Clive Davis of Arista. I've always had a lot of respect for Clive, even though he refused the Mary Jane Girls when I was shopping them before Motown snapped them up. I had shopped the Girls to Arista and a few others. Clive, upon hearing their tape, sent me a letter telling me he didn't think the Girls were going to hit. He later apologized. Even the great Clive Davis can be wrong.

Anyway, here I am sitting in Clive's office while he sat there telling me about how much respect he had for me. He must have played every Whitney Houston track he could get his hands on, and still hadn't gotten to the business at hand. Then he started playing Carly Simon tracks. I'd been with Clive for about four hours, and all I heard was how great Whitney's new album was and how he gets involved with his artists' production. No way. I had never let anyone dictate to me how my songs should or should not be. Clive might be great for Whitney and Carly, but not when it came to me. When I left he said to come back and talk some more about my deal.

My next meeting was with Bob Krasnow, President of Elektra Records. Bob was great. We talked about the old music and the new. He said he'd love to have me on his label and I'd have creative control. We even talked money. I left Bob feeling Electra was a company I could live with.

My next meeting was with Mo Ostin, President of Warner Bros. I was a little afraid of Warner Bros., only because I didn't want to cause conflict with Prince by joining Warner. I've often found that if a company has two superstars, one will get more attention than the other and I didn't want to run the risk of getting lesser treatment from Warner

Bros. Still, Mo had expressed strong feelings about me coming to his company and I was anxious to talk to him. When I arrived I was taken to the conference room, where I was met by Mo and Lenny his Vice President. Both were extremely nice. I was comfortable from Jump Street.

Mo spoke of how with Prince and me at the same company, they'd be non-stoppable. He said he wanted me to start up their old label, Reprise, which was the label Jimi Hendrix was on at Warner. I felt extremely honored. We also talked about drugs. I asked Mo if he was aware of my drug history. He was. He said if I could give him half the records I gave Motown while I was on drugs, he'd love it. That was all he had to say. I'd found my home. We made a deal for eight hundred thousand dollars an album—less than Motown, but fuck it. It would get better. The main thing was I could record again, something I was longing to do.

Mo told me he had a guy named Benny Medina running the Black Department of Warner. I'd known Benny when he was at Motown and his office was right next to mine.

I finally had a home.

Chapter Fifty-nine
Born Again

The future finally seemed bright. I had a new record company and money in the bank. The only problem was the drugs. I was getting high more than ever before.

Lisa and Debbie had come to stay with me for a while and, as usual, the three of us had the time of our lives getting high and fucking around. My life was like a vicious circle, with one thing leading right back around to another. I was getting more and more bored with living. I would sit alone in my room and just cry, even though I didn't have any particular thing to cry about. I guess it was everything: my lifestyle, the drugs, the women, my family, everything. I'd cry and smoke, and when the tears subsided and the rocks were gone, I'd pick up the phone and call for more drugs.

Liz, Lisa's mother, was a devout Christian. Once when I called Lisa at her home Down South, her Mom answered and we started talking. I ended up talking to her more than to Lisa. She's a sweet and dear woman. She'd tell me how my only salvation was through Christ. She read scriptures to me over the phone. It's funny, but with all my knowledge of theology, Christianity was the only religion I really knew very little about. I always looked at it like an offshoot of Catholicism.

In any case I knew very little of Christianity.

Something would happen to me when I'd talk to Liz. I'd hang up the phone feeling better, like there might be hope for me yet. I always looked forward to talking to Liz every night.

One night I was really fucked up and depressed when I called Liz. She knew immediately what was wrong and commenced to pray for me

317

over the phone. She asked me if I believed Jesus was the Son of God. I said I did. Then she asked me to open my heart and let Jesus in and I did. Before I knew it the pain I was feeling disappeared. I mean, I wasn't high anymore, or depressed. I just felt this joy and peace all over. It was a trip. I can't really explain it, but it felt better than any drug.

After Liz and I talked some more, I even remember laughing. I said good night and went fast to sleep.

The next morning I felt great. I immediately called Liz. She was very happy for me. I asked her why I felt so good and she said Jesus was with me, in my heart. I said "Well, if this is how it is with Jesus in your heart, I want him to stay there." I told Lisa I wanted to see her. She came immediately. She saw the joy on my face and I told her that I didn't want to get high anymore. I asked Lisa to stay in the guestroom. I just thought it would be the right thing and she didn't mind.

We flew to New York to see Eddie Murphy and the premier of his movie *Golden Child*. He was glad to see me and I him. I told him of my new experience and he just kind of smiled and said "Whatever it takes to get your ass off drugs, great." I didn't really expect people to understand this new groove. All I knew was that it felt good.

From New York I flew to North Carolina to finally meet Lisa's parents, especially Liz, the woman who brought me to the Lord. I remembered telling Lisa how her father was going to react when he met me. She told me again that her father didn't like anyone and he was prejudiced. I couldn't help thinking about him on the flight down. I was really nervous about meeting her family, wondering about the things they had heard about me. I even felt insecure about Liz.

When we knocked on Lisa's parents' door, the whole family was standing there—brother, Mama and Daddy. They invited me in and then the miracle happened: Lisa's father came up, gave me a hug and asked me if I wanted some coffee or something. Lisa and I almost fainted. Another prediction of mine had come true.

The family and I got along great. I loved them like they were mine. That Sunday they took me to their church. It was wonderful. It was full of people with the Holy Spirit, Blacks and whites praising God with songs of prayer. I gave my first testimonial that day. And I could feel God's presence for the first time. Afterwards the preacher and the congregates laid hands on me and prayed that I would see the Holy Ghost. When they told me what the Holy Ghost was, I couldn't wait. Mostly I prayed for the gift of tongues, I had heard all these people speaking in tongues and I wanted it badly. To me it was a sign that God's spirit was truly with you. I already had the gift of discerning. I would always be able to look at people and discern them, which was a gift from God.

After praying for a few days I hadn't received the gift of tongues, and that meant I hadn't truly been saved. One night in my hotel room I prayed and prayed for the gift. I finally went to bed, exhausted. Some joker rambling in some strange language awakened me, I went to call security when I realized it was me talking. I had been given the gift during the night and had woken myself up with my talking. I praised God all that night.

I stayed in North Carolina for a while longer and then returned to Buffalo, bringing Lisa and her family with me. By now I was filled with the spirit of God. I even joined a church near my house. I spent most of my time in the studio working and when I wasn't I was in Church or bible class. I had proposed marriage to Lisa and she had said yes. I was the happiest man in the world.

My music took a serious change. I was still writing funk, but the lyrics were now all for the Lord. No longer could I write the nasty stuff I had been writing before. I was in God's groove and it suited me fine. Everyone was happy at my newfound faith. I even received a personal bible from Jim Baker. I did this huge *USA Today* article about my religious turnaround. I wanted to let the world know I loved Jesus. My music took on a whole new vibration. People would be in my studio and upon hearing my tracks they would give themselves to the Lord. Tom Flye, my engineer, even gave himself to the Lord. Everyone was doing it. I was on fire for Jesus.

Benny wanted to hear my new album, so he flew up for a visit. Little did I know that Benny coming to Buffalo would be no different than Satan himself dropping by the studio. His visit would lead me right back on the road to hell. Years before Benny had sung in a group called

Apollo, one of Barry Gordy's sons was the leader, and Benny seemed then to be a no-talent entertainer. He was responsible for Fresh Prince.

So now Benny was big shit at Warners, and Mo loved him. Benny had gotten lucky and signed a few hit groups, like the Fresh Prince. Mo was impressed enough to let him head the Black Department. Benny was really a number one asshole with his newfound power. Had I known then what I know now, I would have never signed with Warner knowing that my life would be in the hands of Benny Fucking Medina.

Well, Benny made it to Buffalo, and we sat together in my studio listening to the tracks I had done so far. He loved them, especially the sounds. He even said I'd outdone myself as far as the sounds were concerned. At this point I only had tracks. The vocals were not on the tracks, so I sang them live while the tracks played. I was on fire for the Lord, and the lyrics magnified Him.

Benny listened, then said "Cool," and went back to LA. I was feeling so good just making the album that I wanted everyone to hear what the Lord was doing to my life. Few weeks later, Benny called and asked me where I was as far as the album was concerned. I told him I had a lot of vocal work completed and I let him hear the tunes over the phone. By now, Lisa and her parents had returned home and I was pretty much alone. After Benny heard the vocals he delivered the blow. He told me Warners would never give me eight hundred thousand for what I'd recorded. I asked why. He said he didn't think it was Rick James. It wasn't funky enough. I told him that was because it was music for the Lord. Then Benny went on to say the Lord wasn't giving me the money, Warners was; and if I wanted to get paid, I'd reevaluate the situation or forget the deal.

I was shocked. More than that, I was afraid of being broke again, afraid of losing my fans, afraid of not being good enough. The Devil was doing his work on my brain and it was successful. I needed to regroup. So I did the only thing I knew, I ran to the only refuge where I could find instant solace and peace. The Pipe.

I went to see this friend of mine named T. He was a collector of art. None of my other friends knew him. I kept it that way for times like this when I needed to disappear and get fucked up—and believe me I did—for days and days.

A girlfriend of mine named Kim Fisher came to town to stay with me for a while. I'd known Kim since she was a young girl in Hollywood. She had been born again but was backsliding too, so she knew my pain. She said the things I needed to hear so I'd feel better. She told me all this was a test—I had lost my faith and I'd have to regain it. The important thing was Jesus was with me, living in my heart, and he had a plan. This was only one defeat. She told me to think how far I'd come and not to worry.

Kim made me feel a lot better. She had indeed grown up to be a wise and beautiful woman. Kim's words didn't make the pain of disappointment disappear, but at least I didn't feel like a piece of shit. I now had to deal with my music.

Chapter Sixty
The Devil Rides Again

Now as much as I was on fire for the Lord, I was also on fire for making some money, so I took Benny's words to heart and came up with new lyrics for the *Wonderful* album. After we finished recording and mixing, I went on this mini tour, playing venues like the Apollo, which was fun. We just hit a few dates though, as I was pretty much bored of touring at this point. The *Wonderful* album did reasonably well, going gold, but it was not as successful as my other albums. After the tour wrapped I felt emotionally drained. I needed a change and I was fed up of being on the East coast. I made the decision to head back to LA.

I headed out West with Dave Addison, who was my limo-driver, but also a friend from the early Buffalo days. I felt he was a good influence on me and I wanted to keep someone around whom I trusted. We moved into a secluded house on Laurel Canyon that had once belonged to Mickey Rooney. I had Big Orange, my security man from Buffalo fly out to join us. He was another old-time friend, one who stood six foot five and could move cars for fun.

Warner Bros. asked me to sing on the *Rock, Rhythm and Blues* album that my friend Richard Perry was producing. It was a great concept; the stars of today: me, Elton John, Fleetwood Mac, Manhattan Transfer, Pointer Sisters and Chaka Kahn, singing songs from the Fifties. I picked out two Drifter's songs, "This Magic Moment," and "Dance with Me." They came out really well and I was proud to perform on the album.

I spent many evenings jamming at The China Club, up on stage with cats from The Who, or the Towers of Power horn players. You never knew who would stop by and end up playing. Those jams filled me with a love of music and performing that I hadn't felt so intensely in a while. It was good to just play, without caring what Benny or the record company thought.

When I wasn't at The China Club, I was hanging out at the Roxbury, an infamous nightclub in Hollywood. My addiction had really started to take off again and it was getting demented. I would go to the Roxbury and bring back a hundred people to my house and have them all just hanging out. Pimps, hoes, celebrities, they'd all be there in Laurel Canyon. It was ridiculous; off the hook. There was a never-ending stream of different bitches all the time. Bitches in and out, 24/7. It was a trip.

Dave and Orange tried to help me; but they had no control over what I was doing, no one did. Jim Brown came by and took me over to his house to detox. He came with all these Muslim brothers, and the Crips and the Bloods, and pretty much kidnapped me, locking me in a room in his house. Jim had the Crips watching me, but I still managed to get back to my house, and my drugs in less than twenty-four hours.

At the same time that I was once again losing all control over my disease, my mother was losing control over hers. I thought that the sun of California might make her feel better, so I had her come out and stay with me for a while. I was doing a lot of drugs, freebasing an incredible amount; probably five thousand dollars a week. I had a piece of shit dealer staying with me at that time, Reyes Newman. This brother was a serious snake in the grass, but it was a good way to have a dope dealer near by. He ended up stealing a lot of jewelry and money from me, but what made me really angry was that he stole my mother's morphine and pain medication.

My mother's visit came to an end and I had spent most of it locked in my room, in denial over both Mom's illness and my own addiction. Mom knew what I was doing when I was hiding in my room and her pain at my behavior only made me feel worse. The day she left, she came to my room and I cracked the door, but I wouldn't let her in. We said our good byes through the crack and she left. Since my addiction had taken me over again, I had been determined to OD and die before her, but now I had a funny feeling that she was going to die and I would never see her again, which made the pain even worse.

Things got very bad when Mom left. I started claiming the Devil, going back to the shit I would do years ago when I was studying the occult. The only good thing was that Tanya had come up to look after me. She had heard there were a lot of bad people running around and because she was my friend she came up and stayed in my guest room, trying to protect me from myself and others. One night after she moved in, I took this piece of paper and drew a pentagram in the center and burned the piece of paper. But when I undid it the pentagram was still there with no burn marks. That freaked the girls out, and it freaked me out, because it was then that I realized that the Devil truly was around. It was no longer a game, and The Dark Lord had come to take his place next to me.

Every hour of the day or night, the house was filled with people indulging in orgies, kinky ass sex, bestiality, all kinds of shit. Decadence and perversion ruled and the people who tired of it were easily replaced. I thrived on breaking in women, conquering and destroying, turning them on to freebase. It was like something out of *Caligula*, wild and dark. The evil was thick in the house and thick in my bedroom.

I was taking seven or eight Halycion a day. After taking the Halycion, I would lose my memory and exist in an almost hypnotic state. I would wake up with no idea what had happened the night before. I wasn't taking it to help me forget, but mostly because it was the only thing that would put me to sleep. It was a serious drug, so strong that people were getting off murder raps because of it. At that point my system was so resilient that I had to take a handful of the pills before it had any effect.

In the midst of all this insanity and drug use, a woman named Cathy Townsend, daughter of Ed, who wrote "Lets Get It On," started hanging around. I had met Cathy before and she was a born thief, and a hoe, which is how she paid for her drugs; still, I liked her. She was very funny and always kept me laughing. One day Cathy brought a girl, Courtney, to the house as a gift for me. Courtney was this not too attractive blonde, but she was OK. She was dressed like a hoe, wearing this see-through top and tight skirt, nipples showing. The first fifteen minutes she was there we were on the floor, fucking our brains out. Her pussy was good and I ended up keeping her there as one of my concubines. All I knew of her was that she was from Georgia and she loved smoking coke and she loved bitches. She loved to eat pussy and she loved to have hers eaten, so she was in the right place, cuz there was plenty of that going on.

When she left after spending a month, she went back to her pimp at a motel where they were staying. The pimp was a drug dealer and a drug addict, and was furious at her for being at Rick James' and not coming back with any money. This pimp had a way of punishing the bitches who he felt double-crossed him, burning them with a pipe and so on. That's what happened to Courtney. But because Tanya ended up taking Courtney to the hospital, the police came after me and Tanya. When Tanya and Courtney left the hospital, the people there took down my Jag's license plate number. It was all a fucking conspiracy.

A couple of nights after that, I was hanging with Tanya and I just felt a weird vibe. I don't know what it was, maybe God talking to me, but I felt the sudden need to get rid of the cocaine and all the paraphernalia. We cleaned up the room, vacuumed and everything, and then she and I just sat on the floor in the lotus position staring at each other and just bonded. I really fell in love with her that morning. Ten minutes later, the house suddenly exploded into chaos. We heard a big bamm and the doors got kicked down and about thirty or forty policemen rushed me with shotguns directed at me and Tanya. They even came in through the windows. They let me put pants on and let her get dressed, then they took me to the living room and told me that they had a warrant for my arrest and that I had been charged with assault. My bail was a million and Tanya's was seven hundred and fifty thousand.

We spent the next week in Millionaire's Row at the County Jail. It was a very funky, dirty, fucked up place, and I just passed out and slept for four or five days, detoxing.

Eventually, I was able to post bail for both of us and I went and picked up Tanya. The courts had charged the two of us with kidnapping, mayhem, and aggravated assault, and now that I was straight, I was frightened by what could happen to us. I felt that my life had never been darker. To make things even worse, Penny called to tell me that our mother was on her deathbed. The courts let me go back to Buffalo to see her.

My mother was in the hospital and as deeply as I loved her, I really didn't want to go to see her. I didn't want to face that music. I couldn't deal with seeing my mother suffering or even dying while I was there and I couldn't face seeing even more pain on her face because of what was happening to me.

Me and Tanya arrived in Buffalo and after stopping by the house, we went to the hospital. All my brothers and sisters were there, even William was there in shackles escorted by two prison guards.

All I could think of was maybe I was responsible for some of this because of my association with evil. I walked in and spent some time with her by myself. Even though she was slipping in and out of consciousness I could see tears falling down her cheeks and I felt that she knew I was there. I started crying and reached down and took her rosary and put it around my neck.

I went out into the waiting room and sat down. After a little while, I felt this strange feeling, like I had been jolted out of sleep, and my sister turned to me and told me my mother had passed. I went back to see her one last time and finally found some solace in her peaceful expression.

The church was packed for Mom's funeral. The press was there too, crowding around the entrance to the church, eager for pictures and some insight on what had happened back in LA. Though there was a circus outside the church, inside was calm. My cousin Louis Stokes gave a beautiful eulogy. As I listened, I remembered all the good times with my Mom, dancing all night at the clubs in Buffalo, sharing my dreams of the future with her. I thought of all the times she had helped me and all the kindness she had shown me, and silently I bowed my head and thanked her for her never ending love and support.

Chapter Sixty-one
Witches' Brew

I had thought that things were at a low point, but it turned out there was still some distance to fall. When we returned from Buffalo, Tanya and I decided to go to Maui with her mother. Tanya had just found out she was pregnant and I felt that both women had been through so much for me that they deserved a vacation. In any case, I was longing just to get away and feel free as well.

As Tanya and I drove to the airport I decided we should get high before the flight. So we stopped on the corner of Argyle and Yucca in Hollywood, a serious hangout for dealers. I didn't have any dealer in mind, so we just picked this one brother and bought eighty dollars worth of rock to last us the drive to LAX. As we pulled out, these two white guys with guns jumped in front of us and pulled us over. They were plain clothed cops who had just got off duty. I couldn't believe the dumb bad luck of it. We just sat there numb in the Jag. Tanya was crying, saying she couldn't go back to jail, and I felt the same way, though I wasn't freaking out. So, after a second of hesitation, I took the rocks and I swallowed all eight of them.

The cops searched everywhere, but even though they had seen the transaction, they couldn't find the rock, and eventually, they had to let us go.

So we finally made it to Hawaii and spent two weeks making love to the sounds of the ocean. We didn't even get high, just enjoyed the sun and got to know one another without drugs. I think we were both grateful to God for keeping us out of jail and letting us spend this precious time together.

When we got back we moved into a house in Marina del Rey. Our attorneys found out that we were still getting high and they insisted we go to rehab. Our court date was pending. Tanya was pregnant and our attorneys were no longer willing to listen to our excuses. They decided it would be best to separate us. Tanya went to the Valley while I went to a facility on the beach. Our separation lasted for about 10 hours. I wanted to be with Tanya and I had to be medically and physically restrained to prevent me from fighting my way out of the facility. Our lawyers and the doctors decided it might be more beneficial for us to go through rehab together. We were then placed at the same facility in Marina del Rey.

The first night we were together, we conspired to get high. My old friend Petey took the batteries out of his beeper, replaced them with rock and paid us a visit. Tanya and I got high all night. The next morning, she was spotting blood and she was put in the psych ward for thirty days. We finally graduated rehab and were sent to a sober living house, but we only lasted there until Tanya was too pregnant to stay any longer.

Our son Taz was born and Tanya and I were still getting high. The stress of all that was happening was putting a strain on our relationship. I moved into a hotel. However, our bond was too strong and she ended up spending most of her time there with me. One night I decided I was going to start a record label, so we called this girl named Mary Saguer and asked her over. I had been introduced to Mary by Chris Squire of Yes, who had told me stories of how possessive and strange she was. I didn't pay much attention to his warnings. Besides, I figured she'd have a good mind to start a label with.

Mary came over and after a short while she was pretty drunk and fucked up. She and Tanya started to get in a fight about being on the road. Mary said Tanya was too jealous and would never be able to tolerate the groupies and the sex. The next thing I knew the two of them were in a catfight and Mary was kicking Tanya in the stomach. Now right after Taz was born, Tanya had gotten pregnant again, so when I saw Mary kick her like that I flipped out, and pushed her away from Tanya. Mary swung at me, and I punched her in the eye. We started punching each other, and I slugged her good a few times.

Even though Mary looked like a punch drunk prize fighter, her eyes bruised blue and swollen nearly shut and her lip split in three places, you would have thought we were all just one big happy family as we stood out in the midday smog choking Sunset Blvd., blinking back the blinding sun and waiting for our rides to be brought around. Never mind that two days earlier I'd had every intent of killing her, that she and Tanya had gone at it like rabid animals in a cage or that the things we'd been doing to each other over the past 48 hours would have made the Marquis De Sade weak in the knees. When we said our good byes that afternoon, we were all the best of friends.

The suite at the St James, the second one we'd trashed in that seven day crack run, looked like some kind of medieval torture chamber or the aftermath of a sadomasochist's cell meeting when we were done with it. There was blood splattered on the walls and carpet from the beating I'd given Mary, broken lamps and furniture, a shattered mirror in the bathroom, cigarette and crack pipe burns in the upholstery and the moldering remains of half gnawed meals on foam service trays. A place like the St. James is only too accustomed to the excesses of its more notable clientele. But I think even the jaded maids and bellhops must have done a double take at all the carnage we'd wrecked.

Crack will do that. In a world where the only absolute is your next pull on the pipe, your worst enemy can become your tightest friend and the other way around, all in the blink of an eye. One minute the guy sitting next to you can be Satan's first cousin then, after a long, deep hit, transform before your eyes into the second coming of God's own son, complete with a halo and harp. The murderous rage that had detonated in me was over almost as soon as it started and I had suddenly found myself with my hands around this woman's throat wondering what the excitement was about. I could hardly believe that it I was the one who had done all that damage to her face and, as the anger drained away like water down a drain, I was left with a feeling of sheepish chagrin, like a kid caught tormenting a cat instead of a man who had been one step away from cold blooded murder.

As I look at these words laying out in black and white on the page, I still have a hard time connecting to that man in that ruined hotel room. The image in my mind's eye is more like that of an empty shell inhabited by savage demons, vicious and invisible until they took on a human form, filling that place where my soul once was, clenching and twisting and writhing in my muscles and nerves like they were trying to turn me inside out, forcing all the hate and horror into my fists and clamping down on my face like a rigid mask of rigor mortis. I hear people wondering out loud if the spiritual world is real—whether there really is a realm of devils and angels waging war for hearts and minds of mere mortals. I offer my own life as proof that the battle is real.

But I'm not trying to cop a plea. This isn't about whining that "the devil made me do it." The demons that did their business inside this skin were invited guests—I knew every one of them by name and every time I vaporized a hit up a tube and down my lungs I was opening the door a little bit wider until it finally just ripped off the hinges and blew away. A man who beats a woman must accept the punishments of anger and contempt society serves up and I don't shy away from that. For what I did, I take full responsibility. No one shoved a crack pipe in my mouth, lit the match and waited for me to toke. It's in telling the story, the whole truth and nothing but, that I hope to put the past behind me and reclaim my future.

But if my behavior seemed strange, Mary's was downright bizarre. After the screaming and chaos had subsided, and she was laying on the floor at my feet bleeding into the plush white carpet, I tried to make nice, humbly apologized for beating the shit out of her and tried to ease the pain by offering her a nice fat rock to smoke. Now, any normal person, after getting whipped up one side of the room and down the other, would have run as far and as fast from that scene as their wobbly legs could carry them. But, to a crack addict, the prospect of one more toke, one more chance to feel that rush that wipes away all pain and sorrow, all reason and sanity, is a temptation too powerful to resist. Mary grabbed that pipe like it was her mama's tit, and somehow managed to suck down the smoke through her cracked and bleeding lips.

And that was all it took. For the next two days—although it could have been two hours or two years for all we knew—Mary, Tanya and I stayed holed up in that filthy room, passing around the pipe while on TV, daytime soap operas merged to prime time sitcoms, then into late night talk shows that turned to predawn infomercials and back around in an endless babbling cycle.

It was only when we d smoked up the last of the stash that we finally packed up and checked out and, as Tanya and I merged into the heavy flow of afternoon traffic, surrounded by people whose everyday lives had been taking their normal course while we were hanging in suspended animation, the only thing on my mind was the prospect of a dark room and clean bed. One of the most evil aspects of crack cocaine is the near total absence of any withdrawal symptoms. You can go on a week long run, wear yourself down to the ragged edge, then sleep it off in three days of solid sack time and wake up with only the craving still hanging on. Of course the long term effects will catch up with you sooner than later, but while you re in the middle of it you've got this feeling of invincibility that completely covers up what you re really doing to your mind and body and spirit.

We got to Agoura in the late afternoon and I left it to Tanya to make small talk with her mom and dad while I staggered into the guest room. I was asleep before my head hit the pillow, the kind of dreamless sleep that's the closest thing to death this side of the grave.

I woke up with Tanya leaning over me, shaking me by the shoulders. From the light leaking in through the Venetian blinds I figured I couldn't have been out for more than a couple of hours and I was hoping, for Tanya's sake, that she had a good reason for getting me up. She did.

"It's Mary," she said, shoving a phone up to my ear, her voice slurred with fatigue. In the half-light of that fading day, her face looked pale and puffy, her eyes ringed in dark circles and her hair hanging like stiff straw. I wondered for a moment what would be facing me in the mirror when I finally got the courage to take a look. But I shoved the thought down and turned away to face the wall. "Rick," Tanya insisted, her voice sharp and grating in my ears. "I think you better talk to her."

I turned back "What's the bitch want?" I mumbled, but Tanya's only answer was to hand me the phone like it was a poisonous snake. I took it, mumbling some very pointed suggestions concerning assorted orifices when Mary's voice cut through with a nasty edge that immediately put me on guard. I'd heard that tone—before a woman with an attitude—and it always meant trouble. "We got something to settle motherfucker," she said "I want what s coming to me."

"I'll give what's coming to you, bitch," I said and was about to hang up when she started screaming loud enough that Tanya took a step back from the bed. "You almost killed me, you bastard!" she was shouting, her voice shredding into static over the phone. "I could have died up there. I can bring you up on assault charges and don t think I won't!"

'Assault charges.' That got my attention. Somewhere between the St James Club and home, Mary had obviously gotten some legal advise and it was only later that I learned that her roommate was an attorney and one who obviously knew a lucrative opportunity when she saw it.

"Listen to me you stupid whore," I said while the crack residue set the familiar rush of blood pounding at my temples. "Nobody asked you to come up there. Nobody asked you to get into a fight with my old lady. Nobody asked you to fuck me or smoke up all my rock. You can kiss my black ass."

"I'll do more than that if you don t make this right," she spat back but before I could say anything Tanya, who'd been leaning in close to listen grabbed the receiver and covered the mouthpiece.

"Rick," she whispered, "this bitch is crazy. Maybe you better find out what she's after." We looked at each other for a long moment as, outside in the hallway, a grandfather clock marked time in echoing seconds. I took back the phone.

"So, what do you want?" I said, tuning my voice as low and mean as I could make it. This time, the silence came from the other end.

"You better give me some money," Mary blurted out. "I want—" and in the pause I could hear the wheels in her crack addled brain creaking, "—two thousand dollars."

I almost laughed out loud. Here I was, already up on assault and battery charges, facing down some serious time with this crazy woman threatening to pull me in to some even deeper shit and all she wanted was two thousand dollars? She had me where she wanted and was going to let me go for chump change. "What else?" I asked, hardly believing my good luck.

There was another lengthy silence. "I want you to take me on a shopping spree," she said, like a kid with three wishes. "I want to go down to Rodeo Drive and buy anything I want. Then I want—"

This time I did laugh long and hard. If all Mary was after was some pathetic little Beverly Hills fantasy, she obviously had no inkling of the fact that she really had my balls in a vise and could squeeze me for all I was worth. If she held out for a hundred grand, or a record deal, or a Ferrari, then I would have had something to worry about. But this nickel and dime shakedown was a joke.

"I'm going back to sleep, bitch" I told her, "and when I wake up you better hope I don t remember talking to you." She was still squawking as I handed the phone back to Tanya and pulled the blanket over my head.

True to my word, when I came around, late the next afternoon, I had only the vaguest memory of Mary's lame ass attempt at extortion. In fact the only thing I was sure about was the raw need for more crack grinding in the pit of my stomach. I staggered to my feet, joints aching and eyes crusted from sleep and felt my way along the wall to the bathroom, a taste on my tongue like wet newspapers. A shower, a shave, a little mouthwash and deodorant and I'd be good as new, ready for the next installment of the long running nightmare I called my life.

I found Tanya sitting with her Mom in the kitchen, drinking coffee as the day opened up bright and clear, out the window. It could have been a picture off a Hallmark card, a humble scene of domestic bliss, if it wasn't for that haunted look I immediately caught in Tanya's hollow eyes. It must have been the same look she saw on me, too because within two minutes we'd said our good-byes and were tearing up the freeway, back to L.A. and the quickest score we could make.

That turned out to be Duane, one of my oldest and most reliable connections who ran his business out of a small house on an Inglewood side street where, if the wind was blowing right you could catch the scent of salt air off the ocean just the other side of the freeway. Duane was part of a large and enterprising network of dealers that I'd cultivated over the years, with a relationship that blurred the traditional lines between a customer and his connection. When you're rich and famous, with rich and famous friends, it's to any dealer's advantage to keep you coming back, passing out free samples and generous discounts just for the juice that comes from being in your orbit. After all, if Rick James is buying his shit from you, everyone else is going to know you've got the best. Even at the most totally uncontrolled levels of my crack consumption—throwing down $4,000 or more a week to feed the habit—chances are I'd be getting high for free just as much as I was paying for it, and that made even the thought of quitting not just difficult but damn near impossible. That old cliché' about the dealer giving you the first taste for free just didn't apply. Every time I turned around someone was offering me a hit on the house.

By the same token, going out to score was about more than just picking up your package and paying the man. It was a social occasion where you might stay holed up at your connection's crib for two or three days, getting high, telling stories and holding court with all the other crackheads coming by to hang with the King of Funk. For the dealers, it was all public relations. For me, it was all about staying close to the only thing that mattered.

Duane was a case in point and his place in Inglewood had long since become one of a half dozen homes-away-from-home made available to me on a twenty-four hour basis. And Tanya and I wasted no time making ourselves comfortable, settling in with a pipe and pile of rocks in front of Duane's entertainment center while he went about his various deals and deliveries.

It was late on Friday night and Tanya and I were well into our run, trading hits and drinking Jack Daniels with the big screen TV droning on across the room. I'd just settled back to enjoy a rush when I suddenly felt Tanya stiffen beside me. With all the time we'd spent together, we became very attuned to each other's body language and I immediately knew something was wrong. I turned to see her staring at the TV screen and when I started to ask what was up she waved me off, and lunging for the remote, turned up the volume.

It was then that I heard my name and turned with a sinking feeling in my gut to the face of the blow-dried newsman on the screen. Over his shoulder, I could see a picture of me, some Motown publicity shot at least a couple of years old.

"Rock and roll bad boy and self-proclaimed Super Freak, Rick James is in trouble with the law again tonight," the reporter was saying, as on the screen concert footage flashed by, mixed with pictures of the August arrest up at the Mulholland estate. "Already facing charges of drug possession kidnapping and torture, James and his twenty-one year old girlfriend Tanya Hijazi are being sought by police in connection with yet another incident at a local hotel where James reportedly assaulted a thirty-two year old West Hollywood woman. Police have issued an All Points Bulletin for the capture and arrest of James and Hijazi."

A sudden clatter jogged me back to awareness and I realized that the crack pipe had slipped out of my hands. Tanya turned, her eyes wide with panic and the kind of paranoid certainty that only a crack head can truly appreciate.

"That lying bitch," I seethed and in a sudden almost reflex action, kicked over the coffee table.

"God Rick," said Tanya in a faint trembling voice. "What are we going to do?"

"Let me think," I shot back, but it was no use. It was as if the gears in my skull were slipping like a bad transmission, while my heart raced like an engine with a stuck carburetor. What were we going to do? I knew exactly what to do. Find Mary, cut out her heart and feed it to the fish off the end of the Santa Monica pier. The only thing I wasn't quite sure of was whether they would execute me by lethal injection or the chair. I picked up the pipe where I'd dropped it and loaded in another rock. I needed a little inspiration.

I was still trying to get inspired an hour later when Duane ambled in and we spilled the story in a confused and jumbled rush. When he'd finally sorted out the details, he came up with what seemed like the only viable option.

Lets face it, Duane reasoned; there was no way Tanya and I were going to evade a citywide dragnet for very long. The best thing to do was to face the music, turn ourselves in, and find the best lawyer money could buy. Hey maybe Mary would settle for that shopping spree after all.

Looking back, it was clear enough that Duane's main concern was to get these two fugitives out of his house as soon as possible. But, for the moment, all I wanted was somebody, anybody, to tell me how to duck the shit storm that was brewing over my head and Duane was all I had.

There was only one problem; it was Friday night. If we went to the local precinct and turned ourselves in, we'd have to wait the whole weekend before we could post bail and the thought of forty-eight hours in jail, alone and apart with no crack to keep us company, was a little bit more than we could handle.

There was only one thing to do: cop as much of Duane's crack as we could, find some place to hide out and spend one last lost weekend before we let ourselves get locked up. Maybe only another crackhead can really understand the crazy appeal of the scheme—there s something about being on the lam, cut loose from every tie and carrying a bag of quality rocks that perfectly fits the lifestyle, the outlaw image, that comes with the territory.

And we played it to the hilt. Since we were going underground, we'd have to be able to pass unnoticed. Disguising ourselves made the whole caper that much more like some warped version of a 007 movie. We ransacked Duane's crib until we found a Rastafarian knit hat big enough to hide my braids, some wraparound sunglasses and a trench coat, which together made me look like a Jamaican Secret Service agent. The irony of trying to hide a face I'd spent most of my life trying to get into the spotlight was totally lost on me. I was way into my new role as Fugitive From Justice; the absurdity of the whole situation was hidden in the cloud of crack smoke clouding my brain.

Tanya also got herself decked out with a hat and glasses and, since we were sure they'd have a make on the Jaguar, we stashed the car in Duane's garage and headed down the street on foot. We must have hiked about a mile down Culver Boulevard, ducking into doorways or staring at store windows when people passed us by on the street. We didn't have the slightest idea where we were going or what we'd do once we got there, but it wasn't long before the bag of rocks in my pocket made up our minds for us. We ducked into a seedy motel near an off-ramp of the 405 and after signing the register with our own version of "Mr. & Mrs. John Doe" we locked the doors, pulled the curtains and got back to the business at hand.

But for some reason we weren't getting as much of a thrill from being bad ass outlaws on the run as we'd imagined. The paranoia that comes with prolonged cocaine use was providing its own kind of high and, with every pair of car headlights that swept up the street, adrenaline would surge up our nerve endings and a dizzy panic would parch our throats. Not that we ever considered putting down the pipe. The drug was creating its own insane spiral of fear and frenzy, a pain-and-pleasure response that had no beginning or end. The freakier the scene got, the more crack we craved and with each toke the freak needle peaked higher. Something had to give.

It must have been about three in the morning when our little escapade finally came apart at the seams. We'd been smoking all night, monitoring the TV for more news flashes, as if we half expected to hear a report that we'd actually been taken alive in some desperate standoff. We'd both left on our disguises and the thick wool cap I was wearing was soaked with sweat, my eyes rattling like ball bearings behind the cheap sunglasses and the trench coat balled up around me like a straight jacket.

Suddenly directly outside the window we heard the sound of a car pulling up. Headlights flooded through the blinds and a door slammed. This was it: the SWAT team had arrived. Stopping only long enough to grab the bag of rocks on the table, Tanya and I bolted for the bathroom, pried open the window and climbed out into the night. We dropped down into some shrubbery behind the motel, crouching low and trying not to breathe as we waited for the sound of a police bullhorn to call us out.

We were still out when dawn broke, gray and wet over empty streets of Inglewood. We took a bunch of Valiums, gave ourselves up, and slept in our jail cells for three days.

Once I had posted bond, we moved in with Tanya's mother, Suzanne. Suzanne knew we were getting high, but she was sympathetic because she knew we were addicts and our behavior was out of our control. She didn't approve of it, didn't like it, but she just wanted us to be safe and she knew we were better off with her.

Our court date had finally arrived and it was time for Tanya and me to face the music. We were originally scheduled to be in a courtroom in Malibu, which is a great liberal place to be tried, but at the last minute, we were moved to San Fernando, which had a ninety eight percent conviction rate. I was getting fucked up every night before we went to court. When we got to court in the morning I was so out of it that I was falling asleep in the courtroom—to the point where the judge told me to go and get some sleep if I needed. It wasn't that I wanted to piss the judge and jury off, I was just so fucked up that I couldn't help it. My dope dealer would bring me more dope during the recess and I would be high again for the afternoon session.

Francis Courtney was supposed to be a primary witness. Her lawyers had her in a hotel when they were supplying her with drugs in order to make sure she stayed around long enough to give evidence. In the end, the judge allowed them to tape her evidence, but they had stopped and started the tape, which makes the tape conjecture. When she finally showed up she made so little sense that the jury paid no heed to her. I mean she was suing me for forty five million dollars and she couldn't even be bother to show up in court to sign the necessary documents.

The prosecutors wanted Tanya to testify against me, but she refused. In the end she took a deal and got two years, because she just wanted to get this over with and get back to Taz. Mary's kick to the stomach had caused her to miscarry our second child and now she was determined to be the best mother she could for Taz. Getting her time over and done with and getting back home made sense.

I was convicted of assault and two or three charges after that. I was carted right off to jail. It was a very sad time. I dreaded the thought of being away from Tanya and I wanted to cry when I thought of Taz growing up without me. I went back to Millionaire's row at the county jail and slept for two weeks, just sobering up and detoxing, trying to stay strong for myself and my family. It was a weird time for me, but at least I could talk to Tanya; my friend Dave had hooked up this phone at my house where we could talk to each other over a speakerphone.

My attorneys were trying to negotiate a reduced sentence for me. Every evening they would come and tell me of the latest offer, and, for some reason, a voice kept telling me "Don't take it, I got something else planned." I listened to that voice and sent my lawyer back to fight some more for me. My sentence had been reduced down to eight years from life already and something in my mind was still saying, "Don't take it."

My lawyers were going crazy, trying to persuade me to take eight years and then one day I got a call to come down to the visiting room. Waiting for me was a shorthaired, conservative white guy who smelt like a cop to me. Turns out he was a retired Orange County detective named Tom Owens who was now working as a private detective. I was already agitated and pissed off from the detox. When he started to introduce himself I right away just said "Fuck you, I don't need your help." When he got up scowling and started to walk away, I realized this was really stupid and I apologized. I asked him to sit down. Tom told me that Dwayne Moody had sent him. I had met Dwayne through Jim Brown, and Dwayne had had similar legal problems to mine. Tom Owens explained that he suspected some of the state's witnesses were probably professional witnesses, or at best, very unreliable. He had started to gather evidence on the girls who had testified against me and had found out that in various ways some of them were being compensated for their testimony. This really ended up helping me.

The next time my lawyer came in he said "Rick, because of all of Tom's evidence they are offering you five years." When I asked him how much hard time I would be doing my lawyer said that with good behavior I would probably be incarcerated for two years. Because I was a drug addict I would be able to go to a rehab prison for the first eight months. The rehab prison, CRC, was known as Camp Snoopy to its inmates because it was so laid-back and easy. You played baseball, went to drug rehab classes, and, if you wanted to, sang in the choir. I always used to tell people that a few years in jail would probably sober me up, so all in all, it seemed like an OK deal to me.

Chapter Sixty-two
Folsom Prison Blues

After my attorneys negotiated my sentence, I spent about five months in County. This was a sobering time, both physically, as I struggled with detoxing, and mentally, as I realized I would be spending the next two years incarcerated. I have always understood the value and preciousness of freedom, whether it's freedom of the body or freedom of the mind. I was disheartened to find that something I prized so highly had been taken from me.

One night in County I woke up to find I was on the floor and that the walls of my cell were shaking violently. All I could hear was the screams and shouts of the other prisoners as the whole building shook. It was the Northridge earthquake. As I lay on the floor, locked in my cell, unable to move off of the heaving ground, I felt pure fear and panic. In an earthquake, the Corrections Officers are instructed to leave the prison and go home immediately, leaving the prisoners to take their chances in their cells. I prayed to God to spare me and not let me die without seeing my son again. He must have heard, because eventually the walls stopped shaking, the COs returned and jail life went back to normal. That feeling of being trapped like a rat really freaked me out and stayed with me for months afterwards. I started to get heavy phobias, that the walls were coming in on me, and I'd start to sweat and pray.

Besides praying, I also turned to writing and reading to help me through these new phobias. Over the next few weeks, I read several autobiographies, Ray Charles', Marvin Gaye's, "Inside my Life" by Toni Morrison. Reading these stories helped to put my own situation in perspective. As I read a few more, I decided I wanted to write one myself. That's how I started writing *Confessions of a Superfreak*. It was therapeutic, the act of writing helped me to deal with and exorcise the demons of my addiction and desires. I felt that perhaps God had brought me to this point to allow me to ask for his forgiveness; and in a way, documenting my life and writing about everything I had done was like asking that question of Him. I started to write out my memories out on pencil and paper and sneak it to my lawyer on the sly. He would have it typed up for me and stored away for when I was ready to publish it.

Once I began to write, time passed more quickly and soon I found myself transferred to my new home, CRC, or Camp Snoopy. If you have to be incarcerated, Camp Snoopy is the place to go. Prisoners live in dorms rather than cells and spend the days working on their mental, emotional and physical wellness, playing basketball and baseball and attending classes to help them conquer their addiction. I quickly found myself a pretty popular inmate, with even the warden giving me some respect.

I got in one fight during my incarceration and that was in CRC. This big, tattooed redneck, Aryan-power-fucker got mad at me when I got on the baseball team. One day he stayed back after practice and suck-ered me in the bathroom. Of course, he didn't know I was good with my hands and that I had boxed in my youth in the YMCA, so I fucked him up. He was a bit overweight with a baldhead and he hit the floor like a falling redwood. I was about to really beat him down, but a little prison homie stopped me, saying "Don't, you only got a short time, don't fuck it up for yourself."

After the fight there was a stand off in my dorm between the white and the Black shot-callers. The Crips, Bloods and Mexicans were on my side, and the Aryan Powers were on the dude's side. They asked the dude, who was bleed-ing from the lips and eyes, who had done this. Then they looked at me and I didn't have a scratch, and they said "Well you don't look like you've been in a fight." They asked him did he want to continue the fight and he said no. I had gone straight for one of his eyes, just like I did as a kid in street fights and he knew he didn't stand a chance if he started to fuck with me again.

My reputation grew for that. The next day I was called into the Lieu-tenant's office. The Lieutenant, whom I had a pretty good relationship with said, "So, I guess you didn't have anything to do with this?" And then he added, "I heard whoever whopped him did a good job." They brought the white fucker in and he said he fell on a bucket. In the end I

344

became friendly with the white-power dude. He was going to be in various prisons for the rest of his life and it was hard not to feel sorry for him.

After eight and a half months in Camp Snoopy, I went to a screening in front of the warden so that she could decide whether I was going to serve my full time or if I was going to get off on parole. I already knew my chances of getting out were pretty slim, because the warden had told me that once, when out on the streets, I had dogged her. In the end I guess she got her revenge because she sent me to Folsom, the oldest, most hard-core prison in California.

I was shipped off to Folsom on a bus filled with blacks and Chicanos and some white boys. There were three armed guards watching us and any conversation or communication on the bus was prohibited. It made for a boring ride, but at least it gave me time to think. CRC had been pretty easy for me, because being Rick James finally started to mean something in a real way. I had been able to throw my name around and got a lot of things that the other inmates couldn't get. I always had lockers full of food and goods and by the time I left I was practically running a grocery store out of my dorm. But now I was getting nervous about how it was going to play out at Folsom.

By the time we hit Folsom I was the very last person on the bus with nothing to my name but the two baloney sandwiches prisoners were issued for the ride. As I was getting off, this big motherfucker guard came up and said, "If I'd known you were Rick James, I would have given you three sandwiches." I could've used them too, cause I was starving at this point.

Then I had to walk past The Yard. The Yard was filled with two thousand inmates and as I walked by they all stopped talking or lifting and started singing my songs, cheering me, asking about the Mary Jane Girls, shouting things like "Rick, come to Five building," or "Make them put you in Four." In the end I was placed in Two building, where new inmates go through processing, get shots, find out where they were going to work and so on.

My first day there I told the sergeant that I wanted to make a phone call and he said, "Well, boy, if you want to make a phone call, you'll have to sing for it." Then he tried to pass it off like he was joking and said, "OK, you can make a call." I talked quickly to my lawyers and told them I was OK. Then I hung up and asked him to have my cell opened. He said "Boy, I told you, you gonna have to work for it, now sing." This was starting to piss me off. All the tiers were filling up with guys, all quiet, looking down to see how this confrontation was going to play out. It was my first day and I pretty much knew that my reputation at the prison depended on how I handled this. So I took a guitar from one of the prisoners and started making up some song. Not Funk, not Rap, not Rock. No I played a hillbilly country tune, just for this guard:

> *"Well I guess here in Folsom I gotta figure,*
> *Some people ain't gonna like niggahs, uh-huh*
> *Well he wants me to dance and he wants me to sing,*
> *Me being a slave and everything, uh-huh..*
> *Big fat red-neck, don't like niggahs, uh-huh..."*

In the tiers all the guys were screaming and clapping. The sergeant had a big old frown on his face, but there was nothing he could do. He'd told me to sing. The three female lieutenants came in, one Puerto Rican, one Black and one white. They had heard I was in Two, so they were coming to see me. They were fine as a motherfucker.

So I said, "You want more?" and he said, "Yeah, give me a real one this time." So, seeing these girls, I hit "Ebony Eyes." And them bitches started crying and swooning and screaming, "That's my song!" I sang the shit out of it. And when I finished, every nigga' in the block started screaming and applauding. Then I said, "Now can I go in my cell?" He said, "All right Mr. James, you can go now."

That pretty much set me up for my stay in Folsom. I was moved to a private part of the prison, the "Rich House," because the Warden knew a lot of people would be trying to get to me, but in the end, pretty much everyone loved me. These *Thug Life* motherfuckers would come over and start in talking shit and I would talk shit right back to them.

I ended up having all the shot-callers real close to me and they put a blanket of love around me. The Mexican Mafia, the 415, the Crips and the Bloods, even the Aryan Race. I had heard the Mexicans had a hit out for me, so I called the head Mexican Mafia shot caller to my cell and he said "I've been in prison 25 years and your music helped me get through this shit, I ain't gonna let anyone touch you man. I'd kill one of our people if they fucked with you." So I had a lot of love and a lot of friends that I miss to this day.

Many of the guards hated me, but I just told them, "Fuck with me and I'll have your ass. I'm too fucking rich and I have a cousin in congress, so just go ahead and fuck with me." They had bets going; who was going to be the first to write me up, send me to detention, shoot me accidentally. But soon even the COs were growing fond of me, so I was pretty safe. I started going to the library, which was pretty nice, because the brothers who ran the library let me play guitar in the back room. One of the females smuggled me in a tape recorder that recorded, so I could write and record. Another female officer would smuggle my tapes back out. When I wanted it, I could get steak, escargot, champagne. The CO prison guard bitches loved me, the niggers loved me, the CO motherfuckers and the rednecks even loved me. A few times I even sent fruit baskets to their old ladies out in the street after my people found out their addresses.

So, although I longed to get out everyday, my stay in Folsom was Ok. Me and Tanya wrote constantly and her mother kept me up on Taz. I did my time, wrote close to 300 songs, played basketball and read a lot. And I finally got sober. I hadn't had cocaine in my system since I hit county after the trial. I'd have the occasional drink when a CO would bring one to me, but I felt really clear and I was ready to get out. Me and Tanya were looking forward to getting married.

The day before I got out, Tanya's mother called me to say that Tanya had had a bridal shower and she'd shoplifted a pair of shoes for it. She was being sent back to jail for probation violation. I was heartbroken for her and nervous because now I had to take care of Taz on my own. Taz was four and he had come to see me every weekend at Folsom, so we knew each other. But still, I had been relying on having Tanya there to raise my son with me. I was pissed, angry and sad that she had gotten herself into county jail again.

Finally, my release date came. My lawyers were there to pick me up in my Jag. I was ready to rejoin the land of the living.

Getting Back on Track...

Tom Snyder, the Tomorrow Show (talk show host) and Rick

Rick with Bobby Womack and Snoop in the studio

Rick with friend Roi

Rick with Keith Sweat

Rick…Hangin' Out

Rick…Meeting and Greeting

Mary Wilson, Teena Marie, Rick and Tanya Hijazi

Rick on the set of "Life" with Eddie Murphy and Martin Lawrence

Rick with Raphael from Tony, Toney, Tone

Big Al and Rick backstage

Mark Cywinski and Rick hanging out at Mark's house

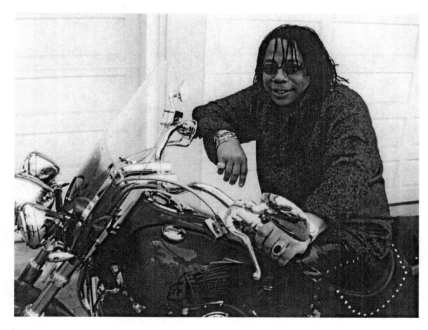

Rick and friends

Loving Family, Friends and Life

Chapter Sixty-three
Urban Rhapsody

Now that I was outside of the prison system I was nervous about my career. I didn't really know how my fans felt about what had gone down and I was very nervous about whether people were still going to like me. I had written over three hundred songs in prison but I didn't know if I had it in me to record them. There was also the stress of knowing that for the next two years I was going to have a drug test every week to make sure I was straight. I really didn't know if I was going to have a career any more and with my new family to support, it was really weighing on my mind.

I had heard so much rap and hip-hop in prison that my concept for this new album was to integrate hip-hop, rap and old school in one album. So I did *Urban Rhapsody*. I basically paid for it myself with the help of a friend of mine. It opens up with a very Cole Porter-ish Marvin Gaye-ish kind of funk thing, with rap and a monologue. I wrote a song called "Someone's Watching You" about COs and how they set you up and basically behave like bitches on the rag. I wrote a track called "Back Again" that was used on the *Money Talks* soundtrack and I did one track with Joanne McDuffie, even though she was a snake. "Never Say you Love Me" says everything that I wanted to say to her which was, don't say you love me when you don't. Finally, I did a track with Snoop Dog, which was very fly. My friend Bobby Womack did a little something, as did Ned from the Five Footers, Charlie Wilson, Teena Marie and Rappin' Forte.

It was a great album I thought. I got a band together with some cats from Buffalo and decided to tour on it. Me and Tanya had really solidified our relationship and we had really fallen in love even more. I appeared on a bunch of TV shows to talk about my time in prison and they all wanted to know about the album and the book I was writing.

We did a few warm-up gigs outside of LA without using our names. But our first main gig was at the House of Blues, in Hollywood. Everybody was there—Denzel, Wesley, Eddie, Chris Tucker, Eddie Griffin. All my friends. Chris and Eddie and Paul Mooney brought me on stage. There were so many people outside they had to put up screens to broadcast the show. There were so many people inside that we broke the in-house record for crowd size. Thousands of people were trying to get in, even Wesley Snipes had problems getting in and I had to go out in my robe and tell the door people he was cool. It was a very big night for me and I was nervous, more so than I'd ever been. I felt like the whole world was watching me and I was worried that I would fail. I felt I was a little over weight and worried that I wasn't what people were expecting. The band did their warm-up and I went on. It was like magic. Nothing had changed. People were screaming and hollering and I was at the top of my voice, in great shape vocally. It was a crazy night. Snoop came up and sang and did his little rap. It was fantastic. The music was hot, the people were screaming, and I was still sober.

Rick James was back.

Chapter Sixty-four
The Next Beginning

Now it was time for Tanya and me to get married. We had been living together in this small house in the Beverly Glen area, but with Taz we decided we needed a bigger place. After a bit of searching we found our dream home. Tanya was a felon and two felons aren't supposed to be together when one is on parole. My Parole officer said, "I know Tanya is staying over with you and I could send you back to prison for it." But then he added, "You should marry her, she's been through a lot for you. You have a child together." It was true, she had sacrificed a lot for me.

Dec 21st 1997 we got married at our house. It was a small wedding, just with our family and friends. And we had a quiet, peaceful cere-mony. I was thinking to myself, "I hope I can change and I hope she's changed. I hope I can handle this. I hope I can do it the way God would like to see me do it." We would have to work hard to get over our past lives, to forget about the drugs and the sex and raise our son happily. After all the years and all the drama, I would finally be a good father and a happily married man.

As we said our vows in front of our families and our friends, I thought of all the people in my life who I had loved and who had loved me back. I thought of my friends from the old days in Buffalo and my beatnik years in Toronto—the people who had been there during the wild years in LA and the crazy months of travels to the far-flung places of the world. I thought of the people who had fallen along the way. Elke, Jay, my Mom.

I knew now that a new chapter in my life was beginning. A life of sobriety but a life still filled with music and passion. I knew that whatever life held for me after this would have to be another book.

Family First

Rick and son Tazman at home doing a photo shoot (Fall, 2002)

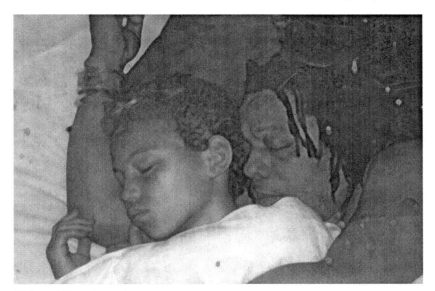

Rick and Taz taking time out

Tanya, Ty, and Rick
Granddaughters Jasmin and Charissma, and son Taz at Rick's home

371

Rick and Tanya

Tanya, Rick and Taz

Tanya and Rick
Sharing a special moment

Epilogue
Looking Back on the Last Days of Life with Rick James through the Eyes of his *Moon Child*: A Conversation with Linda 'Hunti' Hunt"
by Jake Brown with Linda Hunt

Most household dictionaries define soul mate as "one of two persons compatible with each other in disposition, point of view, or sensitivity." Often as intimate without romance, as with it, Linda 'Hunti' Hunt's soul mate was Rick James. As his assistant and best friend for over a quarter century, Hunt was by Rick's side through the heavens and the hells of his career as a Funk Superstar. Living with Rick for the last six years of his life, caring for him following his stroke in 1998, and through the subsequent personal and professional recovery process, Linda was sadly also the one who found him on the tragic day of his passing, August 6, 2004. With Rick from the heights of his stardom to the very end, 'Hunti' shares some of her most personal memories from the diary of her life with Rick James:

"I first met Rick when I was in my teens in 1977; but I officially went to work for him in 1981, from then up until he passed away. Throughout the years, he always had a team of lawyers and financial advisers, but you can bet anything he did, he ran it by me for my opinion. He decided we were soul mates, and people make a mistake when they think of soul mates, that it connotates all this romantic stuff, but it had nothing to do with being a soul mate. We could finish each other's sentences, it was just crazy. 'Hunti' was one of many nicknames he had for me, and the story he loved to tell to sum us up for people was to say, 'She came to my house for a picnic one day and she never left.' I filled a void, and there were a lot of things that needed doing that I volunteered to get done, and before you knew it, I had quit my job and was working for him. As an employer, he was generous. Between he and I, one thing people never

375

understood about us was we could sleep in the same room and it didn't really matter. He'd be on a date, and forget his date, and come sleep with me. That's just how our relationship was. It had been like that since I was a teenager, and still was. It wasn't sexual. Once we sat around and watched the movie Gladiator over and over again for 24 hours straight, no drugs, no drinking, don't answer the phone, we didn't want to deal with people. We sat around and ate, and run our mouths.

Rick was a big gossip, he loved it, and could out-gossip any woman on this earth. I always took the brunt of it, but he'd get in trouble some-times because he ran his mouth too much. Even up till the end, he was loud as ever, he just couldn't move as fast. In terms of his personality off stage, so to speak, Rick LOVED funny a lot. He liked people who could make him laugh, he liked to laugh at stuff. And like I said, he LOVED to gossip, he was one of the girls. He was a drama queen, he really was. If you've ever watched a soap opera, and say 'That would never happen in real life,' with Rick it would. He'd invite certain people to hang out, and then disclose different facts about each of them, and before you knew it, they'd be going at each other, and he'd be sitting back in the middle, smiling. He really loved to start fights, to stir up trouble. And all you could do was laugh at it.

Once, near the end, I came into the room to bring him something and he was visiting with an old promoter friend of mine, and told him his favor-ite song he'd ever written was 'Moon Child', which he'd written about me, and truthfully describes me perfectly. We used to share clothes too, leath-ers, unisex. I remember once in the 80s, we were out in a club partying, and I had this one particular leather jacket, and I LOVED this jacket. And Rick had it on, and Eddie Murphy admired it, and Rick said 'You can have this.' And I said 'Wait a minute, that is my jacket!' Years later, we went to Eddie Murphy's house, and sure enough, that jacket was still in his closet. Rick's friends were loyal: Eddie never left, right up till the end. We visited him a couple of months before Rick died.

Before Rick died, he knew things were happening, because he'd men-tion certain people, saying 'You know how much I love this person?', that type of thing. And Eddie was one of those people he would talk about. He'd say 'I love how he doesn't kiss my ass. He's my friend because he's my friend.' There were others too: Ike and Rick were great friends; they were still scheming, up until he died. Mariah Carey was another who, whenever Rick would see her out in the clubs, she was always so respectful of him, and wonderful to him. And let's face it, she didn't have to be. She would show him so much love and respect. He loved Snoop Dogg, and they'd see each other out; he also loved Jamie Foxx, he really did. They had some things they were planning to do before he died. The month before he died, people showed up in his life that he hadn't seen in years. One of his first promoters, so many people—just showed up out of nowhere—who he had been talking about, wanting to see. A lot of them showed up at our door, and no one was supposed to know where we were living; they just tracked him down.

Some of them he would try to contact, and some would ignore him, or never got back to him, or who could just never get together with him, now all started showing up. He couldn't believe it, and especially the last week of his life, he spent talking to these people about the past, reliving it, a lot of the good things. And he was feeling confident about a lot of things, but then was scared about other things. He was scared about not being accepted, he didn't want to be a laughing stock. He was scared of failure, because he went through that lull right before and after he got out of prison, where he got snubbed by some people who never would have before. That's enough to make you depressed right there, especially if you're insecure, which a lot of artists are. Now, in the last few years of his life, when a lot of rappers started sampling his music, it was great, because he was back to hero-worship with them, which was good for his confidence. He'd even been talking to the old members of his band 'Stone City Band' in Buffalo about planning a reunion tour, heading into 2005. He was really excited about that.

He loved to keep people around who could make him laugh— it could be anyone, from another entertainer to a pimp. And when I say that, two of his favorite words were pimps and hoes. Later on, maybe the last two years, he'd use the word pimp or player, and he spent quite a bit of the last year of his life literally hanging out with pimps and hoes. He liked the rowdiness and to laugh, and the only thing he loved more than a good laugh was a good story. He liked to be pulled into stories, and pimps had plenty of them. With Rick's love for gossip, he got most of it from them about people they were servicing in the business, who shall remain nameless; but we knew more about entertainers' sex lives than we ever should have known. It was Rick's way of keeping his ear to the street, and he liked to know the details of the low-down dirty, and he got a lot of information.

He thrived on it, because near the end, he did like to stay home a lot, and he didn't have to go anywhere to hear what was going on out in the world. He could stay home for a month without going out, and know everything that was going on in Hollywood. There were two pimps in particular that hung out a lot, and one was building a stable again, and he would bring his new girls by to get Rick's approval or disapproval. 'What do you think of her?' And Rick would say 'She's too skinny, she needs to eat, she's too skanky, you gotta get somebody classy.' He liked to pretend almost like it was him, and he liked to live vicariously through other people's lives. Everyone was very respectful though when they were in Rick's home, and if they started acting like that, they had to go. The majority were clean and came over to have a good time, and people weren't judging us, because Rick would treat them all like he had someone really important in his home. I think that's why they were so comfortable with him, because he made them feel good.

He'd go out and spend $800 on dinner for a bunch of people he barely knew, but made them feel good about themselves, so they gave him that respect in turn. One of our biggest contentions—Rick and I—was about his belief in the whole whores-in-the-bible thing, he really took that to heart. He really did, because again, if you really wanted to get to Rick, you'd come to him with a sob story: 'I'm a prostitute because my father molested me,' or 'I'm a stripper because my mom threw me out when I was 15.' That's all you had to do, and for that period of time, he was focused on you; if he could find a way to make your life better, even momentarily, he would. And when it was time to go, Rick would wait till there was a blow-up about something else to get rid of them so he wouldn't be hurting their feelings. Right before he died, one of the last things he did was hang out with one of the pimps who brought his new girls over, and they all went out to eat. Part of that company he kept stemmed back years to 'Super Freak', that was life imitating art. And with his new music, he couldn't wait to play it for the pimps, it was like he sought more approval from them than regular people. Their approval meant more to him because he saw it as real, I think. Another motivation for that was also that, near the end, Rick was really, really insecure and scared to be by himself. He was always saying to me, 'You're not leaving, are you?'

I think that's part of why it took him so long to break it off with his wife Tanya. His divorce from her was finalized six weeks before he died, and he was so happy. He was ecstatic, because she'd moved out in the summer of 1999, but it wasn't until the summer of 2004 that everything finally went through. And they'd been on and off since 1999, because her M.O. was: she would come over, get him really upset, then leave. They'd play house and pretend like they were husband and wife when they'd see each other, until they'd get in a fight and split up again. He had this thing for her, so what can you do, and she kept promising they would reconcile, and constantly held their boy Taz over his head. She was basically another addiction, and he hadn't figured out how to stop it yet. She still wanted to be *Mrs. Rick James*, because that came with a lot of perks. She met people she never would have met, and once she got her introduction, she wouldn't need him anymore. So basically, she would come to use him, and he knew it. Plus whenever he wanted to see his child, Rick and Tanya had to interact. He paid her way beyond what she was supposed to in child support, but that didn't stop her from asking for more. He bought her everything she needed, and she still always wanted more. He saw Taz at Christmas in 2003, and then one more time in the summer before he passed in August.

Relative to Rick's deteriorating health, I could see little signs of things, and we talked about it, and he didn't want to talk about it, but when we were by ourselves, he would say to me 'You know, I'm not going to be here a long time.' And I'd say 'Oh yes you are,' and he'd look at me and say 'You know I'm not,' that type of thing. What his biggest thing was, even though he talked a lot of stuff, was move to an Island and retire. As much as he wanted to be a star, near the end he said 'It's killing me, it's hard.' He was tired of putting up a face, and tired of being Rick James. As much as people loved it, it took a lot of work to be Rick James, whether he was on the radio or not. He'd have to be a certain way around people, always up, ready for a party. Ready for the Super Freak thing, and I told him 'You don't have to do that all the time.' And sometimes he would agree and say 'You're right, I don't.' Still, his last diagnosis from the doctor was 'You're doing great! Lose a little weight, try to stay clean, you're fine. You'll live another 20 years.'

Truthfully, there was nothing in the way of a warning, and when he said he was getting older, what he meant was he knew he had to slow down with the wild life if he wanted to live a long time. He had a pace maker, which we'd just had put in not too long before he died. And the whole time he wore it, it never went off once, he never had to be resuscitated. No matter what you hear: that last couple years of his life working, he only missed ONE concert. We didn't let him get on the plane because we decided he needed to go to the hospital, and that is when we found out he needed the pacemaker. I was one of his entourage on the road usually, and the last couple of years he was doing around 20 concert dates a year. We were on tour when the Dave Chappell Show sketch first debuted, and once Rick came to terms with it, he used it as a stepping stone, to do more interviews, and looked at it like 'Any press is good press.' He'd already had the VH1 'Behind the Music' special to update people on his life story, so he understood the parody for what it was, both as a piece of humor and as an opportunity. His health problems near the end stemmed basically from the wear and tear on his body, even after the stroke.

I know one regret he had before he died was that he couldn't stop doing drugs. He would cry over it at times, and he wanted to, and some days, we would resolve to, 'We're gonna do the rehab schedule,' and then we'd stick to it for a bit, then that one day would come when he'd wake up, and you could just see it in his eyes, that he'd slipped, and go 'Oh damn.' I'm not even talking about weed, I'm speaking of more serious drugs, and it was just the look he would get, and he could see how disappointed I was in him, so then he would take the whole day to make sure things were extra perfect for me. His biggest thing was that he just couldn't stop, he tried so many times: he tried, and tried, and tried. And he would sit and bite his nails to the stubs trying not to go out the door. I've been around alcoholics in my own family all my life, and one thing you just know with some people, no matter what you do, its not gonna change. No matter what you do, if they don't wanna change themselves.

Rick had been to rehab a million times, and everyone has tried the hard love approach, and if at that point he's still using, then he's not going to stop. And I've never done drugs, ever. I've never shared a drink of alcohol with him. So in spite of that, I chose to stand by him. I think you have to accept a person for who they are, not what you want them to be, after you've tried everything else. Then you're not disappointed so much. But in the last year he was alive, if you looked at him, you'd think 'He's getting older, but he's okay,' but he wasn't, he was tired all the time. He had diabetes, he had the high blood pressure thing going on, he was overweight, anxiety. He pretended to himself he was healthy, but he really wasn't, because I was telling him all the time, 'You can't do this, you can't do that.' Not that he listened. He was a homebody, because he could stay in the house for a week, no problem; but also, there were times when he didn't want to stay home, when he wanted to go out and do something, when he wanted to party.

When he went out, he'd go to this place, that place, but he wouldn't stay anywhere long. Sometimes he would wake up from a partying run, then sleep for a couple of days, and get up and record. He always had music on in the house. One of his rituals before going to the studio, on the days when you woke up knowing he was going to work, no matter what, you'd hear classical music. There was incense burning, and everything had to be perfectly cleaned in the house. He had his moments as a neat freak, mainly when it was time to record; everything around him had to be in order when he worked. The house had to be cleaned, everyone looking pretty decent, and he'd freshen himself up to where you'd think he was going out to a concert or something really artsy. He was never too embarrassed to go in my closet and get something if he wanted it. Also, he had to have a real breakfast, a real old-fashioned full breakfast. He had to make his business calls. There was a line of things he did: he got up, he ate breakfast, he started the classical music, he went and got dressed, then made his business calls that he had to make. He wanted to get everything out of the way so that when he was in the studio, no one bothered him.

We were living in a two-bedroom apartment, and he had music equipment set up there to demo with; and then in Woodland Hills, where we lived, he also had a full-fledged studio. We were in Woodland Hills for a little over a year before he died. He could work for two or three days at a time, but other times, he may just want to work for twelve hours straight. When I say work: when it came time for work, he was one of the hardest working people I'd ever met in my life. It was not playtime. He'd always be writing, there would always be a million writing pads lying around. He had guitars at home, a keyboard, some amplifiers, and a recorder. Anything he couldn't do, he had a guy named Barry who would come over and help. Whoever was there was the first person Rick would bounce ideas off of, if you were in the room when he finished a song, you were the first to hear it. Unless there was something specific about that song that he wanted your opinion on only. When he was working, if he knew you were coming by, okay you could come in. If he didn't know you were coming by, once he was working, you'd have to wait till he'd come out and then see if you could come in. I could come in and go as I pleased, but that was his routine.

Rick loved to go to Ralph's market too, he'd get a cart and walk around the supermarket with his date and show her off. He had a rapport with the people at the market, and I'd do the big shopping, but he liked to do the little shopping to gossip and socialize with the employees. Even with his health in the shape it was, his last meal was Taco Bell. He LOVED Taco Bell, and would have it at least once a week. Not Mexican, just Taco Bell Tacos. Even if he'd gone to a Mexican restaurant, he would have to go to Taco Bell on the way back. At home, he liked Chilean Sea Bass, I would make him that and he used to really like it. As much as he loved fine restaurants and things of that nature, at the same time, he liked home cooking. He LOVED home cooking.

Also, he loved to swim. I don't care what shape he was in, if he couldn't stand up straight, he'd still get in that pool. It was just hilarious. He would have bathed in the pool if he could have, and when I'd tell him no, he'd go bathe in the Jacuzzi, and having bubble baths overflowing. Then when it would get into the pool, he'd say 'You can go get it fixed for me Hunti.' In that way, he was very down to earth, almost too nice. When people came up to him, he would really let them interrupt him—even if he was on a business call—he'd put that on hold so he could sign autographs. The only time he wouldn't sign them was if he didn't feel well, then he would be a little agitated, and he'd still do it, but you could tell he wanted to do it and get out of there. I'll say this: he always found a way to have a conversation, or hit on somebody's mama, he loved to hit on people's mothers. He loved it. He was great at making people feel they were the only one in the world.

He loved the attention, but at the same time, it was a reminder of what he was, so it was good and bad at the same time. He loved it, but then after a while, someone would bring up how he used to be, which would bring him back to reality, and before you knew it, Rick would be out of the room. Moodwise, he was much calmer as he got older. He'd have his moments, but nothing like it used to be. It was always constant before, and you never knew, but now, it was really bad if drugs were involved, or if you hurt him really bad. He was really good at putting on a show, and making you think he was really mad at you, and before you'd hang up the phone, he was on the other end cracking up, and you were thinking 'Oh my God, oh my God, he's gonna hate me.' And he was on the other end of the line laughing, and thinking 'I'll let them know one day I'm not mad.' Rick loved to laugh, and he loved to play jokes on people. If he could get a joke across, he would. At one point, I wouldn't eat anything out of the refrigerator, and anyone who did, I'd say 'You're crazy,' because if I picked up something I'd left out and sipped from it, he'd start playing with my mind and go 'Do you know what I did to that?' And most times, he hadn't done a thing, but he was like a little boy, in that he LOVED to stir the pot. To him, there was nothing better than getting a bunch of people around and causing trouble.

One of Rick's biggest flaws, and one of our biggest arguments was Rick's being too sensitive toward women, to the point where they would take advantage. Even though he became a Muslim in prison, he could quote the bible and the Koran back and forth, and the one thing about the bible is he thought he was doing God's work, as far as the whores, etc. And I would say 'Rick, you're just using that as an excuse.' He really actually believed that, that he was supposed to be helping, but I would say 'You know what, you can help, but there is only so much you can do for someone who don't want it. If they don't want to come out of the gutter, they aren't coming out of the gutter.' That was probably the only thing I liked about the apartment better than the big house was that it wasn't big enough to have a lot of people in it. So that downscaling was a fantastic thing for him because it brought him back down to reality. We weren't running a woman's center or a rehab center, but you'd be surprised: we sometimes had twelve people living with us. He was always trying to help this person and that person; if you had a sob story, they knew exactly whose door to knock on in Woodland Hills. And I would have to turn people away. Rick was generous to a fault almost, but if he was being suckered, once he realized it, they were out.

He'd be generous with you, your mama, your daddy. There was one point when we lived in Buffalo, when he had rented eight, nine cars for different people who 'didn't have cars, even though Rick was paying them great salaries. That was the kind of person Rick was, he would still rent them all cars. He'd rent apartments. He even bought a house next to the one he and I lived in for his entourage and band to live in, and not just when we were working, we had people living there off and on for several years at a time. He would have people's whole families living in the houses with us. When I first started working for him, he didn't even know I was living with him for 2 weeks because so many people were coming in and out. He liked his house clean and decorated, even with all those people there, he had house rules. But it was still really laid-back. He'd have certain rooms really nice, but basically, they were living like hippies if you walked into a bedroom. That was the time. If you just walked into the house, and the living room, the foyer, the bar, you'd get one impression; but then if you went up into people's bedrooms, you'd go 'Woah, why are there all these mattresses on the floors?' But that's what they chose, it's how they wanted it. In his room, it was always nice, he wanted his room nice, and he only let certain people in. If he was having a party, at times he'd hold court in his bedroom, and people would flow through to say 'hi', but then after a certain point in the night the door would close and then it was just hand-picked who would come and go.

His children—he had 3 children, and his oldest daughter was in his life most primarily. She was a rapper and great writer, and would look to him for direction and he would give her advice about the business, and if she made a move he didn't like, he would tell her. If she did something he thought made her look like a 'bad daughter', as a father, he would very quickly let her know. They would go out together sometimes, and in some ways, socially speaking, they used each other. Rick liked to party with her because she was always around beautiful women, and she liked partying with him because it was great for networking. They were on good terms when he died, and she would come by often to see him. Rick didn't raise his older children, he and their mother were together as babies, but they were missing out of his life for a good 10 years, to where they disappeared, and he spent thousands of dollars trying to find them.

He reconnected with them at nine and eleven through happenstance by way of a friend of Rick's, so he had gotten to know them again as teenagers and young adults before he died. Things with his daughter could be tumultuous at times, because Rick wanted to be a great father, but in actuality he'd say 'I don't know how to do this.' They had their moments, because she was still exploring and being a single mom, and basically they were both into the *Hollywood Thing*. He would provide financial support when she needed it, but she was independent. And Rick was a firm believer in making your own way. And in a lot of ways, he didn't do his best. He could do his best for maybe up to two to three days, then it would start wavering. He would still be good, but it would start wearing on him. His son Ricky was really artistic, a fantastic artist, and phenomenal. As a painter, but he could draw, illustrate, and all those kinds of things. He also had a child who would be fifteen now. Rick saw him three days before he passed away. We went and got him from his grandmother's, and bought him a phone, and had a big breakfast. He enjoyed the moment, as it was.

Taz would be 15 now. Rick saw his son a couple times a year, and there were times they would talk every day, and times they would talk every couple weeks when Tanya was acting up. They would email back and forth a lot too. When he'd visit, Rick and he would curl up and take little naps together, it was just beautiful to look at. Taz loved his daddy; he walked around with the attitude like he was 'Little Rick James.' He had the whole attitude: I'm the important person here, its adorable. He also has the leadership quality- that star confidence- like his daddy. He's very athletic and artistic like his big brother, they were so alike.

Rick was a grandfather two times over, and he loved that role. His daughter had two daughters of her own—one should be seventeen now, and a little girl who is probably seven now—he loved them. Rick's smallest granddaughter was 'GrandDaddy's Little Girl', she had his big cheeks, and was really like a girly-girl. He LOVED to swim with them. He loved them and they loved him, and it was a freer relationship because he wasn't having to worry about being parental. He could laugh and joke with them more easily. His oldest daughter loved basketball, and was a sports fanatic, so he could talk sports with her.

Passing—It wasn't easy for him at that time in his life to be an active parent, he had so much going on, and with his health. He would say 'I don't feel well,' we'd go to the doctor, they'd find nothing, and I'd say 'Look at your lifestyle, you're not going to feel well.' But he'd been doing all he'd been doing so long, he thought he could do it forever. And he'd say 'As long as you're here Hunti, I can handle it.' I'll always regret that, because I took the day off, and had woken him up for a doctor's appointment he was supposed to have, and he said he didn't want to go.

So he did his normal groggy thing, and he and whoever he was with, neither wanted to get up, so I called the doctor, and he said 'Let them sleep it off, and if anything happens, let me know.' So I went out, had a nice evening, came back, checked on him, and he was fine, so I went to bed. Then in the middle of the night, I felt really strange, like he was watching me, but I went back to sleep, because he'd do this thing sometimes where he'd walk in my room in the middle of the night, and stand over me! And I'd say 'Either get in the bed or leave,' and I fell back to sleep. So when I got up the next morning—it was August 6, 2004, and I went in the kitchen, because he always left a trail of food—even if he tried to clean it up, there was still a trail of food. And I looked around and said 'Hey, wait a minute, nothing's been touched.' So I went in his room, and looked at him, and as soon as I opened the door, I knew. It was my voice on the 911 tape all the tabloid shows were playing in the days after he died. They were very exploitive and disrespectful.

One thing Rick should really be remembered personally for, is his generosity. And how sensitive he was, and how smart he was. And of course how great his music was, but how much beautiful music he wrote that wasn't the wild funk, music you'd never believe he'd written if his name and voice wasn't on it. He was so brilliantly talented, and just such a great guy...he was. He was crazy as a button, and he had his good times; but above all else, he wanted people to love him. I know I did, and always will...

Author Jake Brown, has penned several best-selling Colossus Books, including: *Dr. Dre: In the Studio; SUGE KNIGHT – The Rise, Fall & Rise of Death Row Records; YOUR BODY'S CALLING ME: The Life and Times of R Kelly – Music Love, Sex & Money ; READY TO DIE: The Story of Biggie Smalls – Notorious B.I.G.; 50 CENT: No Holds Barred; Jay-Z and the Roc-A-Fella Records Dynasty; TUPAC SHAKUR (2-PAC) IN THE STUDIO: The Studio Years (1989-1996; Kanye West In The Studio – Beats Down! Money Up!*

R.I.P.

Buffalo, New York

Rick James Discography

Album	Artist	Credit
1971		
Cycle Is Complete	Bruce Palmer	Percussion, Vocals
1973		
25 #1 Hits From 25 Years, Vol. 2	Various Artists	Performer
1978		
Come Get It!	Rick James	Producer, Arranger, Synthesizer, Bass, Guitar, Keyboards, Performer, Mixing
1979		
Bustin' Out of L Seven	Rick James	Producer, Synthesizer, Guitar (Acoustic), Bass, Guitar, Harmonica, Percussion, Clavichord, Conga, Keyboards
Fire It Up	Rick James	Producer, Synthesizer, Bass, Guitar, Keyboards
Gold Rush 79	Various Artists	Performer
Wild and Peaceful	Teena Marie	Producer, Arranger, Guitar (Acoustic), Guitar, Percussion, Piano, Conga, Drums, Piano (Electric), Timbales, Vocals, Vocals (bckgr), Guitar (12 String), Tympani [Timpani], Horn Arrangements, String Arrangement
1980		
Garden of Love	Rick James	Producer, Arranger, Synthesizer, Bass, Guitar, Keyboards
In 'n' Out	The Stone City Band	Guitar, Keyboards, Vocals
1981		
Street Songs	Rick James	Producer, Arranger, Synthesizer, Bass, Guitar, Keyboards
1982		
Reunion	The Temptations	Producer, Arranger, Vocals, Clavinet
Throwin' Down	Rick James	Synthesizer, Bass, Guitar, Keyboards
1983		
Cold Blooded	Rick James	Producer, Arranger, Synthesizer, Bass, Guitar, Keyboards
Come Get It!/Fire It Up	Rick James	Guitar, Keyboards, Vocals
Mary Jane Girls	The Mary Jane Girls	Producer, Arranger

1984

Beverly Hills Cop Original Soundtrack		Producer
Kool Street Videos	Various Artists	Performer
Reflections	Rick James	Synthesizer, Bass, Guitar, Keyboards, Vocals

1985

Glow	Rick James	Guitar, Keyboards, Vocals
Greatest Hits [Motown]	Teena Marie	Producer, Arranger
How Could It Be (Party All the Time)	Eddie Murphy	Producer, Drums, Vocals
Only Four You	The Mary Jane Girls	Producer, Arranger

1986

Flag	Rick James	Synthesizer, Bass, Guitar, Keyboards
Greatest Hits [Motown]	Rick James	Producer, Arranger, Synthesizer, Bass, Guitar, Keyboards, Horn Arrangements, String Arrangements
Motown Time Capsule: The 70's [Video]	Various Artists	Performer
Street Songs/Throwin' Down	Rick James	Synthesizer, Bass, Guitar, Keyboards

1987

Naked to the World	Teena Marie	Vocals

1988

Colors [Original Soundtrack]		Performer
Loosey's Rap	Rick James	Guitar, Keyboards, Vocals
Wonderful	Rick James	Producer, Arranger, Synthesizer, Bass, Guitar, Percussion, Drums, Keyboards, Vocals, Vocals (bckgr), Mixing, Cover Art Concept

1989

Kickin'	Rick James	Guitar, Keyboards, Vocals
Rock, Rhythm & Blues	Various Artists	
This Magic Moment/Dance with Me	Rick James	Guitar, Keyboards, Vocals

1990

'70s Preservation Society Presents Those Funky '70s	Various Artists	Performer

1991

Greatest Hits [Epic]	Teena Marie	Producer, Arranger
Mega Hits Dance Classics, Vol. 9	Various Artists	Performer

1992

Back on the Street	Ron C	
Double Trouble	Roy Ayers	Vocals
Rick & Friends	Rick James	Performer

1993

Bound by Honor Original Soundtrack		Performer
Come on Feel the Lemonheads	The Lemonheads	Vocals
Hitsville USA, Vol. 2: The Motown Singles Collection	Various Artists	Producer, Arranger, Performer
Hot & Sexy, Vol. 2: Passion & Soul	Various Artists	Performer
In Yo' Face!: The History of Funk, Vol. 5	Various Artists	Performer

1994

Title	Artist	Credits
Bustin' Out: The Very Bestof Rick James	Rick James	Producer, Arranger, Vocals, Horn Arrangements, String Arrangements
Emperors of Soul	The Temptations	Producer, Arranger, Clavinet
I Need Your Lovin': The Best of Teena Marie	Teena Marie	Producer, Arranger
In My House: The Very Best of the Mary Jane Girls	The Mary Jane Girls	Producer, Arranger
Jointz From Back in da Day	Various Artists	Performer
Mega Hits Dance Classics, Vol. 11	Various Artists	Performer
Old School, Vol. 1	Various Artists	Producer
Old School, Vol. 2	Various Artists	Producer, Performer
Old School, Vol. 3	Various Artists	Performer
Soul Train: Hall of Fame, 20th Anniversary	Various Artists	Performer

1995

Title	Artist	Credits
Anthology [1995]	The Temptations	Producer, Arranger, Vocals, Vocals (bckgr)
Art Laboe Killer Oldies 2	Various Artists	Performer
Art Laboe's Dedicated to You, Vol. 6	Various Artists	Performer
Art Laboe's Dedicated to You, Vol. 7	Various Artists	Performer
Baddest Love Jams, Vol. 1	Various Artists	Producer, Arranger, Vocals, Performer
Baddest Love Jams, Vol. 2: Fire & Desire	Various Artists	Producer, Arranger, Performer
Class Reunion: The Greatest Hits of 1981	Various Artists	Performer
Deep in the Groove: In-Store Play Sampler	Various Artists	Performer
Disco Nights, Vol. 7: DJ Pix	Various Artists	Performer
Friday [Clean] Original Soundtrack		Performer
Friday Original Soundtrack		Performer
From Hip to Hop, Vol. 1: Funkbots	Various Artists	Performer
Funk Classics: The 70's	Various Artists	Performer
Funk Classics: The 80's	Various Artists	Performer
Funkology, Vol. 1: Got to Give It Up	Various Artists	Producer, Arranger, Performer
Funkology, Vol. 2: Behind the Groove	Various Artists	Producer, Arranger, Vocals, Performer
Mega Hits Dance Classics, Vol. 7	Various Artists	Performer
Motown Legends: Duets	Various Artists	Performer
Motown Legends: Give It to Me Baby	Rick James	Guitar, Keyboards, Vocals
Motown Love Songs: Motown Milestones	Various Artists	Producer, Arranger, Performer
Motown Year by Year: The Sound of Young America, 1982	Various Artists	Producer, Arranger, Vocals (bckgr), Performer
Motown Year By Year: The Sound of Young America, 1985	Various Artists	Producer, Arranger, Performer
Old School Friday Original Soundtrack		Performer
Old School, Vol. 2: Love Songs	Various Artists	Performer
Only Dance: 1980-1984	Various Artists	Performer
Smooth Grooves: A Sensual Collection, Vol. 2	Various Artists	Performer
Soul Classics: Quiet Storm — The 80's	Various Artists	Performer
Soul Hits of the 70s:	Various Artists	Performer, Cover Photo

Didn't It Blow Your Mind!, Vol.

Soul Train 25th Anniversary Hall of Fame Box Set	Various Artists	Performer
Thump'n Quick Mix's	Baka Boyz	Producer

1996

Baddest Love Jams, Vol. 3: After the Dance	Various Artists	Producer, Arranger, Performer
BET 15th Anniversary Music Collection	Various Artists	Performer
Funkology, Vol. 3: Dance Divas	Various Artists	Producer, Arranger
Motown Milestones: The Best of Teena Marie	Teena Marie	Producer, Horn Arrangements, String Arrangements, Rhythm Arrangements
Old School Love Songs, Vol. 1	Various Artists	Performer
Old School, Vol. 6	Various Artists	Performer
Old School, Vols. 1-5	Various Artists	Performer
Old Skoolin'	Various Artists	Performer
Pallbearer Original Soundtrack		Performer
Ragga Ragga Ragga, Vol. 6	Various Artists	Producer, Arranger, Performer
Roller Disco: Boogie from the Skating Rinks	Various Artists	Performer
Slow Jams: The Timeless Collection, Vol. 5	Various Artists	Performer
Smooth Grooves, Vols. 1-4	Various Artists	Performer
Smooth Grooves: A Sensual Collection, Vol. 9	Various Artists	Performer
Soul Classics: Quiet Storm, the 80's	Various Artists	Performer
Strip Jointz: Hot Songs for Sexy Dancers	Various Artists	Performer

1997

4 Tha Hard Way Rappin'	4-Tay	Producer, Performer, Mixing
Classic Funk, Vol. 3	Various Artists	Performer
Cosmic Funk [Polygram]	Various Artists	Performer
Def Jam's How to Be a Player [Clean] Original Soundtrack		Performer
Def Jam's How to Be a Player Original Soundtrack		Performer
Disco's Leading Men: Disco Nights, Vol. 11	Various Artists	Performer
Funky Milestones	Various Artists	Performer
How to Be a Player	Various Artists	Performer
Money Talks [Clean] Original Soundtrack		Producer, Performer
Money Talks Original Soundtrack		Producer, Performer
Sounds of the Seventies: '70s Dance Party 1979-1981	Various Artists	Performer
Ultimate Collection	Rick James	Producer, Arranger, Horn Arrangements, String Arrangements
Urban Rapsody [Clean]	Rick James	Producer, Bass, Guitar, Percussion, Arranger, Guitar (Bass), Keyboards, Vocals, Vocals (bckgr), Mixing
Urban Rapsody	Rick James	Producer, Arranger, Bass, Guitar, Percussion, Guitar (Bass), Keyboards, Vocals, Vocals (bckgr), Mixing
WDAS FM Classic Soul Hits, Vol. 2	Various Artists	Performer

1998

Campus Soul	Various Artists	Performer
Chart Toppers: Dance Hits of the 80's	Various Artists	Performer
Chef Aid: The South Park Album [Clean]	South Park	Performer
Chef Aid: The South Park Album [Extreme]	South Park	Performer
Chef Aid: The South Park Album	South Park	Performer
Disco Nights, Vol. 11: Leading Men	Various Artists	Performer
Funk Classics: The 70's, Vol. 2	Various Artists	Performer
Motown 40 Forever	Various Artists	Producer, Arranger, Performer
O.G. Funk: Locking, Vol. 1	Various Artists	Performer
Old School Mixx, Vol. 2	Various Artists	Performer
Original Players of Love	Various Artists	Performer
Party Time, Vol. 3	Various Artists	Performer
Pure Funk	Various Artists	Performer
Soul Classics: Best of the 80's	Various Artists	Performer
Strip Jointz, Vol. 2: More Hot Songs for Sexy Dancers	Various Artists	Performer
Very Best of Kleeer	Kleeer	Synthesizer, Keyboards, Programming

1999

Funkdamentals	Various Artists	Performer
Monster Funk Party	Various Artists	Performer
Motown Chartbusters, Vols. 7-12 [Box Set]	Various Artists	Performer
Only Soul 1975-1979	Various Artists	Performer
Pure Funk, Vol. 2	Various Artists	Performer
Soul Train: The Dance Years 1978	Various Artists	Performer
Super Freaks	Various Artists	Performer
United We Funk	Various Artists	Performer

2000

20th Century Masters — The Millennium Collection: Rick James	Rick James	Producer, Arranger, String Arrangements
20th Century Masters - The Millennium Collection: The Temptations		Performer
3 for One	The Lemonheads	Vocals
Angel and the Goddess	Jonathan Goldman	Technical Assistance
DJ Masters: Funk Classics	Various Artists	Performer
Funk Box	Various Artists	Producer, Arranger
Funky Grooves	Various Artists	Performer
Jammin' Gold	Various Artists	Performer
Love Funk: 12 Classic Funk Hits	Various Artists	Producer, Arranger
Love Songs	Teena Marie	Producer, Arranger, Vocals
Love Soul Classics	Various Artists	Arranger, Producer
Motown History, Vol. 1	Various Artists	Performer
Party Starter Level 1: The Classics	Various Artists	Performer
Party Time [SPG]	Various Artists	Performer
Reflection Eternal	Talib Kweli & Hi Tek	Producer
Sampled	Various Artists	Producer, Arranger
Shape Fitness Music: Cardio, Vol.3	Various Artists	Performer
Ultimate Collection	Teena Marie	Producer, Arranger

393

2001

20th Century Masters — The Millennium Collection: Mot	Various Artists	Producer, Arranger
20th Century Masters — The Millennium Collection: Teena Marie	Teena Marie	Producer, Arranger, Vocals
20th Century Masters— The Millennium Collection: The Mary Jane Girls	The Mary Jane Girls	Producer, Arranger, Multi Instruments Vocal Arrangement, Horn Arrangements, String Arrangements
70's Soul Experience	Various Artists	Performer
80's Soul Weekender	Various Artists	Producer, Arranger
AnotherLateNight [UK]	Rae & Christian	Producer, Arranger
AnotherLateNight	Rae & Christian	Producer, Arranger
At Their Very Best	The Temptations	Performer
Back to Black: 1900-1999	Various Artists	Performer
Can You Dig It? The '70s Soul Experience	Various Artists	Performer
Daily Disco Workout	Various Artists	Performer
Funk Classics	Various Artists	Performer
Funk Soul USA	Various Artists	Performer
Funkology	Various Artists	String Arrangements
Funky Collector No. 8	Various Artists	Performer
Funky Collector No. 9	Various Artists	Performer
Motown Chartbusters, Vol. 10	Various Artists	Performer
Motown Chartbusters, Vol. 11	Various Artists	Performer
Motown Chartbusters, Vol. 12	Various Artists	Performer
New Millennium Funk Party	Various Artists	Performer
Old School Jams, Vol. 3	Various Artists	Performer
Old School Love Songs [Box Set]	Various Artists	Performer
Solid Gold Soul: 80's Rhythm & Grooves	Various Artists	Performer
Solo Anthology	Smokey Robinson	Producer, Arranger
Soul Classics Quiet Storm [Box]	Various Artists	Performer
Soul Classics [MCA Special Products]	Various Artists	Performer
Strange Games and Things	DJ Spinna	Performer
Street Songs [Deluxe Edition]	Rick James	Producer, Arranger, Bass, Guitar, Percussion, Drums, Timbales, Vocals, Tympani [Timpani], Horn Arrangements, String Arrangements, Cover Art Concept
Ultimate Jukebox Hits of the '80s, Vol. 2	Various Artists	Performer
WDAS 105.3 FM: Classic Soul Hits, Vol. 6	Various Artists	Performer

2002

20th Century Masters — The Millennium Collection: Mot	Various Artists	Producer, Arranger
20th Century Masters — The Millennium Collection: Mot	Various Artists	Producer, Arranger, Horn Arrangements, String Arrangements
Anthology	Rick James	Producer, Arranger, Multi Instruments, Horn Arrangements, String Arrangements, Rhythm Arrangements, Rhythm Track
Hit Me with Your 80's Box!	Various Artists	Producer

It Must Be Magic [Bonus Tracks]	Teena Marie	Vocals (bckgr), Voices, Vocal Arrangement
Jukebox Hits of the '80s [Collectables]	Various Artists	Performer
Like, Omigod! The '80s Pop Culture Box (Totally)	Various Artists	Producer
Love Funk, Vol. 2	Various Artists	Producer, Arranger, Horn Arrangements, String Arrangements
My Girl:The Very Best of the Temptations	The Temptations	Producer, Arranger
Nocturnal Rage	Nocturnal Rage	
Old School Funk, Vol. 4	Various Artists	Performer
Smooth Grooves: Soulful Duets	Various Artists	Performer
Solid Gold Funk Various Artists	Performer	
Soul Classics, Vol. 2 [Collectables]	Various Artists	Performer
Soul Classics, Vol. 6 [Collectables]	Various Artists	Performer
Street Songs [Bonus Tracks]	Rick James	Producer, Arranger, Bass, Guitar, Percussion, Drums, Timbales, Vocals, Poetry, Tympani [Timpani], Horn Arrangements, String Arrangements, Cover Art Concept

2003

Choice: A Collection of Classics	Derrick Carter	Producer, Arranger
Sampled, Vol. 4	Various Artists	Producer, Arranger

2004

20th Century Masters — DVD Collection	The Temptations	Producer, Arranger
All Night Long: Classic 80's Grooves [Universal Inter]	Various Artists	Producer, Arranger, Horn Arrangements, String Arrangements
Funkin' 80's	Various Artists	Producer, Arranger
Greatest Hits [Universal International]	Rick James	Producer, Arranger, Horn Arrangements
Old School Jams, Vol. 5	Various Artists	Producer
Summer of Motown	Various Artists	Producer
Superstars of Seventies Soul	Various Artists	Performer

2005

20th Century Masters - The Millenniumm Collection	Rick James & Friends	Producer, Arranger, Executive Producer, Vocals, Horn Arrangements, String Arrangements
20th Century Masters: The Best of Rick James DVD	Rick James	Producer, Arranger
Best of Smokey Robinson [Motown]	Smokey Robinson	Arranger, Audio Production
Book of Life	Missippi	Lyricist
Complete 80's Soul Weekender	Various Artists	Producer, Arranger, String Arrangements
Funk Gold	Various Artists	Producer, Arranger
Gold	Rick James	Producer, Arranger, Vocal Arrangement, Horn Arrangements, String Arrangements, Rhythm Arrangements, Instrumentation
Gold	The Temptations	Producer, Arranger
Motown Remixed [Australian]	Various Artists	Producer, Arranger
Motown Remixed [Bonus Track]	Various Artists	Producer
Motown Unmixed	Various Artists	Producer

Original Artist Karaoke: Motown – Brickhouse	Karaoke	Producer, Arranger
Original Artist Karaoke: Motown - Superfreak, Vol. 16	Karaoke	Producer, Arranger, Horn Arrangements, String Arrangements
Super Freak Live 1982 [DVD]	Rick James	Guitar, Vocals
Wild and Peaceful [Expanded Edition]	Teena Marie	Producer, Guitar (Acoustic), Percussion, Conga, Piano (Electric), Vocals, Vocals (bckgr, Tympani [Timpani], Horn Arrangements, String Arrangements, Rhythm Arrangements, Syndrum, Guitar (12 String Acoustic)

2006

'80s Soul Gold	Various Artists	Producer, Arranger, Horn Arrange- ments, String Arrangements
Definitive Collection	Rick James	Producer, Arranger, Multi Instruments, Vocal Arrangement, Horn Arrange- ments, String Arrangements, Rhythm Arrangements
Gold	Smokey Robinson & the Miracles	Producer, Arranger

2007

Old School Jams: Gold	Various Artists	Producer, Arranger, Vocals, Horn Arrangements, String Arrangements
Let's Groove [Sony]	Various Artists	Producer, Arranger
Motown's Disco Party Pac	Various Artists	Performer
Deeper Still	Rick James	Producer, Arranger, Composer

Name Index

The index has been organized by first name for ease of finding references.

ORDER FORM

WWW.AMBERBOOKS.COM

Fax Orders: 480-283-0991
Telephone Orders: 480-460-1660
Postal Orders: Send Checks & Money Orders to:
  Amber Books
  1334 E. Chandler Blvd., Suite 5-D67, Phoenix, AZ 85048
Online Orders: E-mail: Amberbk@aol.com

_____*The Confessions of Rick James: Memoirs of a Super Freak*, ISBN #: 978-0-9790976-0-7, $18.95
_____*Kanye West in the Studio*, ISBN #: 0-9767735-6-2, $16.95
_____*Tupac Shakur—(2Pac) In The Studio*, ISBN#: 0-9767735-0-3, $16.95
_____*Jay-Z…and the Roc-A-Fella Dynasty*, ISBN#: 0-9749779-1-8, $16.95
_____*Your Body's Calling Me: The Life & Times of "Robert" R. Kelly*, ISBN#: 0-9727519-5-52, $16.95
_____*Ready to Die: Notorious B.I.G.*, ISBN#: 0-9749779-3-4, $16.95
_____*Suge Knight: The Rise, Fall, and Rise of Death Row Records*, ISBN#: 0-9702224-7-5, $21.95
_____*50 Cent: No Holds Barred*, ISBN#: 0-9767735-2-X, $16.95
_____*Aaliyah—An R&B Princess in Words and Pictures* , ISBN#: 0-9702224-3-2, $10.95
_____*You Forgot About Dre: Dr. Dre & Eminem*, ISBN#: 0-9702224-9-1, $10.95
_____*Divas of the New Millenium*, ISBN#: 0-9749779-6-9, $16.95
_____*Michael Jackson: The King of Pop*, ISBN#: 0-9749779-0-X, $29.95
_____*The House that Jack Built (Hal Jackson Story)*, ISBN#: 0-9727519-4-7, $16.95

Name:_____

Company Name:_____

Address:_____

City:_____State:_____Zip:_____

Telephone: (____) _____E-mail:_____

For Bulk Rates Call: **480-460-1660**   # ORDER NOW

Rick James	$18.95	❏ Check ❏ Money Order ❏ Cashiers Check
Kanye West	$16.95	❏ Credit Card: ❏ MC ❏ Visa ❏ Amex ❏ Discover
Tupac Shakur	$16.95	
Jay-Z…	$16.95	
Your Body's Calling Me:	$16.95	CC#_____
Ready to Die: Notorious B.I.G.,	$16.95	Expiration Date:_____
Suge Knight:	$21.95	**Payable to:**
50 Cent: No Holds Barred,	$16.95	Amber Books
Aaliyah—An R&B Princess	$10.95	1334 E. Chandler Blvd., Suite 5-D67
Dr. Dre & Eminem	$10.95	Phoenix, AZ 85048
Divas of the New Millenium,	$16.95	
Michael Jackson: The King of Pop	$29.95	**Shipping:** $5.00 per book. Allow 7 days for delivery.
The House that Jack Built	$16.95	**Sales Tax:** Add 7.05% to books shipped to Arizona addresses.

Total enclosed: $_____

CPSIA information can be obtained at www.ICGtesting.com
Printed in the USA
LVOW081947220313

325639LV00023B/776/P